TALES FROM GEORGIA'S GNAT LINE

MERCER UNIVERSITY PRESS

Endowed by

TOM WATSON BROWN
and
THE WATSON-BROWN FOUNDATION, INC.

TALES FROM GEORGIA'S GNAT LINE

To Bryan Miller, my friend,
who comes from good stock
and who understands all of
Georgia, including its gnat
line. Best wishes for
interesting reading!
Larry
April 18, 2019

Larry Walker

MERCER UNIVERSITY PRESS

Macon, Georgia

1979–2019

40 Years of Publishing Excellence

MUP/ H973

9 8 7 6 5 4 3 2 1

Books published by Mercer University Press are printed on acid-free paper
that meets the requirements of the American National Standard for
Information Sciences—Permanence of Paper for Printed Library Materials.

Many of the articles in this book were originally published in the *Macon
Telegraph* and *James*, and are used here with permission.

Printed and bound in the United States.

This book is set in Adobe Caslon.

ISBN   978-0-88146-6980
Cataloging-in-Publication Data is available from the Library of Congress

CONTENTS

FOREWORD

"By an Old Raccoon in the Barn"

Many people who have recently moved to Atlanta from New York, Chicago, Los Angeles, or wherever, soon realize that they are not really in the South as they understood it to be. They often ask me, "What can I read to learn more about the South—how it used to be and how it is now?" And my answer is always, "As to how it used to be, read Margaret Mitchell's *Gone with the Wind* and perhaps Pat Conroy's *Prince of Tides.*" Now I make an additional recommendation: "For a close look at the culture of the South, you should read Larry Walker's *Tales from Georgia's Gnat Line.* It's full of stories that have been learned and told and retold over his lifetime, enhanced by the more than fifty years he practiced law in the small town of Perry along with his thirty-plus years serving in the Georgia legislature. This book reflects a lifetime of listening and telling tales of Georgia and the South from the perspective of a well-lived life as a bona fide Southerner. It's a fascinating journey through the people, places, and culture of Georgia."

Larry Walker's perspective on Southern life will help you understand why we call him "a flash of joy in the pan of life." Get *Tales from Georgia's Gnat Line*, read it, and you will began to get it.

Connell Stafford
Former executive assistant to United States Senator Sam Nunn
and vice president of the Coca-Cola Company

PREFACE

When I was writing a column for local newspapers, the best compliment I got came from former United States Senator Herman Talmadge, who told me, "Most everything you write reminds me of my boyhood."

Most everything you write, Larry, reminds me of something, my boyhood or otherwise. Your latest about the loss of the peach crop and your mention of screwworm eradication certainly brought back a memory of my childhood. Screwworms, gobs of them, bored into mule haunches. One of my farm chores was to pick them out with a knife blade and drop them into a can of kerosene. You can't believe how many could get into a hole in mule flesh the size of my young fist. Maybe two dozen.

The mules didn't seem to feel the digging, or whatever it was I poured into the wound when the last of the screwworms were in the can of kerosene. I got very good at picking screwworms out of mules. Today, my parents might be prosecuted for child abuse. I prefer to think they thought the experience would inspire me to go to medical school and become a rich doctor.

And then there was this. Before we got "lights" from the REA in the late thirties, we, of course, had no electricity. My grandparents had it in the twenties via a backyard Delco unit and even piped it across the street to light up the Methodist church. By the time I came along, all that had gone the way of the Great Depression and the boll weevil. All we had were the defunct Delco and light fixtures and wall switches that didn't work.

Without electricity, neither did we have running water. Only hand-dug wells, which were not always good wells. The one at the Methodist parsonage was not a good well. About once a month it would go dry. It had to be "dug out." On those mornings when it yielded no water, the preacher would come knocking on our door, right after breakfast.

I didn't have to guess what he wanted: "Can Jimmy come clean out the well?"

Daddy would get a short-handle shovel and a plowline. The three of us would go to the parsonage. Shovel in hand, I would straddle the bucket. Daddy and the preacher would let me down to the bottom of the well, and I would dig until I had filled the bucket with sand and mud. They would haul the bucket up to be dumped and then send it back for me to fill again. Again and again until water reappeared.

Today, that, too, might be classed as child abuse. At the time, it was only my bad luck to be the smallest Methodist boy in Inman. Thanks, Larry, for stirring these old, great memories. I know that your book will do this for your readers.

Jim Minter
former editor of *The Atlanta Journal-Constitution*

DEDICATION

This book is dedicated to my nine grandchildren so that they will know about life in the South, and how it used to be—the good and the not so good. I want them to know how much I have enjoyed my life on the gnat line. I hope that Ben, Cody, Haley, Gray, Wade, Walker, Sophie, Stella, and Knighton enjoy their lives as much as I have mine.

Special thanks to my law associate, Brooke Newby, who helped put this book together, Matthew Hulbert, my law partner, who did much of the proofreading, and my friend, Avery Chenoweth, without whose encouragement this book would have never been.

TALES FROM GEORGIA'S GNAT LINE

PREAMBLE

This book is about the South, the Deep South and my part of the world. It's about good people, and some not so good, and it's about that part of the United States that was, and is, somewhat different from the rest. And it's about cotton, because in lots of ways it was cotton that caused Southerners to do some of the things that otherwise good people would not have done.

Often, when writing, it's about cotton, even when the word "cotton" is not mentioned. Talk about tenant farmers and mules and, really, most of that writing involves cotton. Talk about the Civil War and cotton is certainly involved as a primary cause of this war. Truly cotton was "King" in my South.

When you have the power and the money, and the two most always go together, you don't easily give it up. And so it was in the South. If you had the cotton and you could get it gathered and sold, you'd have the money and the power; and those who had it didn't easily give it up. The South has paid for this and continues to pay, but it's not as bad as it used to be, and maybe during my children's lifetimes, the debt will be paid.

Let me tell you about my world. You don't practice law in a small town for more than fifty years, serve thirty-two years in the Georgia General Assembly (sixteen of them as its majority leader), and then on the University System of Georgia's Board of Regents for many years and not know about the South—the good and the bad.

When I was a young boy growing up on Swift Street in Perry, Georgia, I would lie on my back in the grass, place my hands together like I was getting ready to pray, then spread them slightly apart, looking upwards through them, and conjure images of fish, boats, mountains, dogs, mules, and all manner of things until the clouds drifted away just like so many things that I love about the South are doing today—drifting away.

Despite the relentless heat and racial segregation and separation,

1

which I learned about at an early age, I was largely content, as content as a boy could be. I knew my people, where I was and where I needed to be, and where I would stay. My place.

The Good Book tells us that the road is long and narrow, and for someone from a small town in Middle Georgia (and I guess always will be), it was and is. And I wouldn't and didn't get on that long and narrow road for California, New York, or even Atlanta.

Oh, I had and have wanderlust, which I am sure I got from my Gray grandparents, Grandbuddy and Granny, who lived in California twice (where Grandbuddy was a cameraman at Universal Studios) and Arizona (where they homesteaded) before they came to Perry somewhere around 1920. They knew that the road was long and narrow.

What is it about this place, this flawed place, that has such a hold on me? I can't answer fully to your satisfaction or mine, but I will try.

Family, first and always, it's family. Early on, I was taught by Daddy that family was the most important. A man who once told me that he had "seventy-four first cousins, living" should and did feel that way. And Daddy knew where most of them lived and what they did. He expected—no, required—that I honor and appreciate my immediate and extended family including, and probably most importantly, my two Gray grandparents in Perry and the two mule-farming ones in deep, rural Washington County, Georgia, the Walkers, Grandma and Papa, who made syrup, killed hogs, and burned wood slabs in the stove, all of which interested and thrilled me beyond words. They epitomized the South of earlier days, and I got to see it!

I've been blessed beyond measure with so many wonderful friends. They are just behind family in importance. I will use "Do-Tricks" as an excellent Southern character example. Let me describe him in his prime. He was about five feet, seven inches, and 150 pounds. His arms looked like short stove pipes and his fingers like ten Vienna sausages. I saw him arm wrestle a state weight-lifting champion, eight inches taller and sixty pounds heavier. It took the big boy about five minutes to put Do-Tricks down. The big boy won the match, but Do-Tricks won the crowd. There was no one else like Do-Tricks, and yet the South is full of characters— all distinctive. Jerry "Do-Tricks" Horton never held an office, not even in the Kiwanis or the Rotary Club, wasn't rich, could do anything with his hands (and did), was loved by children and animals, and had one of the biggest funerals ever in Houston County. He played lots of tricks and practical jokes, but he got his name from Ed Beckham, and it had to do with rabbits. Characters, nicknames, practical jokes—all so Southern, and it's part of what I love.

And it's black people, or African Americans, my friends. It's their home, too, and they've been a large part of my life. I worked with Joe Hodges at the feed store. He taught me lots about life, and I loved him. I worked for George "Big Hoss" Johnson in the cotton field. I was put in his charge by Daddy, and although I was nervous around him, I knew that this giant of a man (reputed to be the strongest man in the area), with part of one arm missing and not a tooth in his head (he could bite an apple in two) would look after me. He did. And Amos and Solomon Brown in Washington County, about five or six years older than me, whom I idolized, and those outstanding and smart legislators with whom I served: Calvin Smyre, Michael Thurmond, Bob Holmes, Kasim Reed, and Bobby Hill come to mind. But most importantly, those black Perryans who helped me get a start in my law practice, became my clients, and allowed me to represent them. Thanks.

Dirt roads. It's hard to find them, but you can. We still have them in the South. Next time it rains, find a red dirt road, take off your shoes and socks, walk in the mud and the mud puddles. Let the mud ooze between your toes. Brooks and Dunn knew. Get their top-hits album and listen to "Red Dirt Road"—over and over. A good wet red dirt road can help with what's bothering you. It'll keep you from needing a psychiatrist.

Barbeque, the best in the world. Tomato sandwiches. Homemade peach ice cream. Caramel cake. Chocolate pie. Sweet iced tea. Boiled peanuts. Fried chicken (wings?). Grits. Grits with redeye gravy. Fried catfish and hush puppies. Cathead biscuits. I could go on, but space prevents. Anyway, you Southerners understand.

Music: country, bluegrass, blues, beach music, shag, gospel. We've got it. Ray Charles playing and singing "Georgia on My Mind." That song is the best in the world for someone who voted, as a representative in Georgia's State House, to make it our official state song—maybe the most exciting vote I made out of thousands during my tenure. I hope my family will have Ray Charles's version played at my funeral.

It's never been easy to be a Southerner—black or white. But it's worth holding on to, and we must. I promise to do my part. I won't let them make me feel inferior because I use "y'all" and do it often, or because I have a drawl. And, by the way, do you think God talks more like I do, or like one of those big Yankee United States senators from up North? I think you know the answer.

Yes, the road is long and narrow. It's wider down here in the South than it used to be, and it is getting wider all the time, but there have been recent problems which will probably have to be addressed. We can't afford to fight the Civil War again—either here in the South or in the whole country.

PERRY PEOPLE

His United States Senate campaign slogan, first-time run, features a catchy tune, "Put Sam Nunn in Washington." And the people of Georgia did it in an election with one of the biggest upsets in Georgia's hstory—Sam Nunn, a four-year member of Georgia's state House, was "put in Washington."

Sam, a native of Perry and the son of prominent attorney Samuel Augustus Nunn Sr. and popular mother, Elizabeth Cannon Nunn, relied heavily on the people of the small town of Perry, Georgia, (probably population of around 8,000 when Sam was elected in 1972) for his support.

Buddy Tolleson, owner of Tolleson Lumber Company, Perry's oldest industry at the time, was Sam's financial chair, and many of the merchants in Perry wrote personal letters of support to their counterparts in other small Georgia communities. For example, my father, Cohen Walker, who was in the farm equipment business in Perry, wrote letters to most of the other farm-equipment dealers in the state. Likewise, Mr. Francis Nunn, another farm-equipment dealer, did the same. Sam will tell you today that without the good people of Perry, he would never have been a United States senator.

Many people all over the United States know about Sam Nunn. But few know that Perry is also the boyhood home of General Courtney Hicks Hodges, boyhood friend of Sam's father, "Mr. Sam," and a World War II European general and commander of the First Army and later the Third Army. The main street into Perry from US Highway 341 is Sam Nunn Boulevard, and the main street into Perry from US Highway 41 is General Courtney Hodges Boulevard.

That's not all. One of the "winningest" high school basketball coaches (boys) in the history of the United States was Eric Staples, whose teams won 924 games and lost but 198. His winnings included eight state championships and twenty-five regional titles. The Houston

5

County School Administration Building is named for 'Fessor Staples.

But that's still not all. Georgia's first Republican governor since Reconstruction, Sonny Perdue, who is now the United States Secretary of Agriculture, was born in Perry, Georgia. He now lives in Bonaire, Georgia, a community about fifteen miles from Perry. Interstate 75, as it goes though Houston County, including Perry, is named for him.

Read this book and learn that there's more to Georgia than just Atlanta. Oh, we're proud of Atlanta, one of the most dynamic cities in the world, but we're proud of Perry, Houston County, and life on and below the gnat line too. Read on and find out what the gnat line is and why it is. You'll be glad you did.

LITTLE SAM MAKES GOOD

One of the drawbacks to growing up in a small Southern town, the son of a prominent citizen, and with the same name as your father, is that, invariably, you acquire the moniker "Little." And so it was that Sam Nunn, son of "Mr." Sam Nunn, the "go-to" attorney in our area, was known for a long time by the adult folks in Perry as "Little" Sam Nunn.

He was Little Sam when he attended Georgia Tech, Little when he came back to Perry to practice law, Little when he became a husband and father, and Little when he chaired Perry's Chamber of Commerce and was instrumental in starting and shepherding a biracial committee which he cochaired with future United States congressman Richard Ray, became a successful lawyer, served on the board that gave us the Houston Lake Country Club, and was a founder and board member of the First National Bank. Then he was elected to Georgia's House of Representatives, where he served for four years. Still, to the Perryans, he was Little Sam Nunn.

But lest I overemphasize this, let me assure you that from an early age, Little Sam was the object of much attention by adults and students alike, and the question was not whether he would be outstanding, but exactly what he would do to make us proud. It was not a question of "if." It was a question of "what" and "when."

And, of course, when Little Sam was elected to the United States Senate, and with the death of Mr. Sam a few years earlier, the "Little" was relegated to the memories of a few old Perryans like me. But it is Little Sam that I write about today, and not the senator Nunn, who could have been, and should have been, president of the United States, with a little luck.

Perhaps a good starting point is 1956. I was in the eighth grade, Perry Junior High School, and Sam was a senior at Perry High School. Academically and athletically, Sam had, as expected, amassed an outstanding record. Let's look at what was going on with Sam at that long-ago time.

A look at Perry High School's yearbook, the Panther '56, is in order. This is part of what was written about Sam Nunn: "Sincere in all he undertakes. Always a great success he makes." "Basketball 2, 3, 4, Captain 3, 4, Allstate 3, 4, Class President 1, 2, 3, Vice-President 4; Golf 1, 2, 3, 4, Low score 3, Beta Club 3, 4." You should be beginning to get the picture.

Let's focus on basketball. I take my information from Billy Powell's book, *Pride of the Panthers*. In the district championship game, Perry defeated its old nemesis, Fort Valley, with Nunn scoring eighteen points, and then in the state tournament finals against Valley Point, Nunn got twenty-seven in a Perry victory, 81 to 52. This is a team that, during the regular season, did not lose a game and defeated the likes of Warner Robins, Middle Georgia College B-team, Southwest (Atlanta), West Fulton (Atlanta), Lanier (Macon), Griffin, Smith (Atlanta), and Murphy (Atlanta).

Outstanding student, good young citizen, and great athlete. In addition to basketball, Perry won the state golf tournament with Sam on the team. As an aside, lots of golfers over lots of years since 1956 have learned the hard way of Sam Nunn's golfing prowess.

And then Little Sam was off to Georgia Tech in the fall of 1956 to be greeted with the requirement that all male freshmen were expected to participate in the "cake race," which, at that time, was a cross-country race.

Sam had never run cross-country and was not on Perry High's track team. But participate in Tech's 1956 cake race he did. Whether he was motivated by winning the cake or getting to kiss Georgia Tech's Homecoming Queen if he won the race, I do not know. But I do know that he won the race, as the archivist at Georgia Tech has a picture of Sam holding his "winning cake" and kissing the Queen all at the same time. Actually, I do know why he won the race: pride, determination, and the desire to win. These attributes were the things that folks in Perry expected of him and qualities he had in abundance.

Lastly, we must mention Little Sam and Georgia Tech basketball, where he played on the freshman team (at that time, freshmen were not allowed to play on the varsity). All he did was to finish the season as Tech's leading rebounder (at five feet eleven inches) and second leading scorer! Pride, determination, and the desire to win.

To quote Sam: "I couldn't pass Mechanical Drawing, so I transferred to Emory." In a rare occurrence, Sam encountered something he couldn't master, but this transfer to Emory was fortuitous, as he characteristically created an outstanding record at both Emory University and Emory's School of Law.

Little Sam was rapidly becoming just Sam, except to a dwindling number of older Perryans. And then it was ultimately US Senator Sam Nunn, and then Sam Nunn, the American who probably knows more about nuclear proliferation than anyone alive.

Little Sam, you did well. And Sam Nunn, you've done well. You've made the folks in Perry look good. They were right about you all along.

SOME DEBTS ARE TOO BIG TO BE REPAID

I had forgotten that I made this speech. If someone had asked me, which didn't happen, I would have said something like this: "Oh, I made a few comments, and I'm sure I thanked my House colleagues, and perhaps others, but I don't remember anything much about it." What I'm talking about is any kind of a farewell speech when I left the state Legislature in 2004.

Last week, the last week of April, Florence Harrison's brother-in-law brought to my office a box with a few books, several photographs, originals of letters, and lots of magazine and newspaper clippings. Most of them were about Sam Nunn or me. Charles Harrison told me that his sister-in-law, Florence, wanted me to have the box and its contents, and that his brother, Willis Harrison, had agreed. Mrs. Harrison had saved the contents of this box for years.

Florence Harrison was Sam Nunn's high school English teacher (he graduated from Perry High School in 1956) and was mine (I graduated from PHS in 1960). Florence died in May of 2014, and, as a lawyer, I handled her estate. Her husband, Willis, died in December of 2016, and I handled his. But back to the box and a newspaper clipping I don't ever remember seeing.

The clipping, half of a newspaper page, was titled "Text from State Rep. Larry Walker's farewell speech" and apparently was from Macon's *The Telegraph*, judging from an ad on the back of the page which had my speech.

A half page! I couldn't believe it. Saved, along with many other things, by my homeroom and twelfth-grade teacher, Florence Harrison. Amazing.

Then I read it. And what struck me as never before was how much I owed Mrs. Harrison, and my first-grade teacher, Miss Frances Couey, and my sixth-grade teacher, Jeanne Bledsoe. I will never be able to pay what I owe. That's what teachers do. They give so much and it can never be repaid by the recipients.

A few excerpts from my speech.

I quoted Thomas Jefferson, who said, "If due participation of office is a matter of right, how are vacancies to be obtained? Those by death are few; by resignation, none." Or, as Jefferson is usually quoted, "Few die, and none resign." In other words, if the politician continues to serve long enough, he will either die or eventually be defeated. None quit. But I did.

I talked about love undeserved and quoted from my favorite hymn, "My Tribute" (and I like it by Andraé Crouch) by reciting these words: "How can I say thanks for the things you have done for me. Things so undeserved, yet you gave to prove your love for me. The voices of a million angels could not express my gratitude..."

I talked of legislative colleagues, including Terry Coleman, Tom Buck, Tom Murphy, Lynn Westmoreland, Bill Lee, Calvin Smyre, and perhaps a hundred or so more. Democrats and Republicans. Friends. Good friends. Lobbyists, clerks, governors, secretaries, my shoeshine man, the press, and three especially close political friends, Allan Stalvey, Clark Fain, and Connell Stafford. I also talked of my wonderful secretary of twenty years, Dianna Lynn.

And then I closed with what Robert E. Lee closed with when he gave his farewell address to the Army of Northern Virginia: "With an unceasing admiration of your constancy and devotion to your country, and a grateful remembrance of your kind and generous consideration of myself, I bid you an affectionate farewell." And so I bid my political colleagues and my friends an affectionate farewell, which I truly meant— the affectionate part.

Frances Couey taught me to read in the first grade, and Florence Harrison taught me to love to read in the twelfth. I call them my bookend teachers. Neither the speech I made in 2004 nor this writing would have ever happened without Mrs. Harrison. She helped to make me what I was when I wrote the speech in the spring of 2004 and helped make me what I am today. I think Sam Nunn would say the same things about her. In fact, I know he would.

WHAT ABOUT GENERAL
COURTNEY HICKS HODGES?

We've done well by Eric P. "Fessor" Staples with the naming of the Houston County Board Administration Building for him, as well as other honors. And we have properly honored former United States senator Sam Nunn with Sam Nunn Boulevard and "Sam's Room" in the Eric P. Staples Building. But what about Perry's native son General Courtney Hicks Hodges?

Walk down the hall at my law office, and at the end of the hall is a photograph of generals entitled, "A Gathering of the Stars." There are twelve of them, and there he sits next to General Omar Bradley, who sits next to the allied supreme commander, General Dwight D. Eisenhower. Pretty good for a little Perry boy, don't you think?

General Hodges was born in Perry on January 4, 1887, and is the only enlisted man on record to rise from private to four-star general in the United States Army.

In 1906, Courtney Hodges enlisted in the army, and in 1916, Lieutenant Hodges served with Gen. John J. Pershing's forces along the Mexican border. He went to France in 1918 as a captain, was decorated twice for valor, and returned after occupation duty in Germany as a lieutenant colonel.

Later, Colonel Hodges served as an instructor at West Point. In 1943, he was named commanding general of the Third Army. On D-Day, June 6, 1944, General Hodges landed at Normandy and on August 1, 1944, assumed command of the First Army. The First Army spearheaded the Allied forces' drive through Europe.

After Germany surrendered, General Hodges and his staff were redeployed to the Pacific to organize another army for the invasion of Japan. En route, when he returned home to Perry to be honored on May 31, 1945, the people of Perry gave their famous son a tremendous "welcome home" celebration. It was presided over by Mayor Sam A.

Nunn Sr., a boyhood friend.

General Hodges was on the battleship Missouri and watched the Japanese surrender. Returning to the United States, he again became commanding general of the First Army. After more than forty-five years of active service, General Hodges retired on January 31, 1949. He died on January 16, 1966, and is buried in Arlington National Cemetery.

General Hodges still has relatives in this area. Edward Mason, Thomas Mason, and Courtney Mason were his nephews. Thomas was married to my mother's sister, Virginia Gray Mason, but both of them and Virginia (Aunt Ginny) are now gone. Courtney, the General's name sake, is still living. John Houser was a nephew. Mr. John Hodges, deceased, long-time Houston County Ordinary (now called Probate Judge), and at one time, owner of *The Houston Home Journal*, was his brother. As an aside, nephew John Houser was a WWII pilot, as was nephew Courtney Mason. Courtney "flew over the Hump." There are probably still a few men who served in one of General Hodges's armies in WWII, and maybe some who remember the great welcome-home celebration in 1945.

THE TIMES, THE TOWN, AND THE MAN

Speech by Larry Walker at the dedication of the Eric P. Staples Memorial Building

It was Mayberry with an attitude. This hamlet of Perry in the 1930s , forties, fifties, and sixties. A "David," as in David and Goliath. "Hoosiers" and "Glory Road," all rolled into one. No one exemplified this "Mayberry with an attitude"—a winning attitude—more than the man whose memory we honor here today. Eric Pierce Staples—'Fessor, to most of us.

Still, I don't come today to talk about the winning. It, the winning, has been and will be told so well by others. They tell of the remarkable record and the many victories and the numerous championships. They talk about his record, unequaled in all of the United States of America. And even after we leave, after the excitement of this day passes, the reminders will remain, emblazoned on these hallowed walls for all to see and ponder and, in awe, consider. It is well that it be this way, because 'Fessor and this town at these times were "winners."

From student and principal, to player and coach, and finally to attorney and client, capped by many hours in his latter years spent by the two of us as just friends, visiting and talking and reminiscing. I believe I had a somewhat unique relationship with 'Fessor. From all of this contact, I have concluded that 'Fessor was not a great man because he was a winner, but that he was a winner because he was a great man. That his positive impact on this little community and during these times was publicly acclaimed because of his winnings, but the winning was not the reason for his greatness.

First, the town and the times. A town and a time when 'Fessor strode over all like the Colossus of Rhodes. A time when those who were allowed to participate, based on genetic fortune of white birth, were united in purpose and spirit as never before, or somewhat sadly, since.

Basketball goals in the backyards of almost every white, male

14

youngster in Perry. Dreams of wearing the maroon and gold jacket. Accurate knowledge that the millionaire's son and the mechanic's son had equal opportunity to be a "starter" for 'Fessor's Panthers. It was ability, attitude, and work ethic that mattered, and not chance of birth. Assumption that Perry would win—both by Perry and its opponents. That the Giant Killer would dispose of the Laniers, and the Willinghams, and the Griffins, and the big Atlanta schools, and even the "small giants"—the Viennas, and the Montezumas, and the Cochrans, and the Fort Valleys. That glory for the players and school and community would follow, and there would be pride in a united community and certainty of recognition of players by the community leaders.

But, you say with all truthfulness, there were other towns with better athletes and outstanding coaches—the Glen Cassells, and the Norman Faircloths, and the Bill Martins, and the J. B. Hawkinses, and the Jimmy Maffets, and the Selby Bucks, and the Tom Porters, and the Henry Middlebrooks, and the Bobby Gentrys, and the Country Childs—and still 'Fessor and his Panthers won. And we ask, why? And the jaded answers come: great teacher, great psychologist, outstanding knowledge of the game. Great assistants in Mr. Frank Holland, Paul Hartman, Bob Shuler, and Herb St. John. All of these answers being absolutely true. But let me suggest different and other answers to compete with and supplement those so often given.

'Fessor was a fundamental man. He was fundamental in his religious beliefs as evidenced by his faithfulness to the Perry Methodist Church as a member and as a men's Bible class teacher over several decades. He was fundamental in his job as principal of Perry High School as evidenced by the order and discipline he demanded and his school's outstanding academic and literary achievements, again over several decades. 'Fessor was fundamental in his coaching—always back to the basics of passing, bounce-passing, get the open shot, play defense, and don't let 'em get the baseline. Whether dealing with starters from a state-championship team or a completely new starting five, at the beginning of every season, he always went back to the basics.

And 'Fessor never forgot the little boy or girl, the student ignored by most, the country boy shunned by many, the frightened and lonely girl just moved to the new school. Oh, on the basketball team his strongest, smoothest, and best prevailed. But in the school, in the classroom, in the halls or lunchroom, he was quick with a kind word for a homely girl or a pat on the poor, small boy's fanny. All the while encouraging and including so that all felt a part of his school and their school.

Was he great because he won? Or was he a winner because he was a great and a good man?

Then my time came. My time to play as a starter. I had been on the 1959 state-championship team, playing little, and none, as I can recall, in the state tournament. But then it was the 1959 to 1960 season, and I became one of the starting five. A starter on a team about which this is written in the 1960 Perry High School yearbook, the Panther: "Following Perry's most exciting football season in six years, which proved to be the downfall of our basketball team by injuries to Wilson and Lee Martin and by forcing the Panthers to play a three game a week schedule, came an off year for Perry's Hardwood Aces."

An off year indeed! 'Fessor's only losing season in thirty-six years! And yet I learned so much, about myself and about the little boy or disheartened girl. A man who won because he was great and wasn't great because he won.

Try as I may, what I am trying to say was put so much better by Pat Conroy in his book *My Losing Season*. Listen to Conroy's words:

> There is no downside to winning. It feels forever fabulous. But there is no teacher more discriminating or transforming than loss. The great secret of athletics is that you can learn more from losing than winning. No coach can afford to preach such a doctrine, but our losing season served as both model and template of how a life can go wrong and fall apart in even the most inconceivable places.... You have to take the word "loser" and add it to your resume and walk around with it on your name tag as it hand-feeds you your own stuff [*sic*] in dosages too large for even great beasts to swallow. The word "loser" follows you, bird-dogs you, sniffs you out of whatever fields you hide in because you have to face things clearly and you cannot turn away from what is true.

My team, the 1959–60 Perry High School Panthers, won nine and lost twelve. The record says "losers." The reality was "winners." We were exposed to greatness. A living legend was our coach. He made this basketball loser a "dealing with life" winner.

And so, like every boy who ever wore the maroon and gold and played for 'Fessor, it ended for me. But his lessons to me live on: it's the basics that count—the fundamentals, eat right and get rest, practice hard and often, stay in shape, wait for the open shot, the church and spiritual things are important, don't let 'em get the baseline.

Good lesson for life. And isn't that what 'Fessor was all about?

'Fessor wasn't great because he won. He won—on the basketball court and the golf course and at Perry High School and in the community and in life—his life and so many other lives—because he was a great man.

I

GNAT LINE LIFE

GEORGIA BELOW THE GNAT LINE

When I went to the Georgia House of Representatives in 1973, my district number was 100. What this meant, in part, was that there were approximately eighty house members in Georgia who lived south of me and approximately ninety-nine house members who lived north of me.

When I left the Georgia House in 2004, my district number was 146. That would mean that there were thirty-four house members in Georgia south of my district and 145 north.

In 1973 we had not fully "weaned" ourselves from the effects of the old county unit system, and the 1973 numbers were probably skewed in favor of south Georgia to some extent. But there was no doubt about the strong political influence and clout south of the gnat line.

Jimmy Carter from Plains was governor when I got to Atlanta. He served the final two years of his governorship, and then the people of Georgia elected George Busbee from Albany for two terms, eight years. Georgians haven't had a governor from south Georgia since George Busbee in 1982 unless you count Sonny Perdue, who lived on the gnat line in Bonaire. We've had some great governors since 1973, including Nathan Deal, from Gainesville, but none from south of the gnat line.

Ah, the "gnat line." It's that imaginary line that follows the fall line, splits the Piedmont plateau, and is a line running from Columbus, just south of Macon, to Augusta, south of which there are abundant gnats, and upon which there are sometimes gnats and sometimes not, and with the "sometimes are" usually prevailing. The political power in this state is now north of the gnat line. The gnats are on or south of the gnat line.

We have fourteen US congressmen from Georgia. Five have substantial districts south of the gnat line. The other nine are to the north. The congressional districts in the south are, geographically, very large. In fact, there is a tremendous amount of geography south of the gnat line. And while there are "pockets of prosperity," many communities, once prosperous and vibrant, are dead or on life support and have little hope for anything better. Many of our colleges to the south are losing enrollment. Some of the hospitals in the south are in financial trouble.

When I was in the state legislature, I was close friends with Joe Frank Harris, one-time chairman of the House Appropriations Committee and later governor of Georgia. He was, and is, from Cartersville in north Georgia. I was also a close friend to Marcus Collins, a big, burly farmer (his arms were bigger than my legs) from Cotton, Georgia, Mitchell County, in deep, south Georgia. Marcus chaired the House Ways and Means Committee.

Joe Frank and Marcus were good friends. Joe Frank seldom allowed any agitation to show, even if he was irritated. Marcus was constantly saying to Joe Frank, "We never get any money south of the gnat line." One day, in an exasperated tone, Appropriations Committee chairman Joe Frank responded, "Exactly where is the gnat line?" Marcus retorted in his deep Southern drawl, "Well, it's that line below which we never get any money."

South Georgia, at least most of it, needs help. The solutions are difficult and perhaps financially impossible. But at a minimum, in my opinion, something must be done about the inadequacies of many of the public schools and some of the hospitals in the southern part of our state. I know that work is being done, but more needs to be done.

It seems to me that it will be very difficult to get new industries, with the much-needed jobs, to locate in south Georgia communities where there are many marginal public schools and much non-sustainable healthcare.

I've talked to lots of people about this matter. Most all agree that something needs to be done, but few have ideas of anything that possibly could help. An exception to this is Lindsay Thomas.

Lindsay, who lives on his family homeplace in Wayne County, is a former member of Congress (ten years) and later the executive director of the state Chamber of Commerce. Lindsay can articulate the problems much better than I. He has realistic ideas about things that might help.

One of Lindsay's intriguing suggestions is that there be a concentration on ecotourism, with our state parks being expanded and improved to the extent that they become tourist destinations. Lindsay envisions such things as river rafting, fishing, quail hunting, camping, hiking, and similar opportunities to entice Georgians and non-Georgians to spend time and money in south Georgia.

My idea is that the state, through tax and other incentives, encourage ag industry—fertilizer plants, equipment manufacturers, feed plants, etc. In other words, try to pair industries with agricultural interests and workers who know about agriculture. And, by the way, we do have some of the best farmers in the world south of the gnat line, as is evidenced by our state's leadership in pecans, peanuts, peaches, timber, blueberries, cotton, onions, and other crops.

What about some government consolidations? But I won't go there this time. However, I do think it's like Marcus tried to tell Joe Frank many years ago: we are going to have to spend some more money south of the gnat line.

FROM MULES TO THE MOON

I take my title from Frank McGill's little book *From the Mule to the Moon*, which I found to be not only interesting but also something to which I could really relate. Especially the mule part.

A mule does not reproduce. And while there are male mules and female mules, it is actually a hybrid, being the offspring of a mare (female horse) and a jackass (male donkey). Theoretically, there could be no mules in the world for 100 years, and assuming you had female horses and male donkeys, you could have a mule in approximately eleven months.

My grandfather Walker (Papa) was a mule farmer. He and my grandmother owned about 400 acres in Washington County, Georgia, but Papa actually cultivated about 150 acres. As I can best remember, Papa usually had about four mules, and the 150 acres were cultivated with these mules. I can specially remember the names of three of them: Molly, Dixie, and Kate. Molly was stubborn and had a mean streak. Kate was gentle and kind and was Papa's favorite. I cannot remember much about Dixie's personality. I do remember that all of his mules were important. Without the mules, there would be no crops. Without crops, there would be no money. Without money, there would be no survival.

It is now difficult to comprehend how important mules were to the economy of the South and Georgia, in particular, even as recently as the 1950s. I have made a speech in which I said that "in the 1930s, there were almost as many mules in Georgia as there were people." While this was a bit of hyperbole, there were literally hundreds of thousands of mules in our state at one time. Now you would be hard-pressed to find a mule in our county of Houston.

One of the last Perry mules that I remember was owned by Mr. Lawrence Bannister. In my mind, I can see him in his mule-drawn wagon winding his way through the streets of Perry. Exactly what he was doing, I do not know. Perhaps he was hauling firewood or other commodities for sale. In any event, he and his wagon and mule were part of the local scene. I suspect he would have a difficult time out on Sam Nunn Boulevard today (or maybe the motorist would have a hard time), if he and his mule were still alive and operating.

Much of the economy of the South, prior to the 1950s, was dependent on the mule. They are good, sturdy, indefatigable animals. They have never gotten their just recognition. That is why I secured money for the Mule and Tenant Farmer Statue at the Georgia National Fair and Ag Center.

And now to the "moon" part of my title. Everyone knows about the moon and man's exploration of the moon. Many, including myself, think that the moon affects the way people act and react, as well as crops, animals, etc. We know that the moon affects the ocean tides. People in my law office know that the "crazies" come out when the moon is full. I can add little to this, and, after all, I guess that I am just more interested in the mule. Enough said.

PAPA WAS A TRUE RENAISSANCE MAN

For those of you who know or knew us—Daddy, David, Lynda, Charlie, and me—it might come as a surprise to you that all the Walkers are not short, small people. In fact, my Grandfather Walker, Papa, had a brother, Uncle Charlie (one of fifteen brothers and sisters), who was a tall, large man, as were his children. Several of Papa's other siblings were above average in height. So, there are some big Walkers, although Papa himself was a small man. About like Daddy.

Daddy came to Houston County in the late thirties and left when he died, March of 2002. He used to say "I weighed 135 pounds when I came here, and I will weigh 135 pounds when I leave." Papa was about five feet six inches and maybe 150 pounds or less. He was a small man. It is about Papa that I write today. Papa died on January 30, 1958, and these are my memories of him, the accuracy being tested by the erosion of time.

I've told you he was small. He was also quiet, largely uneducated, and unsophisticated. Except on Sundays, and when he went to Sandersville or Sparta on Saturdays, he wore overalls and sensible brogan shoes. I don't know for sure—I've never heard it discussed—but I am confident that he did not graduate from high school. It wouldn't surprise me to learn that he never even attended high school.

The only thing I ever saw him read was a newspaper and, perhaps, *The Progressive Farmer*. He listened to Grandma or me or another grandchild read the Bible, but I never saw him read it himself. To my knowledge, he never held any kind of an office—not even one in the church or a farmer's organization. Until I wrote about him, other than his obituary, I doubt that his name ever appeared in print. All in all, an unimportant, not particularly significant person? I don't think so. Let me tell you why.

Papa could do so many things. Often, he did most of these things in a single day. Let me give you some examples. He could hitch up the mules to the right plows for the day's work. He could plow a mule—planting, cultivating, fertilizing, or whatever it took to get the job done. He ran his and Grandma's tiny country store, keeping it supplied and turning enough of a profit, small though it was, to help with the living. He could build a birdhouse, a rabbit box, or a porch on the house. He could, and did, make many slingshots out of tree branches, and rubber inner-tubes, and strings. He hand-milked the cow every evening and strained the milk for drinking, cooking, and making butter. He killed hogs, made soap, and cured meat. He could barbeque a hog—and did every Independence Day. He could, and did for me, identify all the birds and trees. He always had a ripe watermelon for us by July 4 (although I've eaten a few on that day that weren't completely ripe!) He cut and kept wood for the stove and oven. He kept a good garden—every year! He made syrup. He could fool you into eating a green persimmon—one time! He could fix most anything and did.

Evidence of this gift is still with us. He kept fishing poles (cane) "rigged up" (black nylon line, cork, lead, and hook) at Grandma's request—although I never remember him doing any fishing. He had a fish bait-bed and catalpa trees. He could cut an absolutely perfect hole in an orange for sucking or strip sugarcane for chewing. He grew the cane but not the oranges. He could cure most any cut or scrape or hurt with kerosene. He once killed an alligator in Alligator Creek (was that the creek's name before or after the killing?) and hauled the amphibious reptile out with a mule.

He worked every day except Sunday, regardless of the weather or how he felt. I guess he even milked the cow and fed the livestock and brought wood to the stove on Sunday. He could sharpen an ax or knife or hoe. In short, it appeared to me that he could do most anything. A true Renaissance man.

Uneducated? Unsophisticated? Unimportant? I hardly think so. In fact, I believe that he is one of the most important people that ever lived—at least to me. Thanks David Flournoy Walker of Warthen, Georgia. Thanks, Papa. I loved you, miss you, and even after all these years, think of you often.

II

MY SOUTH, MY MEMORIES

PERRY IS WHERE I WANT TO BE

I'm where I want to be.

I'll be here for the rest of what's left, and then my folks will have me placed in beautiful Evergreen Cemetery next to whoever beats me there. So far it's just Daddy. Momma is ninety-eight, but she still lives in her own home with someone to look after her. It's not a stretch to think I might go to Evergreen before she does.

I've always wanted to be right here in Middle Georgia, Perry to be exact. I never had that "can't wait to get out of here" feeling.

I guess I could have gone to Atlanta and probably made more money. "More money" would have been nice, but not nice enough to spend a large part of my life trying to get from where I was to where I wanted to be. As it is, I'm ten to fifteen minutes, at most, to the dry cleaners, church, fishing ponds, children and grandchildren, and even the doctor and our fine little hospital.

Truthfully, I've spent lots of time in Atlanta tending to my business and the people's business. I've been there enough to know I could have competed up there. I just never wanted to spend my life anywhere but where I started.

I graduated from Perry High School in 1960. It was a good school. In fact, it was an excellent school. It had outstanding teachers. I was coached by three Georgia Sports Hall of Fame coaches—Eric Staples, Herb St. John, and Bill Chappell. Not many student athletes can truthfully claim this.

Perry, though certainly not perfect, was and is a fine town. It's clean—physically and politically—and the many strong churches have a positive influence. The same people who run the schools and churches run the government. It's not that way in lots of places.

I went to the University of Georgia about two weeks out of high school in the summer of 1960. I was back in Perry in 1965 with a business degree and a law degree. Come next June 25, to be exact, I will have been practicing law in downtown Perry for fifty-four years, and I have been in the same building that I built in 1969 since Labor Day that year. I am now working harder than I ever have.

Janice and I have four children and nine grandchildren, all of whom except one (he's in Decatur and one that's at University of Georgia) live within fifteen miles of us. This is really nice.

When I started in Perry years ago, we didn't have air conditioning or television. Now we have both. In fact, I believe that Janice and I have six televisions, although all but two are pretty old. It's nice to be cool in the summer, warm in the winter, and to be able to watch the Georgia Bulldogs when you are not even at the game.

I still talk slowly and with a drawl. I talk the way most folks who lived on the Piedmont Plateau used to talk. Most folks that live here today learned to talk from television. I learned to talk from listening to good people talk in the feed store and the tractor place. If I had gone to Atlanta to make a living, I would've had to speed up and enunciate better, and that just wouldn't have been me.

There's been lots of progress in our area during the years I've been here. I've been a part of this progress. Thanks to those who let me participate. I'm where I want to be.

EARLY WORK WAS GOOD FOR ME

Our government periodically reminds me that I paid my first Social Security in 1957. I was fifteen years old. Supposedly, I didn't pay in 1958, but I've paid every year since, and I intend to for at least a few more years.

I played Junior League baseball until I aged out. I played high school football and basketball, but I didn't play golf. Daddy had me working, and he didn't think too much of me hanging out at the country club.

There is lots of emphasis in our society on recreation, and "our government" puts lots of money into recreation. I know recreation can be good, but in looking back on the young part of my life, I know that my work experiences, when young, helped me much more than my play experiences. Let me make my case.

When very young, I mowed lawns. I mowed our lawn for free but had several paying (not too much pay!) customers. Very few youngsters "mow for the public" today. Do you ever have young boys coming around asking to mow or rake yards? Probably not. Why?

First, lots of people have expensive mowing machines and mow their own yards. And there are many lawn services that mow and rake leaves, etc. There's not much yard work available for twelve- to fourteen-year-old boys to do even if our government would allow it.

My brother David and I boiled and sold peanuts on the streets and in the stores of downtown Perry. In season, on Saturday mornings, we'd prepare and sell around 120 bags for ten cents a bag. It would take about three hours to get 'em ready and about one hour to sell 'em. We'd put the money in the bank. We learned a lot—about commerce, saving, and people. This knowledge has served us well.

It would be hard for youngsters to sell boiled peanuts in Perry today. Hardy Farms, a large company with a very good product, about has a corner on the market. And would store owners and those in charge at the courthouse and city hall let youngsters hawk peanuts in their domains? I doubt it. It's not like it used to be.

I worked at Tabor's packing shed up on US 41 in Peach County for two years. Later, it burned to the ground. The first summer I made sixty-five cents an hour helping Charlie Etheridge put peach labels on the baskets. They don't put labels on baskets today. In fact, they don't use baskets today. The next year, Pierce and Porter Staples and I put liners in basket tops for eighty-five cents an hour. They don't do this either anymore.

I picked cotton two seasons at Daddy's farm—all day, every day, for several weeks and with the other cotton pickers. Nobody picks cotton by hand anymore—at least, nobody in this country. I'm glad. I despised picking cotton, but it was probably good for me.

I helped haul chicken feed to hot, stinky chicken houses one summer. The work was hard (a 135-pound boy loading and unloading 100-pound sacks of Purina Layena) and there was an odor that couldn't be cured by OdoBan. Now, all the feeding is mechanized and is probably furnished by one of the big companies that buys the chickens. Too bad, young, willing boys.

Do you think there is a steel mill left in this country? If so, do you think they would hire four college boys with no experience to help make steel? I doubt it, but it certainly is a loss to helping boys turn into men. Four of us did this in 1963.

I worked at Billy Bledsoe's Swank Shop in downtown Perry. It was a men's clothing store (very nice clothing), and I learned lots from Billy about style, how to dress, and how to sell. I also learned how to talk! Work for young people in retail mercantile business is hard to come by today.

Interestingly, there was a column in an old issue of *The Washington Post* by Richard Cohen called "The Price of the Great Disruption" that has these words: "Technology is killing the American middle class.... [C]ar companies and Google are working on driverless cars that could... eliminate the jobs of 3.5 million truck drivers, not to mention cooks and waitresses at thousands of truck stops."

Young people trying to learn about commerce and the capitalistic system while trying to make a little money are at the very bottom of the hire chain. I doubt they will ever have the work experiences I had. How unfortunate and sad.

CREEKS WERE BETTER THAN
GO-CARTS AND PONIES

I never had a go-cart. Some of my children did, and the aggravating things stayed broken more than working. I never had a pony, but I had a cousin who did—and a saddle plus a full Roy Rogers outfit, including hat, shirt, pants, a cowboy guitar, cap pistols, and most anything else he wanted.

But I did have something that was better, much better, than a go-cart or pony. I had access to creeks in which I could play, and what a joy it was. Let me write of a few examples.

I've been mudding in Alligator Creek. "They" say that Papa killed an alligator with his shotgun in a creek on his farm in rural Washington County. That was many, many years ago. I wonder if that's where and why Alligator Creek got its name. I suspect so.

Back to the mudding. It was the children of the lady who lived on Papa's farm and me. We dammed up the creek and muddied the water with our feet. Then we caught the fish that swam to the top. They kept 'em and ate 'em. What excitement and fun.

Pierce Staples and I caught crawfish in Fannie Gresham Branch (a branch is a junior creek, at least that's what I think). Fannie Gresham runs into Big Indian Creek at the Dr. A. G. Hendrick Bridge. Fannie Gresham was partially on Mr. Whit Traylor's property. Mr. Whit Traylor was Pierce's granddaddy. The place where we caught the crawfish is right across Washington Street from the Perry City Hall and just below Jake Goddard's State Farm Agency. I'll bet there are still some crawfish there. One day I might go down there and check it out. I wonder who owns that land now.

It's a wonder we didn't keep the crawfish and eat 'em. Mrs. Staples would cook most anything that Pierce brought home, including robins and pigeons that Pierce (and occasionally Pierce and I) killed and cleaned. Pigeons weren't too bad, but I didn't like the robins.

I've grappled for redhorse suckers in Mossy Creek with Jerry "Do-Tricks" Horton and Jerry Wilson. Do-Tricks wasn't afraid of anything. I was afraid of lots of things, including riding, one time, on the back of his motorcycle with him. But back to grappling. Every time I put my hands under the water next to a root or rock, I thought for sure I would pull a big moccasin out from its hiding place. But I couldn't let the other two do it and me not do it. And what fun I've had telling about it for well over fifty years.

A couple of years ago, Janice and I, along with Dink and Pam NeSmith, went to Mississippi and Tennessee, ending up on Saturday night in Tunica, Mississippi, to see Jerry Lee Lewis in concert, and what a show "The Killer" put on. But this is not another article about Jerry Lee Lewis; it's an article about creeks. That's why we tried to write down the name of every creek we crossed that had a sign on the highway, from Perry to Atlanta to Oxford, Mississippi, to Memphis, Tennessee, and back.

Well, here they are: Big Indian Creek, Mossy Creek, Echeconnee Creek, Tobesofkee Creek, Gum Creek, Reeds Creek, Mantachie Creek, Mud Creek, Hurricane Creek, Horn Lake Creek, Hell Creek, King Creek, and Tulip Creek.

Interesting creek names. If you count "Big Indian" as an Indian name, five of the creeks are Indian names. And what about Gum? The tree? Mud Creek is pretty evident and, apparently, Horn Lake Creek was named after Horn Lake. Is this lake shaped like a horn? And what about Hell Creek? Your guess is as good as mine. Then there's Tulip Creek, which, again, is probably named after the tree.

We probably crossed over fifty creeks or branches between Perry and Memphis, but the one's listed above were the only ones that merited a sign with the name on it. There were very few creek name signs in Alabama.

And, yes, as some of you will remember, several years ago, Larry III and I turned a canoe over in Big Indian Creek three times on a cool spring day to the ultimate delight of several onlookers. It was some kind of Chamber or Development Authority deal to see if Big Indian was navigable. Larry (the older) and Larry III proved that it was not!

So many creeks, so much fun. Oh, to be fifteen years old again.

LORDY, HOW DID WE EVER GET GROWN?

"Don't cross your eyes like that, they might get stuck and you will be cross-eyed the rest of your life." If you are as old as I am, you've heard it, haven't you? Our parents and grandparents warned us, we listened, and the advice worked. I don't know one soul who got their eyes "stuck," even temporarily, much less for a lifetime.

"Getting your eyes stuck" was a fear, but perhaps not even in the top ten of our concerns. For example, it wasn't even close to "being careful of snakes." I mean, I know that snakes (a few of them) can be dangerous, but I never knew hardly anyone who got bitten. I used to say "I didn't know anyone" until my friend Riley Hunt told me about getting struck by a rattler when he was young. With me, it was yellow jackets and wasps and "stumped toes." I once got stung by a bumblebee in the middle of my back (didn't have my shirt on). Man, it hurt! But Grandma never said to me, "Be careful and watch for bumble bees"—it was always snakes. The "Garden of Eden experience" may have affected her thinking.

Speaking of the Garden of Eden, what about tithing? We were taught it was very important—in fact, mandatory. We had those little white envelopes at church, and 10 percent of our boiled-peanut money was inserted and given. I looked up "tithe" in the dictionary. It says "a tenth part of one's annual income." I've always thought we were fortunate. What if 11.2735 percent had been called for? Never would have figured it out, would we? Apparently, most folks today have trouble calculating the 10 percent. In our family, and unlike "getting your eyes stuck," I would put tithing in my top ten.

Lockjaw was talked about a considerable amount. It, and ground itch. About the same amount of concern given to both. "Be careful that you don't step on a nail, you might get lockjaw. Don't walk in the dew, you will get the ground itch." I'm proud to say that I never knew anyone to have lockjaw. And I never heard anyone admit to having the ground itch. Ringworms, yes. Athlete's foot, yes. Jock itch, yes. Ground itch, no.

I'm not saying they didn't have it, but I never heard anyone admit to it.

Speaking of admitting to things, regularity has become a major concern. Or is the concern irregularity? Lots of talk about it on television. When we were young, castor oil was about the only answer. Now, a whole industry has grown up around it, and I can tell it is a major concern. Folks don't come up to you and say, "I have irregularity." But you can just tell by how so many of them act. Good thing that there is so much help available. Too bad more of them, and especially store clerks and fast-food employees, don't take advantage of what is available. It might help their attitudes.

White teeth. That's become extremely important. It seems to have replaced lockjaw as a major concern. And efforts seem to be working. Have you noticed that so many of the young men and women have such white teeth? I believe that the effort to whiten teeth is meeting with more success than the regularity effort.

But back to an earlier-in-time top-ten concern. It was "you can't go swimming right after eating." You had to wait a couple of hours. I think the fear was that you might get cramps and drown. This was serious. Not quite up to the concerns about snakes. After all, the Bible-based snake fear trumped the American Red Cross swimming concerns.

While on the swimming subject, what about the correlation between public swimming pools and polio? Perry used to have a concrete swimming pool (I think they filled it with a garden hose) down by the National Guard Armory, which is now the Perry Arts Center and across from the Hollands' house (which now sits at Henderson Village). Vaguely, I seem to recall that polio concerns caused it to be closed. Was this in the early fifties? In any event, this was definitely a "top ten concern."

We've had and have lots to be worried about. And I haven't even mentioned red bugs. Now you want to talk about something that will make you miserable. Especially with where they chose to embed themselves. This was a major concern when I was a boy, and if these chiggers get on you, it will be a major concern with you today. No medicine, including Chigger Rid, seems to do any good. If we could just get the regularity folks working on this, perhaps they could come up with something. I would like to remove this as one of my major concerns. Red bugs, that is.

JUST ANOTHER SILLY LOVE SONG

Often, you cannot help what you think about. Oh, you can force yourself to think about something—what do I need to get at the grocery store, did I leave the keys in the car, am I supposed to speak at the Kiwanis Club next week or the week after, etc. But just as often, maybe more often in my case, things just pop into my head, and there they are for me to ponder. The thoughts won't leave me alone.

Recently, I've been thinking about our little yellow house (and yes, it's still yellow) at the corner of Swift and Third, where I grew up. Let me be more specific. It's the little room, my room for a while, when it smelled new and was new, that Mama and Daddy added on the back of our house when I was a teenager. Probably about fifteen or sixteen years old. I do remember "my" room, but, again, that's not my main reoccurring memory.

I had a 45-rpm record player. One of those that accommodated little records with big holes in the middle and with the capacity to hold, what, ten or so records, to drop down one at a time, until all ten had played. But that's too general for what I've been thinking about. Specifically, it's one of the songs, really the only song I can say with certainty that I played over and over.

"Lavender Blue" by Sammy Turner. Most of you have never heard of it or don't remember it, but I do. I was just getting interested in girls, and I knew I liked to dance, and I loved "Lavender Blue" by Sammy Turner. As I say, I think about it often and with good, warm feelings when I do. And it, and others, made me know I loved music—most all kinds, excusing jazz and opera.

And then it was Elvis. Controversial Elvis. Would my folks let me listen to his music or watch him on our little black-and-white television? Then, before we knew it, Elvis was too big to be avoided or ignored. You had to watch him. Next, the Beatles burst on the scene with "I Wanna Hold Your Hand" and "Hey Jude." And the black artist began to dominate—Chubby Checker and "The Twist," Marvin Gaye and "I Heard It through the Grapevine," and Ray Charles and "I Can't Stop Loving You."

Then, before I knew it, I was out of UGA Law and back in Perry practicing law, and then to the legislature and with Carly Simon, Barbra Streisand, and "Silly Love Songs" by Wings. But, mostly, for me, in the 1970s, it was the Bee Gees with "How Deep Is Your Love" and "Night Fever" and Andy Gibb and his "Shadow Dancing."

With little thought of Sammy Turner's "Lavender Blue," the eighties were here with Diana Ross's "Upside Down" and "Endless Love," and "Lady" by Kenny Rogers. I noticed that the decades were getting shorter, but the music was still good: Toni Braxton's "Un-Break My Heart" and Whitney Houston's "I Will Always Love You."

And all the while, it was old and new: the Platters, Frank Sinatra, the Four Tops, Willie Nelson, George Strait, Garth Brooks, "Crazy" by Patsy Cline, the Dixie Cups, the Tams, the Swingin' Medallions, Little Richard, Chicago, Ray Charles and "Georgia on My Mind," Shania Twain, Reba, Conway Twitty, etc., etc.

Now, we were beginning a new century, and the computers didn't crash and the music kept coming. But for me, it was more of the old and more country. "Motown" and "Small Town." That was me.

But without a doubt, the music that has influenced my life the most was and is what I broadly refer to as "church music." And I was in a good place to be influenced: the Perry Methodist Church.

My friend Bob Messer says it best when he talks about our church's long tradition of great choir leaders that go back for 100 years or more and includes Francis Nunn, the volunteer choir leader, and before him, his mother, Bessie Houser Nunn. And today, Jane Kimbrel as director of music ministries, who is excellent in all respects.

So, "church music" has had the most influence on me. I've heard wonderful gospel music sung at Homecoming, Pinehill Methodist, the Mormon Tabernacle Choir in Salt Lake City, and the Blind Boys of Alabama in concert. This church music has marked me. But, of late, when I lie down at night, I hear Sammy Turner singing "Lavender Blue," and you can see here the flood of memories this one little 45-rpm record player has spawned, and how long it has lasted.

THINGS I'VE LEARNED AS
I'VE GOTTEN OLDER

I've learned that you can leave your problems at work and pick 'em up the next morning. Seldom do I take problems home with me.

I've learned that family is the most important thing in my world. Daddy told me. Daddy was right.

I've learned that next to family, friends are most important. I'm blessed to have lots of friends.

I've learned that from the most powerful to the meekest, all people want to be recognized and appreciated.

I've learned that if you'll let the other fellow do all the talking, you'll be surprised at how smart he or she will think you are.

I've learned that the four most important words in dealing with people are: "What do you think?" Then listen. You'll be surprised at what you'll find out, and you'll be pleased at how much they will like you.

I've learned that as to lots of things I really wanted, when I got 'em, they didn't give me nearly the pleasure I thought they would.

I've learned that my work experiences as a youngster have meant much more to me than my play experiences.

I've learned that I've learned much more from my failures than I have from my successes.

I've learned that much of my success is because I have surrounded myself with folks who are smarter than I am.

I've learned that life is fast. Daddy liked to say that "the days get longer and the years get shorter." Again, Daddy was right.

I've learned that the church or mosque or synagogue or whatever you call yours is what helps to hold society together and keeps us from having anarchy.

I've learned to slow down as life has speeded up. You can get to Atlanta almost as fast at 70 as you can at 79—and you stand a better chance at getting there safer.

I've learned that dogs are a lot smarter than I thought they were and that our national leaders are not nearly as smart as they need to be.

I've learned that wisdom and common sense are rare commodities in today's leadership market.

I've learned that too many folks are against more than they are for and that it's easier to tear down a house than it is to build one.

I've learned that athletes are bigger, stronger, and faster today but not necessarily tougher, smarter, or have more heart.

I've learned that technological advancements don't necessarily make things faster or easier or make their users happier.

I've learned that everyone wants peace of mind and that so many don't have it and never will.

I've learned that the most powerful thing in the world are the words "I love you" from someone who means them.

I've learned that most of us want mercy and not justice and, fortunately, that's what most of us get.

I've learned that I will never understand why I was born of good parents in the most affluent country in the world when so many were not.

I've learned that there is lots of style but much less class and that class has nothing to do with money, position, intelligence, or style.

I've learned that a smile and words like "please," "thank you," "please forgive me," and "I forgive you" will take you a long way in life.

I've learned that the busier I am, the more things I get done.

And lastly, *I've learned that* "the sun don't shine on the same dog all the time!" That's about the way it goes, isn't it?

DADDY HAD HIS RULES

I wrote something very similar to this several years ago, and about two weeks after, I wrote an article I called "Grandma Had Her Rules Too." So, now it will be about Daddy's rules and then another about Grandma's.

Yes, Daddy had his rules. They were probably Mother's rules, too. At least, she adopted them and helped enforce them. She might have formulated some of them, as far as I know. There was no "divide and conquer" in the Walker household. The rules were the rules, and we four children were expected to abide by them. And we did.

You didn't wear a hat inside the house, much less at the meal table. Today, I see wedding announcements in the newspaper and the picture of the grinning couple shows the "man" wearing a baseball cap. It wouldn't surprise me to see the bride-to-be with a cap emblazoned with a large Atlanta Braves "A" on her pretty head. Perhaps my revulsion to this grows out of Daddy's rule.

We didn't slam doors in our house. Well, that's wrong. I should say that if we slammed a door, we were admonished.

You didn't eat before the blessing was asked. You could sip your tea, but you didn't start eating until someone returned thanks. No exceptions. This was the rule.

I wasn't allowed to play marbles "for keeps." It was gambling, according to Daddy, and I was forbidden to gamble. Good thing. I wasn't a very good marble shooter and didn't own a very good "toy." Marble shooters who played for keeps will understand. Maybe if I had played for keeps, I would've gotten better.

Daddy (and Mother) saw to it that I kept my hair cut. And woe unto me if I dyed my hair or tried to grow a ducktail. I won't even get into tattoos or body piercing. I might as well have tried to rob a bank.

"Strong" language was a big no-no. Probably, I was the only child in the family who ran afoul of this rule. The last spanking I ever got was when an aggravating youngster (and he was!) reported to my parents that I had used the word "damn" by telling them, "Larry told me they would take my 'd-a-m' pants off if I didn't leave them alone." His exact words and spelling!

We, my brothers, sister, and I, were expected to work. Around the house, yes. But as we got older, "for the public." And you should know this: I was expected to get to work on time, regardless of whether I had played football the night before or had gone to the prom, getting home at a late time—like, midnight.

The Bible says we (meaning good, God-fearing Methodists) were to keep the Sabbath holy. Daddy took this literally, as well he should, and we followed suit. We didn't go to the movies, fish, hunt, work, or wash the car on Sunday. We could watch television when we finally got one. I generally don't quail hunt (the only hunting I do today) on Sunday. And when I fish on Sunday (which I frequently do) or go to the movies (which I have done, but seldom), I still have a feeling that I am violating one of Daddy's rules.

Now, do I have to tell you how Daddy and Mother may have felt about drinking alcohol or smoking or premarital sex? I don't think so. We shouldn't violate the little rules, much less the big ones.

I'm not saying we didn't ever break the rules. What I am saying is that there were rules. We understood them, and we knew that we were expected to abide by all of them. There were consequences for rule-breaking.

Am I complaining? Absolutely not! I am proud that my parents had rules. They set the parameters, explained the rules, and expected us to do what they said. There was much love and support and, in retrospect, tolerance. Isn't that the way it is supposed to work? At least, isn't that the way it works best?

'Fessor Staples had discipline and rules. He became the "winningest" basketball coach in the country. Bear Bryant was a good coach and a great disciplinarian. Look at his record. The Roman army ruled the world for thousands of years. They knew about discipline. What about the United States Marines? I could go on and on. But the point is: you can't have anything of much value without discipline. You need rules and discipline to have a successful football team, army, government, church, school, or family.

We've lost lots of discipline in our society. It's scary. But perhaps my view is a little distorted. For, after all, Daddy had his rules, and I was expected to abide by them. Thanks, Daddy and Mother. You did good. Better than I did, at times.

GRANDMA HAD HER RULES TOO

I wrote that I would write about Grandma's rules. Well, here they are. I think you'll notice a difference in the nature of her rules and how they were enforced. Actually, it's probably the difference in fathers and grandparents, and since I'm now a grandfather nine times over, I understand better than I used to.

Here they are, as best I remember them, the rules from my kind, gentle grandmother, Josephine May Walker.

Almost all of Grandma's rules had to do with either my safety or, loosely speaking, my cleanliness or hygiene (which, when I stayed with Grandma and Papa out in the country in rural Washington County, Georgia, left much to be desired).

* WATCH OUT FOR SNAKES. She must have told me this at least a thousand times. It was never spiders, yellow jackets, or dogs. It was always snakes. No, I'm not paranoid today about snakes. It's a wonder, though. I can see why many people are—I'll bet their grandmothers warned them to "look out for snakes."

* DON'T LOOK IN THE WELL. She was afraid I'd fall in. She whipped me once (not hard enough to break an egg shell) for looking in the well. Within three minutes of her telling me not to, I was looking in the well. Then for years after and until her death, she apologized and always ended with, "You're the only grandchild I ever spanked." Well, I deserved it, and it should've been administered with more conviction.

* DON'T WALK IN THE DEW (WHEN BAREFOOTED). Grandma said I might get the ground itch. I never knew anyone to get the ground itch, but Dr. Dan Callahan did, and he straightened me out on this. Like snakes, this was an oft-repeated warning.

* DON'T JUMP ON THE BED. Well, it was in the main living area—combination bedroom and den—and the temptation was mighty great. Sometimes, I jumped on the bed. So, what did Grandma do, she just repeated the rule: "Please, 'Lally boy,' don't jump on the bed." I quit,

at least temporarily.

* WASH YOUR FEET AND LEGS BEFORE YOU GO TO BED. Now, I had been out all day long on dirt roads and in the fields with Papa and jumping ditches looking for maypops and building toady frog houses, and all I had to do was wash my legs and feet (in a little white porcelain pan on the back porch) before I went to bed. I didn't have to wash my ears (which Mother said were "scaly" when she and Daddy came to Washington County to get me after, say, a two-week visit in the country) or my face or my little tanned stomach or back—just my feet and legs. That was it, and it was nice. Better than at home!

Two more I can remember. I'll call one "medical" and one "safety." First, hygiene.

* GET THE KEROSENE. When any injury occurred, such as stumped toes and mashed fingers or cut fingers and toes (on two separate occasions I cut my foot with the hatchet), it was always, "Get the kerosene." And it worked. A rag was soaked in kerosene and tied around the injury. It took the pain away, and it kept infection in check. That's one reason I keep a can of kerosene on the farm today.

And lastly.

*SAY YOUR PRAYERS BEFORE YOU GO TO SLEEP. That was after we'd read the Bible together. I'd call that "safety." Wouldn't you?

Yes, Grandma, like Daddy, had her rules. Grandma's were easier to live with, and if you didn't exactly follow the rules, the results were not as severe. I sure did love her.

MEMORIES OF WASHINGTON
COUNTY, GEORGIA

I originally wrote this article on December 17, 2001, and I reread it recently. I like the article and feel stronger about what this experience did for me than when I first wrote it seventeen years ago. For good or bad, and I think mostly good, I was marked by my time in the country in Washington County. Here it is.

My Walker Grandparents lived "out in the country," even by rural Georgia standards. Their house in Washington County was between the Sparta-Davisboro Road and Centralia Rachels Road. Both were dirt until the Sparta-Davisboro Road was paved sometime probably in the 1970s. I loved to visit my grandparents and spent many summer days, portions of Christmas holidays, and other times with them.

Papa, my grandfather, was a mule farmer and had a country store. In the summer, most days started with instructions to the tenants ("hands") as to which mule to use and where to go and plow (plant, get the grass and weeds out of the crop, lay-by, etc.). This was followed by visits to the store from saw-millers and others for their daily supply of groceries (Vienna sausages, potted meat, cheese, crackers, cookies, and more). About 8:00 A.M., Papa would close the store and we would be off to the various fields to check on the hands. Sometimes we rode a mule-pulled sled with guano (fertilizer), sometimes we rode in the wagon pulled by Papa's two mules, but as often as not, we walked. It was not unusual for Papa to spend most of the rest of the day doing his share of the plowing or planting with an implement pulled by a mule.

But it was not all work. Papa had a pond, and my Uncle Eugene and Aunt Ila had a pond about a quarter of a mile down the road, and my Uncle Carlie and Aunt Mary Lizzie had a pond about a quarter of a mile down the road. These ponds are where I learned to fish and where I learned to love to fish. And let me tell you, my first cousin James Maddox and I caught lots of nice fish out of these ponds.

In the fall or early winter of the year, when the weather was "right" (cold but not freezing), Grandma and Papa, with the help of my Aunt Lillian, killed hogs. Oftentimes, I was there. What excitement! This is where I learned that our meat came from the farmer and the farmer's hogs and not the Kroger store.

Papa and Uncle Eugene made syrup—the unfortunate mule going round and round, crushing the cane juice into a large vat for cooking. Papa and Grandma burned wood in stoves for cooking and heating, and Papa and I would ride the wagon to the sawmill to get slabs (the bark sides of the trees not fit for lumber) for the wood-burning supply. I squirrel hunted in Washington County with my Uncle Jim Maddox and visited the kinfolks in the area with Grandma. They would sit for hours on the porch talking—mostly about the church, weather, and other relatives—but sometimes about politics and world events. I was all ears. I learned a great deal from these smart, industrious, good, and kind people.

On Saturday, we would go to Sandersville and sometimes I would get to go to a movie at the Pastime or Arcade theaters. Yes, Sandersville had two picture shows! Once a year, we would have to get a typhoid shot at the Washington County courthouse in Sandersville. I really dreaded that! It hurt and made your arm sore for a few days.

Pinehill Methodist Church was our destination on Sunday for Sunday school and then singing and preaching. Rarely did we miss a Sunday when I was visiting. Once a year was homecoming at the church, with delicious food and great gospel singing. Grandma and Papa and Uncle Jim and Aunt Lillian now rest at Pinehill United Methodist. Also, my Daddy's brother Clyde, who was killed in a hunting accident at age fifteen, is buried there. I try to visit the cemetery when I am in the area.

Often, when I lay down in the bed at night, my thoughts turn to Washington County. It was all so wonderful and did so much to mold my life. Thanks, Papa, for trying to answer all my questions. Thanks for telling me what kind every bird was and the names of all the trees. Thanks, Grandma, for your constant and unfailing kindness and love. I miss you very much and I love you very much.

WALKER COUNTRY STORE

There it sat, hard next to two dirt roads, Centralia Rachels Road and Sparta-Davisboro Road between them, with Centralia Rachels at the rear and side, and Sparta-Davisboro at the front-door side, the door that was seldom used. Papa and Grandma and almost all the customers used the back door with the step, which was really about three feet long and two feet in diameter of a tree trunk, probably oak, with the sides shaved off smooth and flat so that the "step" wouldn't roll over when those brogans and granny shoes touched it as the would-be customers gained entrance into the little store.

My first remembrance of the Walker Country Store was probably around 1949 or 1950. I would have been seven or eight years old. As much as anything, I remember the dust that the occasional cars and mules and wagons kicked up as they made their way to the store, or more likely, as they went on by to Warthen, Sparta, or maybe Sandersville.

I spent lots of time playing in Centralia Rachels. In front of Papa and Grandma's house, it was sandy and had little pea rocks that washed out of the ground when a good rain settled the dust and watered the crops.

My recollection is that Sparta-Davisboro had redder dirt, at least in front of the store, and it had a ditch across the road from the store that in late summer was usually loaded with maypops that were fun to play with—throw at playmates or make pigs with stick legs and tails and stomp them hard with your bare foot and make them pop.

The store was probably, at most, about fifteen feet by thirty feet. It had a little porch on the front and a tin roof. It was made of rough wood, probably pine, on the outside, painted white. I'm no carpenter, but it appeared to me that there were two boards laid with a strip between to cover each seam. It was heated by a pot-bellied stove in winter, and it was heated, very hot, by God in the summer.

I don't remember a sign as to ownership or names on the store until it was no longer operational. I put one on it around 1989 which read, "Walker Country Store, David F. Walker & Josephine May Walker."

When Papa was running the store it didn't have regular hours. Generally, if you wanted a "co-cola" and cheese, or snuff and chewing tobacco, candy and maybe fatback or kerosene, plus some plow line and nails, or anything else, you came to the house, which was immediately adjacent to the store, and hollered out, in a loud voice, "Mr. David, I want to go in the store," and either Papa or Grandma would come out, unlock the store, and let you in to buy what you wanted. Those that Papa considered worthy were extended credit with appropriate entries made in a long, gray and blue, slender book.

I wrote that folks hollered out, "Mr. David..." Actually, lots of them hollered out, "Uncle David, I want to go in the store." I never gave the "Uncle David" any thought until I was older and Daddy told me that he had living at one time seventy-six first cousins. It dawned on me why so many of Papa's customers called him "Uncle David." You can figure it out.

As I said, I owned the store later in my life and was proud of it. Of course, I never ran it as a store, and when I sold the "Walker Homeplace," I offered the store building to my cousin Johnny Swint, who lived right down the road from Grandma and Papa's house. A condition was that he would have to move it off the property I had sold and by a certain date.

Johnny Swint is a really handy man and smart. He figured out how to move the store and set out to do it, but when the moving started, the store fell apart and all that was left was a pile of termite-infested wood and some old, weathered tin. It was sad.

The Sparta-Davisboro Road is paved today. There is a big power-company easement through the farm and close to where the store used to be. The Walker Country Store signs, Papa's candy case, the kerosene pump, and the Coca-Cola box are in Perry. All I have now of the store building are memories, and wonderful memories they are. It was a more exciting place to me than Wal-Mart could ever be. Sometimes, I wish it were still there, and folks would holler out to me, "Mr. Larry, I want to go in the store." It won't ever happen.

THEY LOVED HIM MOST WHO
KNEW HIM BEST

Clyde Walker was fifteen when he died in 1927. This past Sunday, Janice and I visited his grave at Pinehill United Methodist Church out in the country, Washington County, Georgia. There it was, his little marker with his name, date of birth and death, and the words "They Loved Him Most Who Knew Him Best." I would suspect, but do not know, that my grandmother, who was Clyde's mother, was responsible for the poignant words on his tombstone.

My understanding of what happened is based on bits and pieces learned over the years from Daddy, Clyde's five-years-younger brother, and Aunt Lillian, Clyde's three-years-older sister, and not from my grandmother or grandfather, who, to my recollection, never talked about Clyde's death. When I explain the circumstances, you'll understand why they didn't discuss it.

It was November 12, 1927, and Clyde was going squirrel hunting. A perfectly natural thing for a fifteen-year-old Washington County, Georgia, boy to do on a fall afternoon. Not only for the sport involved, but also for the opportunity to provide part of a meal or meals for the family.

And so it was that Clyde was still gone when the sun set and the darkness came. I can imagine that there was apprehension but not panic when the men (exactly whom, I do not know) decided that they needed to go and look for him. And so they set out. It's hard to imagine that what they found could've been worse. There was Clyde, hanging on a fence that he had tried to climb but couldn't get over. Dead.

This is what the men surmised. One of the hammers on the double-barreled shotgun caught on a root or vine and discharged, with the shot striking Clyde in the stomach. Clyde tried to walk and crawl from the big tree, under which he had been waiting for squirrels, to the house. He got as far as the fence but was unable to climb it. A trail of blood clearly marked his path. Clyde was gone. Fifteen years old and loved by all, but especially by those who knew him best.

Why do horrible things happen to good people? It's one of the great mysteries of the ages. I've heard ministers and great Christians try to explain, but I've never heard a completely satisfactory answer. In our finite understanding, maybe there is no answer. Perhaps we don't understand because we are humans and not God.

Some of the happiest times of my life were spent out in the country with my Walker grandparents in Washington County. As a youngster, maybe about fifteen years of age, Papa used to let me take his .410 caliber single-barreled shotgun into the woods, alone, to hunt and shoot at birds and squirrels and rabbits. Never once did he or Grandma mention Clyde's death. As I got older, I realized that they must've thought about Clyde and the dangers involved when I trudged down that little dirt road with Papa's gun on my shoulder. But they let me do it because, at least at that day and time, it was a part of growing up. A part of becoming a man.

Can you imagine what Thanksgiving and Christmas must have been like at the Walker homeplace in 1927? And now they rest—Clyde, Papa, and Grandma—on a hill at Pinehill United Methodist Church in Washington County. Or are they together somewhere in a happier time and place?

Clyde Walker never made it to manhood. He was only fifteen when he died. But they said of Clyde, "They Loved Him Most Who Knew Him Best." The words are chiseled in granite and are still there for folks to see. What wonderful words. Would be unto God that someone would say that about me when my time comes.

Clyde Walker died many years ago. I never knew him, but I do remember him.

WISHING BOREDOM ON MY GRANDCHILDREN

It tickles me to death when a sophisticated magazine like *Southern Living* has a writer such as Rick Bragg, the best in the South and maybe the best in the country, and they let him do his thing. How do I know? Well, let's look as his article in *Southern Living* titled "Return of the Goat Man," with the synopsis, "For years, one small Alabama town had a sure sign that spring had sprung."

Brothers and sisters, if you don't know about the Goat Man, Ches McCartney, it's time for you to learn. Find Bragg's article and get educated. If you did see the Goat Man, and you were over five years old, then you do remember and you are prepared to share your "Goat Man story" with anyone who will listen.

Recently, Janice and I, along with our guests, Carol Horton and Faye Wilson, plus about 800 others, attended the reunion of Fort Valley High School's 1960s band the Malibu's. What a show it was! Part of the conversation at our table grew out of my mentioning Bragg's article and everybody in hearing had a "Goat Man story" to tell. Everyone who had ever seen him, and smelled him, had a story. And let me add that the Malibu's crowd was mostly over fifty years old, so most everyone had at least one story to share.

Enough about the Goat Man. Let me quote a couple of lines from Bragg's article that had to do with his growing up in the rural South. "Some people, unaccustomed to the long, rolling nothing of a cotton field, would have said that there was not too much to do in Spring Garden, Alabama, in 1965. We fought boredom, my brother and I, the best we could."

Most folks would have said the same thing about Perry or Fort Valley, the Malibu's notwithstanding. Well, if what we did in the fifties and sixties was boredom, I wish we could call back some of it, or almost all of it, so our grandchildren could be bored.

Do children still play out at night? Do they catch lightning bugs and put them in a jar? Do they tie a thread around a June bug's leg and let it fly round and round until both the thread holder and the bug are exhausted.

I must have played in at least a thousand games of basketball with other youngsters in my backyard on Swift Street in Perry, often with one of the Perry Panthers—maybe Sam Nunn or Percy Hardy—and I'll bet that some of that Fort Valley Greenwave crowd, my age, played with Ed Beck or Pat Swann.

By the way, basketball was really something in Middle Georgia in the fifties and sixties. We had outstanding coaches, great players, and really close games. Fort Valley had Tee and Perry had Lee. Roberta's John Matthews could shoot as good as Larry Byrd, but probably not quite as good as Perry's Dwayne Powell. I could go on and on, but let me just say that for Perry and Fort Valley folks, this was almost as memorable as the Goat Man.

We had a science club at our house. We had jars full of all kinds of insects that we kept at the club's location—a big fig tree in our backyard. We must have had six or eight active members.

I must have been Roy Rogers 500 times. And I was Lash LaRue and Hopalong Cassidy a few times. I could shoot, rope, and ride a horse—at least in my mind I could. I could shoot a pistol out of a black-hatted cowboy and not even hurt him.

I played Pop the Whip and Red Rover, Red Rover. I even went to a few prom parties when I was in the eighth grade. Teen Town dances at Perry's National Guard Armory will never be forgotten. In fact, the Malibu's brought back memories of Teen Town.

I helped dam up a creek and "muddied" for fish—and caught a few. I hunted rabbits at night and dove and quail in the daytime. I even hunted and ate squirrel. Pierce Staples and I killed and ate some pigeons and robins that Mrs. Staples cooked for us.

I worked. I did many different kinds of work. Daddy was serious about me working. The lessons of work have meant much to my life.

I could go on and on but must close. But let me say this: if this was boredom, I wish it on my grandchildren and today's young people. What I experienced would mean much to their lives. I really wish they could have seen the Goat Man and his goats. It would have given them a lasting memory and good tales to tell their grandchildren.

REMEMBERING MR. HUBERT HAWKINS

My aunt Lillian Walker Maddox, Daddy's sister, could just about outwork anyone I ever saw. Efficient, too. She could shell butterbeans faster than a machine, and although she lived in Atlanta, she came back to Washington County and helped with the hog killings and the syrup makings. She could sew and cook. And on and on. Also, she was smart—very smart. She had been a school teacher. Not that this in and of itself made her smart. But trust me, she was plenty smart.

But this is not about my aunt Lillian. It does start, however, with something she used to say: "Little pitchers have big ears." I didn't then, nor do I now, understand the reference to "pitchers" and "ears." But I do know that it referred to me and my inclination to listen to everything the adults were saying.

Now, I finally get to the beginning. At least my beginning. Aunt Lillian and Grandma, and to a lesser extent Papa, were talking about Grandma and Papa's neighbor Hubert Hawkins. Specifically, talking about the fact that Mr. Hubert "had to go off for a while" because he got caught making non-tax-paid whiskey. Moonshine.

Prison. Liquor. Their neighbor, right up the road. Believe me, this "little pitcher" was suddenly very interested in seeing this Mr. Hubert Hawkins. To my knowledge, until I heard about him, I had never seen him. It could be that he wasn't around for me to see because he had been "detained" for some period of time. But see him, I eventually did.

He came to Papa's store riding a mule. He had on overalls and brogans. He squatted on his haunches or sat on a nail-keg or wooden Coke crate by the pot-bellied stove. He rolled Prince Albert tobacco in OCB paper and did lots of smoking. Lots of quiet talking, too. To my surprise, Papa seemed to like him. If he was a bad man—you know, liquor and prison and all—why did Papa like him? I was a little scared and fascinated.

Time goes on. Not big time, but big time to a ten- or twelve-year-old. Maybe two or three years. I saw Mr. Hawkins on many occasions. It was usually the same, with the squatting and the smoking and the talking. I kinda liked Mr. Hawkins myself. I knew I wasn't supposed to, him being a bad man and all, but I couldn't exactly help it. And, like I said, he and Papa seemed to be good friends. Even more surprising, almost shocking, was that Grandma acted like she liked him. And Grandma was a pillar of the Pinehill Methodist Church! What was I to think?

Time goes on. Time being, like I said, two or three years. And being smart, but not as smart as Aunt Lillian, I learned that Mr. Hawkins lived right up the dirt Sparta-Davisboro Road about a mile and that he grew cotton and lived by himself in an unpainted shotgun house. Or was it a dog-trot house? He had many yard chickens, peacocks, guineas, and many, many dogs. Grandma and I actually drove up to see him in Grandma and Papa's 1950 Chevrolet. I was astounded—and still frightened.

This is a pretty long story. I cannot tell it all in the short space allotted. So let me end it with this. If you think Aunt Lillian was smart, you should have known her husband, Uncle Jim Maddox. He was about the smartest person I have ever known. Near genius. Perhaps he was a genius. Well, when I was about fifteen years old, he asked if I would like to go squirrel hunting with Hubert Hawkins and him! Go squirrel hunting with a man who had been in jail? I said, "Yes, sir," and we went. Uncle Jim, Hubert Hawkins, all those dogs, and me. Must've killed ten or twelve squirrels. It was a great day. Hubert Hawkins acted fine. Matter of fact, he was really nice to us and his dogs. Matter of fact, it was one of the best days of my life. I liked Hubert Hawkins myself. I wish I could go squirrel hunting with Uncle Jim and Hubert Hawkins and those dogs one more time. Especially Hubert Hawkins, even if he had been forced by the law to "go off for a while."

DOES FORT WORTH EVER CROSS YOUR MIND?

Whether it was on the free juke box at the original Longhorns on Peachtree Street in Atlanta, or on public television's *Austin City Limits*, or just on the radio, I never heard George Strait's wailing "Does Fort Worth Ever Cross Your Mind?" without thinking about the two Jerrys— Wilson and Horton—and the one Bobby—Jones—and that summer in 1963 that the four of us spent working at Texas Steel Company in Fort Worth. I never hear "The Old Rugged Cross" that I am not transported back to that little country Methodist church, Pinehill, in Washington County, Georgia. I can see Grandma fanning and singing and Papa fanning and sitting and the memory is both warm and melancholy and there is nothing I can do to stop the feelings or change the memories. Funny how songs do that to me—and I expect to you, also.

Perhaps it's Nat by himself and maybe it's Nat and Natalie, but I bet you have memories—unforgettable thoughts—when you hear "Unforgettable." It may be one of the most unforgettable songs of all time. It might be a man or a woman or a high school dance or a certain period in your life, and it may be sad or it may be the song that brought you and your wife together, but I bet lots of you have memories of this song.

The Snack Shack was the gathering and eating place when I was at the University of Georgia back in the 1960s. It was located on Broad Street about a block from where the Holiday Inn Express is today. When Charlayne Hunter and Hamilton Holmes integrated the university, you could go to the Snack Shack any time of the day or night and Ray Charles's voice would be emitting from the Wurlitzer, "Georgia, Georgia, no peace I find, just an old sweet song keeps Georgia on my mind." I never hear "Georgia on My Mind" that I am not back, though briefly, in Athens during those stressful and tumultuous times. Ray Charles did that to me. And then it is to the floor of the Georgia House of Representatives with Ray Charles himself, there on the floor, playing and singing, and then with our voting unanimously to make the classic

"Georgia on My Mind" our official state song. I never made a vote I was more sure of and of which I was more proud.

It is not our song, though, my wife's and mine—even if we have one. "Hold Me, Thrill Me, Kiss Me" by Mel Carter or "Build Me Up Buttercup" or "I'll Be Seeing You" or Alabama's "Old Flame" would come closer to being "our song." But I never hear "Wind beneath My Wings" and the line "Did I ever tell you that you're my hero?" that I don't think of Janice. For those of you who know Janice and me well, listen to the words and you will understand why.

It was probably in January or February 1960, and Jerry Wilson and I were supposed to be at home, after school, resting for a basketball game that Tuesday night. Instead, we went to Fort Valley to see Sandra Dee and Troy Donahue in *A Summer Place*. When I hear Percy Faith and his orchestra do the theme from *A Summer Place*, I always think about Jerry Wilson and his 1956 Ford convertible and our trip to Fort Valley. I'm glad we violated one of 'Fessor's rules and went to the movie—the memory is always that good.

I could go on and on. The Reverend Al Green and "I'm So Tired of Being Alone." The Tams and "Be Young, Be Foolish, and Be Happy." "Traces" by the Classic IV, and Frank Sinatra singing "Summer Wind." One of my favorites is Barry White's "The First, the Last, My Everything," and two others are "If You Don't Know Me by Now" and "Lady in Red," and what about Jack Green's "Statue to a Fool" or Jackie Wilson's "Lonely Teardrops"? My favorite "church song" is "My Tribute," and for country music, you can't beat Patsy Cline's "Crazy" unless it's George Jones's song, "He Stopped Loving Her Today."

Lots of great songs. Lots of memories—some good, some bad. Some sweet, some sad. But there is nothing you can do when the song comes on except to remember.

YOU'LL NEVER GET OUT OF PERRY

This is a true story. Correction. It's as true as it can be, given it's based on my memory. It's about events that took place starting on Labor Day, September 1962, more than fifty-six years ago. To my immense sorrow, I am the only one involved who is still here to report what happened during that carefree and "what will happen next" week.

The main characters in this comedy/drama were Jerry Wilson, one of the quickest and cleverest people I've ever known, Jerry Horton, "Do-Tricks" to his legion of friends, whose nickname says it all, Tommie Sandefur, eventually the CEO of Brown and Williamson Tobacco, and me.

Who made the suggestion? Probably Jerry Wilson since his brother, Mark "Bo" Wilson, and Bo's wife, Sara Beth, lived in Charleston, where Lt. Col. Mark Wilson, USAF, a C130 pilot, lived.

Let's hitchhike to Folly Beach for the week (for us, a "dead" week between summer work and school). So, that's what we decided to do. Four young guys with luggage on the side of the road? I can remember it vividly. Eunice Scoggins Wilson, Jerry's mother, a wonderful person, opined, "Well, you'll never get out of Perry," as she let us out of the 1956 Chevrolet on the side of the road in front of Mr. Robert Tuggle's house on the Hawkinsville highway.

There we stood, with soliciting thumbs outstretched, standing in front of our luggage. Five minutes and we had a ride. He, who will go nameless, was on his way to Hawkinsville to buy liquor (Houston County was dry). Within thirty minutes, we were twenty miles down the road.

Next, it was Jim Hooks from Perry and his fiancée who picked us up and took us all the way to Jesup. So far, very good!

At Jesup, we ate at a Jaycee's-sponsored Labor Day rest stop. Several doughnuts each. Living off the land, as would characterize the week.

Then a soldier took us all four, and our luggage, all the way to Savannah. We were doing good and moving fast. Eunice was wrong, wasn't she? We did make it out of Perry.

Jerry Wilson's Georgia Tech roommate lived in Savannah, so somehow (no cell phones) we got in touch with him (pay phone?). Lee Smith came, we spent the night in Savannah with him and his parents, and we ate a ten-pound ham for dinner (supper). So far, we'd spent almost no money.

The next morning, day two, Lee took us across the Savannah River into South Carolina. Things got a little dicier on day two. We had a long wait, but finally a preacher, with no hands, driving a pickup hauling eggs, picked us up (one in the front and three in the back) and took us to Two Egg, South Carolina, and let us out.

Four young men (boys?) with suitcases on the side of the road at Two Egg and the darkest cloud (like night) heading our way (later newspaper accounts told of tornadoes). What were we to do? This is almost unbelievable: A Greyhound bus driver stopped his bus and picked us up. We all paid one dollar each. The dog to Charleston!

Night two with Bo and Sara Beth, a free supper, and the next morning, after breakfast, Sara Beth took us to Folly Beach. We were there!

We found a house basement for rent and paid the owner four dollars each for two nights. We had shelter.

We hadn't been there long when we spotted her, a "robust" young lady in shorts and a halter top. Quickly, we made friends with Faye Lee, and she fed us (pimento cheese, peanut butter and jelly and mayonnaise sandwiches).

A place to stay, food (we paid a few dollars, probably less than ten dollars total for our share of the groceries), and Wednesday and Thursday were taken care of.

Friday came. Time to go home. I think Faye Lee took us to our departure place. We were off and headed west, or were we?

We thumbed and waited. Thumbed and waited. No ride. We decided to split up and drew lots. Tommie and Do-Tricks to the bushes, and Jerry and me on the roadside. The plan: Jerry and I would get a ride, and after we were gone, it would be Do-Trick's and Tommie's turn.

In just a few minutes, someone stopped. But Do-Tricks and

Tommie didn't follow the plan. Out of the bushes they ran (almost scaring our to-be driver to death), and all four were together again.

Last leg, as it turned out. Some of you will remember those red linen trucks. Well, a driver of one picked us up. Tommie in the passenger seat up front, and three in the back on the soiled linens. Said he was going to Macon, but he liked us, so he took us all the way to Perry and let us out at the Perry High football field. We got there just before kickoff, and we strolled in, proud as peacocks.

Tommie spent ten dollars from Monday to Friday. I spent fourteen dollars, Jerry eighteen dollars, and Do-Tricks thirty-eight dollars (those pinball machines, you know).

I didn't write of everything that happened. Space limitations? But we did have a grand, exciting, unforgettable time. And, yes, Eunice, you were right in a sense: I never did get out of Perry.

LISTENING TO THE OLD FOLKS TALK

In the spring and the fall, and sometimes when it was overcast and cool, and particularly on Sunday afternoons, the old folks (at least what I thought then was old, although mostly they were younger than I am today) would sit on the front porch, rocking and talking. There was no television and driving an automobile to anywhere cost money, so talking and visiting was what they did.

I listened. I listened closely, seldom speaking, following Daddy's admonition that "you can't learn anything when you're talking." I learned a great deal—at least about the few subjects that captured most of their interest and their talk.

Later, much later, when my black hair had a good deal of gray, I thought back and tried to analyze. I came to the conclusion that a handful of subjects earned 90 percent of the talk.

These were farm folks. Oh, my aunt had taught school in Atlanta and my uncle was an engineer, but in the marrow of their bones, they were of the soil, having been only recently removed. Daddy started off teaching high school agriculture and had slipped over to the farm-equipment business. He had, with Mother's help, fully inculcated me into the rural, ag mindset. So, as I sat on my mule-plowing, chicken-growing, hog-killing, syrup-making grandparents' porch, I understood the talk and especially the "main" subjects.

I'd say first as a topic of choice was the relatives. It was never critically unfavorable, at least in my presence, but was of concern ("Did you know that Aunt May is sick") or laudatory ("Joe Walker got a job with the power company") or braggadocios ("Betty's daughter finished first in her graduating class"). Daddy told me that at one time he had seventy-six first cousins living! There was lots of material for talk about relatives.

Next, probably, was the church. My grandparents and parents were regular in attendance and were proud of their church and kept up with the other members and their joys and tribulations. I never heard anyone say anything bad about the preacher or his sermon. Frequently, the preacher came on Sunday to eat with my grandparents.

There was also lots of talk about the weather. Now, for you youngsters, you should know that other than looking at the sky, and perhaps other signs such as the temperature and humidity, no one, not even the so-called radio weathermen (I never remember a female radio weather person) could accurately tell you what the weather was going to be. And, of course, there was more talk about "rain" and when it was going to rain than anything else.

Frankly, I wasn't afraid too much of the devil or much of anything else except Papa not getting any rain on his cotton or corn. That, the lack of rain, worried me considerably. I knew if he didn't get it, there would be bad consequences.

There was a little "political talk," but not much. Grandma's brother, Carley May, worked for Fred Hand at his huge store, Hand Trading Co., in Pelham. Mr. Hand was also the speaker of the Georgia House. Hand ran for governor in the 1950s, and, of course, we were all for him because our kin worked for him. He didn't get elected. Marvin Griffin did. In any event, this was about the most political talk I ever heard on the front porch.

Other things discussed in my presence were what the Holy Bible said and meant and how you spelled certain words or what was the grammatically correct way to say or write something. All of them wanted to talk and write correctly.

Now, that was most of the talk. Still, if someone caught lots of fish, that would have to be fleshed out, and if anyone saw a snake, especially "a big rattler," that would take up some time and would be mighty exciting to me. All of us were wary of rattlesnakes but weren't too worried about the "coach-whip" Papa kept in his corncrib to keep down the corn-eating mice and rats.

I don't believe that young folks talk about much of the same stuff my parents, aunt, uncle, and grandparents talked about. Most children today don't talk about much of anything; they just punch those hand-held devices.

Still, if you see a big snake, especially a rattler, that brings on lots of talk. But folks don't see many rattlers anymore because the wild hogs eat up most of the snake eggs or the snakes themselves.

I wish I could spend a breezy Sunday afternoon on that porch with these kin one more time. To me, the talk was really interesting and important. It helped make me what I am today.

SOME THINGS I'LL ALWAYS REMEMBER

What's important, if anything, about this article is what you remember in and about your own life. I hope that some of my memories, those little things that make life sweet (or interesting), will help you to recall some of yours.

• We lived in a modest home at Swift and Third streets in Perry. It was heated by a floor furnace in the little hall between the bedroom and the "other" room, which I could call a dining room or a den, or just a room. When it got cold, it was really cold in our house. What I will always remember is Mother's warming a blanket on the floor furnace and wrapping that warm blanket around my little legs and feet when I got in that cold bed. Thanks, Momma.

• I remember going to Sparta, Georgia, with Papa (I believe in 1950, and I would have been eight years old) to get a new, black Chevrolet automobile at Davis Chevrolet. How we got there (fourteen miles), I do not know, but we came back on Highway 15 to dirt Sparta-Davisboro Road in that new car (the only one I ever remember my Walker grandparents owning). The car had to be dusty when we got to the house. I wonder if Papa washed it off or if he even had a hose and running water to do the job.

• Back to our house. Daddy and Mother let David and me play basketball in our bedroom. We would shoot at the top part of the doorframe, and if the ball hit the top of the frame in a "certain way," it would bounce back a "certain way," and that would be a score. David and I must have made at least 1,000 points each in our basketball arena.

• My parent's handy man/painter was a person, as they used to say in the country, who "was bad to drink." Most Perry old-timers know exactly of whom I write. Once, when commissioned by Mother or Daddy to paint our bedroom/basketball arena, he decided to also paint the light fixture in the ceiling and the light switch plates. When Mother questioned him about this, he responded, "They look better this way." At least he didn't paint our one bathtub like he did the tub of one of our friends!

• I remember my first kiss. I know who it was, where it was, and why it was. Of course, a gentleman doesn't tell, but I will say that I was in the eighth grade, and it was at a prom party. The prom party was "why it was." Do any of you remember prom parties? And, by the way, it was the only kiss I ever got from this nice girl. But I do remember it. I'll bet you remember your first kiss!

• I remember the McCroskey twins (girls) who came to Perry High School but left in about the tenth grade. I remember the Austin twins (girls) who came to Perry High School and, I think, graduated but left, seldom, if ever, to return. I remember John Whitworth, the big football tackle, who came as a senior, helped us to win the region and play for the South Georgia Championship, and left the night after Quitman beat us, never to return (at least as far as I know). I'd like to visit with all five of those folks one more time. I doubt it will ever happen.

• I remember "pound parties." You had to take a pound of something (bread, sugar, cake, coffee, etc.) to gain entrance to the party. I guess the "pounds" were given to someone in need or for some good cause. I must have been twelve to fourteen years old when pound parties were in vogue. Do any of you remember them? And, by the way, I do not remember what "went on" at the parties—just talking and visiting, I assume.

• I remember playing basketball in the Macon City Auditorium against the Lanier Poets. I believe they, at times, played five left-handed boys (in the days when high school players didn't dribble with both hands) and ran the "shuffle" (wasn't that Joel Eave's invention, or was it Garland Pinholster's—I can't remember). Perry lost. I also remember going to rock-n-roll shows in the Macon City Auditorium. This was probably in the late 1950s. How exciting! Both the basketball and the rock-n-roll shows.

I'm just getting started, and I'm out of space. So, I'll stop with a load of memories not disclosed. Sometimes that's probably for the best. Still, I hope I've stirred up some happy memories that will help brighten this day for you.

BOILED PEANUTS

Saturday morning. Seven o'clock. September 1955. Daddy, David, and I are in the pickup and headed to what we call "Daddy's Farm." Actually, it was jointly owned by my grandfather Gray and Daddy. We have already had a hot meal, breakfast, thanks to Mother. At our house, we have three hot meals a day—bless her heart. It is already hot, and Daddy, as is his nature, has his left arm hanging out the open window. This arm is very tanned, especially when compared to his right arm. No car air-conditioning for us in 1955, and this is how you try to stay cool. David is eight years old, I am thirteen, and Daddy is thirty-eight. Thirty-eight seems very old to me. I am sleepy but talkative. David is sleepy and quiet. Daddy is all business because we are on an important mission—getting the peanuts washed, boiled, sacked, and ready for sale.

Daddy's farm seems to me to be "out in the country." In fact, it is only a couple of miles from our house on Swift Street. We arrive in a cloud of dust and are greeted by Daddy's tenant, George Johnson, better known as "Hoss" or "Big Hoss." Today, I would call him Mr. Big Hoss. He was a very big man and reputed to be the strongest man in our area in those days. "They" say he could pick up the end of an automobile by himself. What size car and what end, I do not know. One hand was missing, having been shot off in a hunting accident, and he doesn't have a tooth in his head but can bite an apple in two. I like him very much but am somewhat afraid of him, even though he is always nice to me.

Hoss has the dug peanuts ready to be picked off the vines, and David and I start this task. It is not hard work, although you have to be careful to remove the stems and the leaves from the picked-off nuts. In a short period of time, we have a large quantity of peanuts ready for washing. Hoss, with a water hose, helps us with the washing. By now, Daddy has gone, returning to town to work. We carefully clean the peanuts and put the cleaned nuts in a large black wash pot, along with an ample amount of water and salt. Hoss then starts a fire under the pot, and soon the peanuts are boiling. We help keep the fire going—this is the fun part—and stir the peanuts with a stick. Periodically, the three of us sample the nuts.

About 12:45 P.M., Daddy arrives in the pickup, and the three of us, with two or three large buckets of peanuts, return home, where Mother and my brother and sister, who are twins, Charles and Lynda, await our return. After another hot meal, Mother, Daddy, David, and I bag the nuts—120 large brown paper sacks full. We keep four and put the rest in the pickup to be taken to town for selling. Daddy supplies us with change (coins and dollar bills) so that we will be ready for business when commerce commences. By now, it is 3:00 P.M. in downtown Perry, Georgia, and the streets are full of people. Everything looks encouraging, and we are anxious to start our selling venture.

Our sacks of boiled peanuts are tightly packed into cardboard boxes. It takes several large boxes because the large sacks are full—Daddy believes in our giving full measure for the ten cents—yes, ten cents—that the customer is going to pay for these "Georgia ground peas." We take our supply of peanuts to Gray-Walker Supply (later to be known as Walker-Thompson Supply), which is located in the middle of Carroll Street, and store the peanuts under the watchful eyes of Ed Thompson and Glea Gray. We are going to work out of the feed store until we sell all of the peanuts. David and I receive some good-natured ribbing from these two—"You boys probably won't be able to sell all these peanuts, where have you been all day, your customers have all gone home"—but then both of them become our first customers, and we have grossed twenty cents! In a smaller cardboard box, I place twenty bags and David gets ten bags, and we are out the front door—a little apprehensive but ready to go to work.

TWO THINGS I'M PROUD OF

First, yes, I know that you're not supposed to end a sentence with a preposition, at least that is what I was taught in the Perry public schools, but to title this part, "*Two Things of Which I am Proud*" just sounds a little too pretentious for me.

I am proud of the two articles in this section. First, my speech on the floor of the Georgia House of Representatives when the Georgia House passed the flag changes, removing the St. Andrews Cross (a part of the Confederate battle flag) from our state flag in 2001. I was the non-metro legislator Governor Roy Barnes needed to speak on this controversial issue. We needed ninety-one votes and I believe we got ninety-three or ninety-four. I think my speech was important to passage. Governor Barnes recently told me he thought my speech changed twenty votes. By the way, I think changing our flag was one of the three or four most important bills enacted during my thirty-two-year legislative career.

Secondly, I am proud of the Solo and Small Firm Lifetime Achievement Award I was given by the American Bar Association in 2014.

Frankly, I was completely surprised that I had been nominated, much less chosen, for the award. All of this was clandestinely orchestrated by law partner, Kellye C. Moore, and what a superb lawyer she is. With Kellye's help, my nomination was supported by Connell Stafford, former chief of state for US Senator Sam Nunn; Sam Nunn himself; Dink NeSmith, president of Community Newspapers, Inc.; and Bryant Culpepper, Macon Judicial Circuit Superior Court judge (now senior judge).

Read my speech on the flag and remember that it was given many years ago. See "About Larry" on my firm's website for my American Bar Association Solo and Small Firm Lifetime Achievement Award.

By the way, we have a beautiful flag today that incorporates the old but no longer has the Confederate battle cross that was offensive to many. Thanks to those who risked political defeat to make the changes, and especially to Governor Roy Barnes, who initiated the effort that resulted in the changes, and to Governor Sonny Perdue, who gave us the flag we have today.

SPEECH ON "THE FLAG"

I just made the longest walk that I have made in my twenty-eight-year career in this House—it is the six and a half feet from my desk to this well. Politically speaking, it might be one of the last walks I will ever make. For many reasons, I consider this walk as politically dangerous and maybe ill-advised but certainly significant. I did not make the walk without certain knowledge of the possible political consequences.

Despite the personal gravity of the walk, it pales into almost nothingness when compared to the walking done by my Gray ancestors and Walker ancestors and May ancestors and Nichols ancestors—on both sides of the conflict—during the War between the States.

It is absolutely nothing when compared to the twelve-mile forced march—without food or water—that General Stonewall Jackson's men made at Chancellorsville to help assure a great Confederate victory—a victory that many true Southerners still remember with pride and almost reverence to this day. I am among this group.

July 3, 1863. Gettysburg, Pennsylvania. The turning point in the Civil War. What about the walk that General George E. Pickett's men made across that open field and up the slopes of Seminary Ridge? I read from portions of Edward G. Longacre's book, *Pickett*, and from that chapter entitled "Grand but Fatal Day." Longacre is speaking of Pickett:

> But nothing could have prepared him for the sights and sounds that beset him as this "grand but fatal day" came to an end. His once mighty division had been reduced to incoherent clumps of leaderless men...in some outfits manpower losses approached 90 percent. At the regimental level, at least, Pickett's command had virtually ceased to exist as a fighting force.... It was all too much for Pickett, who, upon making his way back to Seminary Ridge, gave way to anguish and despair. One of the first to meet him upon his return was an English-born artillerist. "With tears in his eyes," the man recorded, Pickett stared at the line of guns through which his men had passed

at the start of the advance, then exclaimed to their crews: "Why did you not halt my men here? Great God, where, oh where is my division?"

I am a son of the South—as Southern as anyone in this body. In a sea of Southern drawls, mine is one of the thickest and most pronounced. I make no apologies for it. I am from Georgia's Piedmont Plateau, or the "black belt"—so named for the richness of the soil and for the black people that have tended the soil. I talk the way that the natives from my part of the State talk. I am a Civil War "buff"—not a historian, but a "buff." I believe that my ancestors who fought for the Confederate States of America were brave and honorable men—not totally right in their cause, but then again, not totally wrong. When I watch the movie *Gettysburg*, I want Pickett's men to reach the top of Seminary Ridge. I think that Robert E. Lee was one of our greatest Americans. I do not judge 1863 Georgians and 1956 Georgians by 2001 standards. I will resist efforts to rid "us"—native Southerners—of our great and honorable heritage. I will fight to keep our statues and monuments and memorials. I want my grandchildren to love their Southern heritage. I love the South.

Then I think about other Georgians. Georgians who were forced here and who are just now beginning to share in the wonderful bounty of this country. Georgians who have done the grueling work and the heavy lifting and the dirty jobs and who, at least until recently, have received little respect and much ridicule and deriding. I think about some of the walks they have made.

1832 to 1860. The "underground railroad." What about the thousands of slaves that made this walk—a walk out of slavery and to freedom? A walk that contributed to the hostility between North and South that led to the Civil War.

And what about the walk made by Nat Turner, a Negro slave and preacher, who led the most famous slave revolt in United States history. A rebellion that caused Southern states to pass strict laws for the control of slaves, especially those who were preachers.

Then there was the walk over the bridge at Selma, Alabama, and the marches in Birmingham and Albany and Washington, DC, and Jackson and Perry, Georgia.

There was and is a slave market in Louisville, Georgia. I hope it won't be torn down. It should stand as a reminder of what man can and will do to his fellow man if his better nature does not control. Some went to that place in Louisville, years ago, as families, only to see their husbands or wives and children for the last time. What of this walk?

In 1961, our predecessors had to vote as to whether or not the schools in our State would be closed. Had I been a member of this body, I hope that I would have had the courage to vote to keep our schools open. In 1984, a vote was taken to honor, with a holiday, the birth of Dr. Martin Luther King. With increasing pride, I can say that I cast a vote in the affirmative.

My five grandchildren call me Grandbuddy. I like the name. They tell me it is the same name I gave to my Grandfather Gray when I was four or five years old. I wish my Grandbuddy was here, today. He was a Methodist, but more importantly, he was a Christian. He was a Republican—a delegate to the Republican National Convention, and in 1948, the only Republican mayor in the State as mayor of Perry. But more importantly, he was tolerant. He was fair. He was a friend to black people when being their friend was not necessarily the thing to be. He would be proud of me today. He would applaud my vote to change our flag. He would tell me not to forget my heritage but to reach out and reach across and try to heal and try to love and to try to persuade you, my friends, to do the same. I want my Grandbuddy to be proud of me, and I want my five grandchildren to be proud of their Grandbuddy. I want them to be able to say, forty years after my death, that Grandbuddy was fair and tolerant and he did the right thing. For, after all, isn't this much more important than whether we might be allowed to return to this place? And so I, for one, intend to make the walk—maybe the long walk, perhaps the last walk, maybe the walk up towards Seminary Ridge, but, most certainly, the right walk.

I urge you to join me in this walk—a walk that can change the world's image of this State and its people—and most certainly will if we make the right decision. Like those young black college students who crossed that bridge in Selma, Alabama, and like those courageous young soldiers crossing that open field at Gettysburg, Pennsylvania, 137 years ago, let's do what we have to do—let's do the right thing.

In the Bible's Old Testament Book of Ecclesiastes, chapter 3, verses 1 through 3, are these words:

To everything there is a season, and a time to every purpose under the heaven;

A time to be born, and a time to die; a time to plant, and a time to pluck up that which is planted;

A time to kill, and a time to heal; a time to break down, and a time to build up.

Now is the time for us to pluck up what has been planted.
Now is the time for us to build up.
Now is the time for us to heal.

TRIALS (MAYBE NOT THE KIND YOU'RE THINKING ABOUT: GROWING OUT OF PRACTICING LAW IN A SMALL TOWN

Many years ago, perhaps when I was a forty-nine-year-old lawyer, and not seventy-six, as I am today, I participated in a program at the University of Georgia School of Law. As I recall it, the program featured an attorney from *A Large Law Firm*, one from *A Medium-Sized Law Firm*, and one from *A Small Law Firm*. When my turn came, I was introduced as "Larry Walker, who has a small law practice." Perhaps pride more than the introducer's lack of truth compelled me to respond, "I have a small law firm, but not necessarily a small practice." I might not have even included the word "necessarily."

And so I come to you today to talk about the trials, and the sometimes immense satisfactions, of being an active lawyer in a small town. Those of you who practice in a town of 10,000 souls or less, or have ever had such a practice, will understand. Those who immediately left law school and went, as a young lawyer, to Atlanta or some other large city, just don't know what you've missed. In the next few minutes, let me talk to you about practicing law, first as a sole practitioner, and now with seven other great lawyers and fine people, in a small town—in my case, Perry, Georgia.

I was twenty-three years old when I returned home fresh from UGA law school, ready to right wrongs, help the less fortunate, and make my mark in my small world in Middle Georgia. It was June 1965, and during that month, I graduated from law school, found out that I passed the bar exam, took a job (my first, other than mowing lawns, packing peaches, selling boiled peanuts, picking cotton, working in a feed store and a men's clothing store, working in a Texas steel mill, etc.), and, along with my wife, Janice, had my first child, Larry Walker III. Yes, June 1965 was a really big month for this little Walker family.

I looked it up for this paper. After renting it for about six months, I bought from a local bank the building I was occupying: the price was $5,000. It had a small restroom, a small reception area, which my half-day, five-days-a-week, receptionist/secretary occupied, and my small office. The total of all of it was 28.33 feet by 18.5 feet. Parking was on the street. I paid $1,000 down and financed $4,000. Mr. Tuggle, the bank's vice president, wanted my father to guaranty or cosign the note, but my father, who was also a director of this same bank, forcefully refused. Mr. Tuggle let me have the money without Daddy's signature. I paid it back! This is the way that small-town banks used to operate, before our country went broke. Generally, the only people who could borrow money were those who didn't need to borrow, and even then you needed about five times the collateral to debt to get the money!

And there was my shingle, with the words "Larry C. Walker, Jr., Attorney at Law" on it. But it's not the office or the shingle that I remember most. What I remember most is the excitement and nervousness—I was excited about helping others and nervous about how I would do. Often, I felt that the client knew more about what they were talking about than I did (I was probably right) and that I was getting ready to charge them (the hardest thing for this young lawyer to do) pretty good money for my advice and efforts. Was it really worth what I was charging?

Again, I looked it up: my first two files (I still have all of my files, and our firm has all of its files). My first real property file resulted in a certificate of title on a lot ninety feet by thirty-five feet minus 0.27 acres taken in a right-of-way deed by the Georgia Department of Transportation. I probably was paid thirty-five dollars for this work. Until just recently, my client's estate or the person the property was left to still had this tract of land. It's hard to sell a tract ninety feet by thirty-five feet minus 0.27 acres unless you want to put a bowling alley on it!

My first non-property file was a dispute the local furniture dealer had with Graybar Electric, Inc., the manufacturer of Zenith products. He wanted me to sue Graybar Electric. Can you imagine a twenty-three-year-old lawyer, about thirty days out of law school, suing this corporate behemoth? I didn't, and despite some research and correspondence and other efforts, I never billed for my services. My client did give my wife and me a very small cedar box that we still have, and I ultimately handled, about forty years later, the estates of both of my first two clients.

Yes, I remember the nervousness and the excitement, but I also remember their faces. Faces of people who had little hope and what little they had, they had placed with me. I remember their faces when I was successful for them. It was like they had never had anyone fight for them before, much less with their ending up on the top. Likely, they had never prevailed in a significant dispute before. I miss that very much. The kind of folks I generally represent today (there are exceptions that I will expound upon) pay well and expect "to end up on top." And if they don't, they'll find someone else to represent them. Yes, I remember the faces from the past, and I miss how I felt when I helped these good people.

She was old and black in a time and place when being old or black, and especially both, was not a helpful thing when there were legal disputes. She had borrowed money from a small loan company, and despite making payments for years, was about to lose her house. As far as she and I could tell (and it was very difficult to figure), she was a little behind on her payments but had paid back twice what she had borrowed years before. I was her last hope and wanted to help but saw little I could do until I went to the Houston County Courthouse and read the loan company's deed to secure debt—a deed to secure debt that they had prepared without the help of a lawyer. The company had used a proper security deed form but copied the legal description from a prior warranty deed, verbatim, onto their instrument, which was signed by my client, the grantor in their instrument. These are the words in addition to the legal description in which they also included: "Grantor, herein, reserves a life estate in and to the above described property." I wanted to shout when I saw these words, and I would have done so except for the absolute decorum, at all times, required by the clerk and deputy clerk in the Houston County record room. I worked it out with the company, and my grateful client kept her home. It wasn't an Atticus Finch moment, but it was pretty good, pretty doggone good! Again, I remember, and will never forget, my client's face when I told her she could stay in "her home" until she died. She did.

Murder was the charge in a day before spousal abuse counted for much, if anything. It was July 4, and my Waffle House waitress client shot her husband, who she contended was abusing her, through the heart. As they say, he was "graveyard dead when he hit the floor." We argued "abuse" to the jury and that "the pistol accidentally cocked and fired during a struggle." The district attorney argued that the pistol could not accidentally cock as he "fanned" it during his closing to the jury, when, suddenly, it cocked. You could have heard a pin drop when this happened. The jury convicted my client of involuntary manslaughter, and she was sentenced to five years and served a little more than two. I felt like a real lawyer. It's a feeling that's harder to get with what I do now.

And then there are the aggravations and vexations of small-town law practice. Mix a law practice with politics (I served in the state legislature for many years), and it really gets interesting. Let me give you some examples.

I've done "stuff" off and on for this "client" for years. I'd wager that his fees, added together, have never totaled $200. Here are my latest two "cases." The call comes in about his city water bill (not a Perry resident, and thus not a Perry water bill) that has him charged thirteen dollars "too much." Yes, "thirteen"! I explain to him my hourly charge, and that it might cost him "$500 or more." He says he wants to pursue it. I make several calls and finally got the town's city attorney to "take care of it for me." I call him, tell him it's taken care of, and tell him I cannot in good conscience charge him anything. He thanks me, and I think all is well. I actually feel pretty good about what I've done. Case is closed. Unbeknownst to me, a new one is coming!

About sixty days after I handled the water-bill case, I get another call from this same man. His complaint: a company that recycles televisions parts from televisions it finds in landfills charged him $300 for some parts that did not work. He wants me to sue the company. I adamantly refuse. He says, "You mean you are going to let this company take advantage of senior citizens?" My reply: "I guess I am!" He is not nearly as happy as he was when I handled the "thirteen-dollar water-bill case." And, yes, all of this is very real, and very recent.

Then there is the City of Perry that our law firm has successfully and happily represented for forty-six years, after I served for six years as its municipal court judge beginning at age twenty-three. And the City of Hawkinsville. And my high school teacher who called and wanted me to help him get back six or seven dollars for a magazine he subscribed to and never got. And the man who wanted my opinion as to what he could do about his neighbor's cat walking on his car. And our representation of

Ray Goff when he was terminated as Georgia's head football coach (the most interesting representation I ever had). Frito-Lay, Heileman Brewery, Tolleson Lumber, and the Houston County Hospital Authority have been long-time clients. In a small town, you get the big, sometimes the very big, the small, and sometimes a "thirteen-dollar case," and maybe all on the same day.

We represented *The Boston Globe* in a precedent-setting case, and we have for years represented the Georgia Sheriffs' Association and the Georgia Beer Wholesalers. We've had years in which we probably closed $300 million dollars in loans but saw loan closings virtually stop in September 2007. Practice in the area of loans, contracts, leases, formations of limited liability companies and corporations, etc., is considerably better now than in September 2007, 2008, and 2009, and perhaps better than it's ever been. Consequently, I have two cases pending in magistrate's court (one is in Walton County), which will be the first cases I have ever tried in magistrate's court, and I'm a seventy-six-year-old lawyer with fifty-three years of experience.

You sue 'em, and see 'em at church or the post office and at the grocery store. That probably rarely, if ever, happens to attorneys with King and Spalding or Troutman Sanders. Well, at least it keeps you alert and on your toes.

I've had two "land-line cases" where the parties were carrying guns. I knew all the parties personally, and in at least one of the cases, as the years have rolled by, ended up representing both sides in other matters. I've represented one side (four children on one side, and four on the other) in a dispute over their mother's estate. It was a highly charged and emotional case. I was in school (one a grade above me, and one two grades above me) with two of them. The older one, my client, was our next-door neighbor. I had been his lawyer for years. I had never done anything for the other, or if I had, it had been years before. I've had a man to call that he was coming to our office to see me in a case where I was representing his wife and that resulted in our entire staff being cloistered in the library and the police coming. Fortunately, there was not a shooting. Recently, we had a much older man come to the office barefooted and in what appeared to be his underwear. He was highly agitated. We were highly nervous. And so it goes in an active, small-town law practice.

I mentioned politics. Involvement in the political arena adds an additional dimension to a small-town law practice. I know. They come to see you, and let's say they have a driver's license problem. Are they talking to you as an attorney or as a legislator? I always came down on the side that they were coming to see me as a legislator, but often it evolved into much beyond my legislation responsibilities. Still, I always handled the problem "as a legislator." It probably cost me money, and often I felt that I got taken advantage of. Still, I think my decisions were the correct ones. In fact, I know they were.

Then there are those who start off by telling you that "I've always supported and voted for you" before trying to get you to do something for them. Several of them who told me some form of this never lived in any district I represented, and I've told more than one of them that "I'm surprised that you didn't get locked up, as it's against the law to vote outside the district you live in, and I never ran in the district where you live."

Double-first cousins to the "I've always voted for you" crowd are the "I've always been a friend of your family," as if we don't know who our friends have been throughout the years. It's hard to turn 'em down, even when you can't make any money doing what they want you to do for them, whether they were real friends or just friends for expediency.

There is nothing like an active, small-town law practice. I've loved it for now going into my forty-seventh year. I wouldn't trade what I've done for anything. I can't imagine doing anything else. I'm still enjoying it.

Eleven years ago, Janice, my wife, and I built a new house about five miles out of Perry. It's on a tract of land that had three fishing ponds on it when we bought it. We've built another one and now have four ponds. I can leave my office and be fishing or on the tractor mowing in about twenty minutes. It's three or four minutes to the laundry and about the same amount of time to the bank or restaurants. We have four children, eight grandchildren, and another on the way. Two of my grandchildren played high school football last night. All of my children, my active, sharp ninety-one-year-old mother, two brothers and a sister, two aunts (one is ninety-three years old), cousins, and many, many nieces, nephews and great-nieces and -nephews live within fifteen miles of where we live.

No, I wouldn't swap my small-town practice and my small-town life. The money may be better somewhere else, but it's been mighty good to my family and me in Perry, Georgia. And my practice has changed as it has grown throughout the years.

He was about five feet four inches and weighted about 240 pounds. I used to do legal work for him, and he would stand in front of my desk. He never sat. One day, he said to me, "Mr. Walker, I've got the highest accommodations in you." I knew exactly what he meant. I was always very appreciative of his words. I'm glad he thought I could get the job done for him. If you practice in a small town, you understand. I haven't heard anything like what he said to me in many years. I miss it. I guess that small-town practice is not like it used to be. I don't guess it will ever be the way it used to be. That's a shame. And if it is gone, I'll still remember his face, and that of the lady pursued by the small-loan company. Those were the days when I felt like a real lawyer. The memory of his words is good. I wish someone today would express "highest accommodations in me."

THE SUMMER OF '63

Our experiences in the summer of '63 deserve a book and not just a story. The book may never get done. This story, such as it is, will. By "our," I mean the experiences of Jerry Wilson, Jerry ("Do-Tricks") Horton, Bobby Jones, and myself. I will try to give you a taste of what it was like in that now seemingly distant time.

The date was June 10 or June 11, 1963. My little turquoise and white Corvair was crammed full and had luggage tied to the top—enough to last us for eleven weeks. We had made signs, which were attached to the sides of the car—"Texas or Bust!" And so we were off to Fort Worth, Texas, and Texas Steel Company on Hemphill Avenue, where we would work—and I mean WORK—for the summer. $1.95 an hour, and time and a half for overtime.

Within forty-eight hours of our leaving Perry, Wallace would "stand in the schoolhouse door" at the University of Alabama in Tuscaloosa, and Byron De La Beckwith would shoot and kill Medgar Evers in Mississippi. Governor Wallace stood in the doorway at the University of Alabama on Wednesday, June 11, and Medgar Evers was killed shortly after midnight on Thursday, June 12. Such was the dark and scary situation in the South in the summer of '63.

Times were so different. Let me give you an example: I was twenty-one years old; the other three, Jerry, Do-Tricks, and Bobby were twenty. Our first stop was in Selma, Alabama, where after eating lunch, we tried to shoot pool in an adjacent billiard parlor. We were kicked out because we weren't all twenty-one years old!

We spent the night in Meridian, Mississippi. That night, Medgar Evers was killed. The next day when we drove through Jackson, Mississippi, there was demonstrating in the streets. I had no feeling that we were witnessing history. I did have a feeling of being frightened.

No sooner had we arrived in Forth Worth than we were stopped by a Texas Ranger in an unmarked car wanting to know "what we were doing." Apparently, our explanation was satisfactory because not only did he let us go, he gave us one of his cards with a comment that "we would probably need it before the end of the summer." This time, the feeling was not of anger but relief.

Jerry Wilson's brother, Durward ("Will") was, at that time, vice president of Texas Steel. Later, he would be president and chairman of the board. With Durward's help, we were able to get a small, hot garage apartment close to the Texas Christian University campus. From what I have been able to read, we lived very close to Lee Harvey Oswald and his family. I wonder if we ever saw Lee Harvey while we were there. We also lived close to an elderly lady whom we helped get into her apartment when she, on more than one occasion, locked herself out. One day she brought us a cake for what we had done and announced to us that she was the mother of the legendary golfer Ben Hogan. We were all impressed, but Bobby Jones was thrilled!

The work at Texas Steel was hot, hard, loud, constant, and scary. The initial reception for four nonunion college boys by hardened union steel workers was less than cordial. I suspect that the first day we worked was the highest production day in the history of the company—they wanted to see if we could cut it. Sometimes, I didn't think we would make it, but somehow we did. It did not take them (or us) long to figure out that even though we were connected to Durward Wilson, we were labor and not management. They soon understood that we were "with them." When we left to come home, I know that they were sad to see us leave. My friend Newby, for whom I had daily completed his time card, actually had tears running down his cheeks. I miss these men and think of them often.

We worked six days a week but managed to do some interesting things in our limited off time, including eating at the Cattleman's Steak House, seeing the movie *Cleopatra* at a theater in Dallas, going to the Fort Worth Zoo, and water skiing on Lake Worth. Also, we did some other things that by today's standards are rather mild but that I am still not ready to confess.

I read the book *All The King's Men* by Robert Penn Warren while I was in Texas that summer. I made and saved enough money to buy an engagement ring, which I gave to Janice. I learned to love country music from hearing Do-Tricks play his guitar and sing—sometimes when we should have been sleeping! I followed with interest Senator Richard Russell's leading the Southern senators in fighting the Civil Rights Bill. I learned how to work—hard—and learned to admire and appreciate people who worked like this for a living. I got a good education about life.

We left Fort Worth to return to Georgia sometime in August. Lee Harvey Oswald shot and killed President Kennedy in November. I will never forget the summer of 1963.

ROLL A PEANUT DOWN CARROLL STREET—
WITH YOUR NOSE!

Republicans in Houston County are not new; today there are just so many more of them. Passions about politics did not start during the 2000 presidential election, but, generally, differences used to be handled in a more genteel and clever way. Take the case of the bet between Perryans Charles P. Gray (my grandfather) and local businessman Wendell K. Whipple, as written to me by Mr. Whipple on August 26, 1976, some fifteen years after Grandbuddy's death. This is verbatim, as given to me by my grandfather's friend, and my friend, Mr. Whipple.

"I arrived in Perry in the middle of the depression following the stock market crash of 1929. In this area, it was just beginning to be felt in earnest. The Republicans were truly the minority party in Georgia and throughout the South, but in Perry and Houston County, there were enough Republicans to have a county Republican committee, and chairman of that committee was Charles P. Gray, owner of Union Motor Company.

"I came in early 1931 to join my brother, Allen P. Whipple, in the Whipple Bros. Funeral Home and to work for him in his drugstore, Whipple Pharmacy. In the summer of 1932, Allen sold his drugstore, and Joe Beddingfield, S. L. Norwood, and I formed a partnership and opened the Houston Drug Company in September of that year. At that time, the population of Perry was about eleven hundred people.

"The Republicans had been in office since the turn of the century except for the two terms of Woodrow Wilson. Although President Hoover's handling of the veteran's bonus march on Washington had dimmed his popularity, and there was widespread dissatisfaction with the economy in general, there was little optimism for a Democratic victory in the 1932 election.

"As the campaign began to heat up, however, the drugstore was the popular gathering place for the crowd that gathered, as they do in every small town, to settle world problems. A great deal of good-natured banter was the order of the day, and as the town's leading Republican, Charlie Gray came in for a lot of ribbing from all sides.

"In one of the drugstore pow-wows, an election bet developed between Charlie Gray and me on the outcome of the election. The wager was that the loser would roll a peanut with his nose from the Houston Home Journal office (located at the present site of the office of Dr. J. L. Gallemore) to the Houston Drug Company store (present site of Jones Jewelers). The bet was to be paid off three days after the election.

"The bet was made all in fun and probably would never have been carried out, but the drugstore crowed picked it up and kept it going. One of the leading ones in promoting it was S. L. Norwood, a leading Democrat, a good friend of both of us, and a partner in the Houston Drug Company.

"When Roosevelt won, of course, the town went wild, and S. L. phoned the story of the bet to the *Macon Telegraph and News*. It made the late edition of the news and the Associated Press picked it up. Copies were mailed back to us from as far away as Oregon.

"When the story came out in the paper, it appeared that Charlie would have to pay off, but he thought he had a perfect out because he was on the federal grand jury in Macon. He underestimated S. L. Norwood, however. The election was on Tuesday, so the bet was due to be paid on Friday. S. L. slipped a copy of the newspaper story to the judge, so on Thursday afternoon, the judge called Charlie to the bench and said, "Mr. Gray, I understand that you have a commitment in Perry tomorrow, so you are excused from jury duty."

"The day—November 11th—was Armistice Day and it dawned bright and clear. The crowds began to gather an hour before the appointed time. School turned out, and the street was lined with cars and people so that traffic had to be diverted for several hours. Some brave souls even climbed on top of buildings to get a better view.

"Charlie showed up in coveralls wearing a handsome (?) false nose and with a toy elephant strapped to his back. I was at the starting point, and I carried a toy donkey.

"By the time he got started, Charlie had acquired quite a cheering section, and leading it were two of his daughters who were in high school. They were walking along beside him fanning him all the way, and Virginia, the older daughter, was crying. She thought it was terrible for anyone to treat her father that way, but now she remembers it as a hilarious occasion.

"After the first one or two passes at the peanut, Charlie discovered that he could blow it along, and after that, his progress was faster. By the time he reached the end, he had everybody in the crowd cheering for him, and probably if the voting could have been done over in Perry, that day the town would have voted Republican just for Charlie's sake.

"As I said, it was Armistice Day, so of course the American Legion Auxiliary ladies were busy selling poppies in the crowd. After the peanut rolling ending, the peanut was auctioned off. It brought three dollars, which was a very good price in those Depression days. Claude Andrew, then vice president of the Bank of Perry, was the high bidder, and the money was donated to the Legion Auxiliary Poppy sale. Then the donkey and the elephant were auctioned and brought a dollar each—also donated to the poppy fund. W. I. Greene and Louis Harper were the high bidders.

"Charlie lost the bet that day, but he won a multitude of friends who never forgot his good sportsmanship. Some years later, he was elected Mayor of Perry, and he was probably the first Republican after the Civil War to be elected Mayor in any small town in Georgia."

Presented to Larry Walker, grandson of Charles P. Gray, on August 26, 1976.

Does anyone want to bet on any future political race? Are you willing to risk rolling a peanut down Carroll Street with your nose? Even if you lost, you would probably win.

SENATOR RICHARD RUSSELL AND THE
KENNEDY ASSASSINATION

I have always been an admirer of Georgia's long-time United States Senator, Richard B. Russell. Like all of us, he was not perfect, but he did lots of good things. And, he knew how to get the job done. Presidents came and went, but Senator Russell was a constant. When Senator Russell spoke, everyone in Washington, even presidents, listened. He was "the man."

Let me tell you about a day in 1964 that I spent with Senator Russell. I believe it was 1964 because President Kennedy had already been killed, and I have a letter from Senator Russell dated February 22, 1964, which refers to our meeting. I was in law school at Georgia in Athens. Richard Russell IV, the senator's nephew, was a good friend of mine. He invited me to go with him to the Russell homeplace in Winder, Georgia. Winder is thirty or forty miles from Athens. We had a lunch at the Russell home with Senator Russell, my friend Dick, the senator's aide (I believe her name was Martha Tate), and the Russell's cook, whose name was Modene—just the five of us. It was a typical Southern-cooked dinner ("dinner" is what we used to call the meal in the middle of the day that was usually the main meal of the day).

After lunch, Senator Russell drove Dick and me all over Winder and Barrow County. I remember that we visited the Russell cemetery and one or two businesses in Winder, but what I remember most is what Senator Russell told us that day. I will never forget it.

First, a little background. Remember, Senator Russell was not only chairman of the Senate Armed Services Committee, he was also chairman of the CIA "watchdog" committee of the Senate. If anyone in the United States government knew what was going on in the world, as far as surveillance, intelligence, and counterintelligence was concerned, it was Senator Russell. This is what he told us: that we (the United States government) had put more than eighty CIA agents into Cuba and all had either been captured or killed by Fidel Castro and his people, and that we had tried, without success, to assassinate Castro.

I was flabbergasted and astounded by Senator Russell's statements. I had no direct contact with Senator Russell after that day in Winder. I heard no confirmation of his statements for years. Then, a few years ago, in stories about President Kennedy, his statements were confirmed. What he told Dick and me that day—which I never doubted—was true!

Now, bear in mind that Senator Russell was a member of the Warren Commission that investigated President Kennedy's assassination, concluding that Lee Harvey Oswald shot and killed President Kennedy acting alone. All members of the commission signed the report except one. You guessed it—Senator Russell! The one person on the commission who knew more about what was going on than any other. Since that 1964 day in Winder, Georgia—which was one of the most interesting days of my life—I have been intrigued by what Senator Russell knew and what he took to his grave that we will never know. Could it be that he knew of a conspiracy or involvement of other governments? Could it be that he knew that Lee Harvey Oswald did not act alone? Perhaps what he knew we will never know.

WATCHING FOLKS EAT DIRT

As best as he can remember, he was about ten years old. He could have been as much as twelve, but he suspects he was about ten. In any event, it was somewhere about 1952 to 1954.

He was a curious little fellow, not curious in the sense of being odd, but curious in wanting to acquire information and knowledge. Later, as a grown man, his mother told him, "You asked more questions than just about any child I ever saw." Whether she thought that was good or bad, he did now know.

But back to 1952, or whatever it was. He remembers lots about that day, but of course not nearly everything. But he does remember that his grandfather and some other men were going to dig a new well for the tenant farmer family that lived across the dirt road and down a field road and by a creek—Alligator Creek, he thinks—at the edge of the woods. And more importantly, at least to him, he was going to get to go with the grandfather and see this digging done.

Now, so as to give you a better picture of his remembrance of this day, I think I need to tell you what he recalls about this tenant farmer family. There was a mother, but as best as he knows, no daddy. Now he knows that there really was a daddy, but there was no adult male living in the house. There were six to eight children, with a couple of handsome boys four or five years older than he was. These boys did field work for his grandfather, and the mother worked in the house for his grandmother. There were also three or four pretty girls and some smaller boys about his age. He was very impressed with this family and considered the children as his friends.

Funny thing, he can't remember anything about any well before the new well was dug. Was there an old well that "filled up with dirt" or "played out?" Or did they haul their water from somewhere else? He guessed that for the purpose of this recollection, it didn't matter. Still, he was curious about this and wished his memory were better—if he ever even knew about their water source prior to the men's digging the new well.

He was so excited. And, as it turned out, rightfully so. He was going to experience two or three things that he never experienced before, or since.

Believe it or not, the men dug the well with shovels. The just started digging and made a hole six or eight feet across and went straight down. As the hole got deeper, one man stayed in the hole digging, and the dirt was hauled out in a bucket and was piled by the hole. The dirt towards the bottom was clay and had lots of chalk or kaolin in it—it is important for this story that you know about the chalk.

Then two things happened that he would never forget. He might have forgotten the first had it not been for the second. But the second made such an impression that he could not forget the first.

First, when the hole was about fifteen or twenty feet deep and water was beginning to seep in, his grandfather asked, "Would you like to go down into the well?" He did! In the bucket—down and up. First and last time he ever went down into a well. And, of course, back out.

Well, the well was built and he thought it was all over. What an exciting day. But then it happened. What he really will never forget. There was a pile of chalky clay by the side of the new well. First-dug dirt on the bottom and last-dug clay bucketed-out and on the top. And as casually as they would pick up a piece of hoecake, the family for whom the well was dug started eating the clay! Of course, he was astounded. His grandfather and the other men didn't try to stop them—they seemed to think it was all right. So, he decided he would try some dirt himself. And he did! But he quickly spit it out—not giving it much of a chance— just like the family that the well was being dug for didn't have much of a chance. He wished he had tried to like it a little more and vowed that one day he might, again, try to eat some dirt.

Seeing a well dug "by hand." Going down into the well in a bucket. Watching folks eat dirt. What a day. Such that he remembers it sixty years later.

REMEMBERING MR. BIG HOSS

His skin was black—really black. I want so say "like charcoal," but that's not right. Because it had a shine to it. Maybe more like burnt motor oil or a fresh clump of blackberries. Onyx. A black snake. Like the black ink that's making these words. Black and shiny.

He was big. To a twelve-year-old boy, really big! Thinking back on it, probably about six feet tall and 220 pounds, which is big. Not huge, but big. Even bigger in the 1950s than he would be today.

So, he was really black and he was really big. But that's not all. His hand and the lower part of his arm (left, I think, although time had negated certainty) was missing. Blew it off with a shotgun. Actually, the gun discharged when he had the stock butt in one hand and his other hand over the end of the barrel. Big hole in the hand. Dr. Weems had to remove what remained of the hand and part of his arm.

Big and black and with sometimes an artificial arm and hand (his "hook") and with no teeth. Right, no teeth! Not a one in his head. And he smiled a lot. Especially to and around me. And even in this strange social relationship, odd as it was, we had a good time together.

He got in trouble occasionally. It was rumored that he liked to play cards (did they call it skinning?) and do a little drinking. And sometimes Chief Dennard or Sheriff Chapman would have to come to Daddy and talk to him about some trouble he was in—nothing big, you know. A little gambling and perhaps a little too much to drink and maybe a fight. Daddy would do whatever he had to do to get him out of jail and everything would return to normal. I was aware of all of this.

He and his wife, Frances, and his considerable number of children (was it eight or ten?) lived on our farm. I thought he was wonderful. Still do. Even though he's dead and it's been probably forty-five or fifty years or more since I last saw him. Let me tell you why.

Rumored to be the strongest man in our county, even with one hand and part of an arm missing, he could pick up the front end of an automobile. He could bite an apple in two. And he would—just to amuse me and others. In fact, he could eat anything he wanted to—boiled peanuts, corn on the cob, etc.—you get the picture.

And Daddy would put me in his charge. We would go off together and work together, and I knew Daddy had confidence in him. Otherwise, he wouldn't have left me with him. Even though he occasionally got into trouble with the law, Daddy knew that he would take care of me and he wouldn't "cut up" while I was with him. I sensed a kindness and protectiveness, which made me feel good and safe when I was with him.

Get the picture. This little twelve-year-old white boy, who didn't know much, in an old pickup truck, windows down, being driven by a large, black, one-armed, no-teeth man using a hook for steering. And with the driver eating apples, laughing and talking, and telling the little white boy some things he had never heard before. Not awful things, and things the little one probably didn't need to know. But definitely things he hadn't heard before. Probably things he hadn't even thought about.

And he liked me. Probably realized that he was one of my heroes. And I liked him. Still do. We would ride and laugh and talk, and I thought he was wonderful. This, the strongest man I had ever known. The white folks called George Johnson "Hoss." And some of the black folks called George Johnson "Mr. Big Hoss." I called him "Hoss." But I should have called him "Mr. Hoss" or "Mr. Big Hoss." Wish I had. But it wouldn't have made me love him any more, which I did, this "Mr. Big Hoss."

III

MY ATTEMPT AT FICTION, BUT IT'S MOSTLY TRUE

PO BOY AND BUBBA

This is true, more or less. Unfortunately, although some would say fortunately, few folks around here remember these people I write about, and most of the others are disinterested. I think this is a shame because most of the ones I write about are worthy of remembrance, whether first-hand or because someone told you about them. And, by the way, generally speaking, they used to be well-known in our community, before it grew to what it is now, and when people used to talk with each other about Jesus and what He wanted us to do, whether or not it was going to rain, who had been seen, their car or otherwise, at Thelma's house, and people who lived here, including the people I write about.

Let's take Mr. J. C. Freeman, one of the most prominent people in our town. At one time, almost everyone knew Mr. J. C. Some knew him as Mr. Freeman, but the natives and people who had been here a long time called him Mr. J. C. to his face and his wife's face, or "Just Cash" to his or her back. A little more information is in order. Folks said Mr. J. C. was Jewish, although he attended the Methodist church downtown and taught the men's Sunday school class. Now that I have your attention, let me tell you more about Mr. J. C., his businesses, and the folks who worked for him.

Prior to the war, Mr. J. C. was in the shoe business. He sold Jarman's, Florsheim, and Nunn-Bush and had a real nice store, but during the war, he couldn't get shoes and he got out of the shoe business and got into the feed, seed, and fertilizer business. It was while he was in the shoe business that he got the name "Just Cash." Folks didn't have any money and they, or their children, needed shoes, so they would ask for credit. Mr. J. C.'s answer was always the same: "Just cash, just cash." And that's the way it was. Then when he got in the feed and seed business, Freeman Supply Co., the answer was still, "Just cash, just cash." It could be that the fact that his initials were J. C. kept "Just Cash" going, I don't know. By the way, I never knew what J. C. stood for.

There were other things that the people in the know said about Mr. J. C., and generally it was this: "Mr. J. C. knows how to make money, but even more, he knows how to hold onto it." None of this is to say that people, in general, didn't like "Just Cash, Just Cash" or Mr. J. C. They did. He was honest, a hard worker, gave to the church (but few, if any, other charities) and was pleasant to the other folks at church (he wasn't a member) and his customers. He had a good feed and seed business. I haven't already said it, but he had good products, Ralston Purina feed, and supplies, knew how they worked and what you needed ("for the tomato wilt, to kill rats, etc.") and charged a fair price. So, even if it was always, and I mean always, just for cash, Mr. J. C. was respected and liked in a distant and non-close sorta way.

Now, that brings up two other people who worked at Freeman's Supply Co. One, Junior Pinkston Jr., came right early to the feed store and the other, Bubba Ottwell, sometime later. Now, I never asked Po Boy, who is Junior Pinkston Jr., or Bubba what they thought about Mr. J. C., but had I done so, I think both would say something like this: "Oh, Mr. J. C. was a mighty good fellow, but he sho' did know how to make money and he had a special gift for holding on to it."

I'll get to Bubba later, but let me tell you right now, he wasn't one of those rich Ottwells from Fort Valley. Frankly, I don't think anyone, at least anyone who lived around here, knew much, if anything, about Bubba. But let's talk about the one that lots of folks knew about and the one that Mr. J. C. hired first, and that's Po Boy. I used to think Po Boy was related to some of those Pinkstons in Macon, but he said he wasn't, as far as he knew, and that his folks came out of Wheeler County, but his grandparents, he didn't say which side, although I thought it was his mother's, came from Washington County. He didn't seem to know much about his family background so I didn't press him.

I know you are wondering about "Po Boy." Po Boy was a nickname that Junior Pinkston Jr. got in the seventh grade, about the time students start giving and receiving names, and his stuck because Po Boy used to tell everyone who would listen that he was just a po' boy (he never said poor). It stuck. And he liked it and called himself that, and that's why I feel free to use it instead of Junior Pinkston Jr.

I'm getting ahead of myself, but I'm telling you that back then, Bubba and Po Boy were known around town and were generally well-liked. And, of course, the fact that Mr. J. C. had a good business that almost all the folks in town patronized (remember this was before Wal-Mart, Tractor Supply, Ace Hardware and the like) gave them lots of exposure to lots of people, from all walks of life.

I did hear one person say one time that she didn't like Po Boy. That was Mrs. Mary Sue Blasingame, formerly Mary Sue Ransom. Her reason was that Po Boy once put a live toady frog down the back of her dress. But someone who was in their class, hers and Po Boy's, whose name I won't reveal, tells me that the real reason she didn't like Po Boy was that she had a crush on him and he never paid her any attention except that one time with the frog. Even if Po Boy had paid attention, it wouldn't have done either one any good because Mary Sue's parents, who lived on one side of the tracks, wouldn't have stood for Po Boy, who lived on the other.

I think I need to tell you a little more about Po Boy. I'm sure no one will ever write about him again, so this is my chance and, in a way, his chance and probably his only chance. So here goes.

I told you that Po Boy called himself Po Boy and the other students called him Po Boy and it got so common that even the teachers called him Po Boy. When he graduated after the eighth grade, they gave him a little certificate saying that Po Boy, Junior Pinkston Jr., had met all requirements for this eighth grade diploma and that he had, in fact, qualified for the diploma. He never got a high school diploma because he dropped out in the tenth grade when he turned sixteen, after his folks got killed by a train when they ran their car across the track in front of the train. But if he had his name on a diploma, it would have been Po Boy, Junior Pinkston Jr., inscribed right on the paper, because that's what everyone, including Po Boy, knew and wanted.

Po Boy got a job in Mr. J. C. Freeman's feed store the same day he got his driver's license from the Georgia State Patrol. Po Boy wasn't dumb. Quite to the contrary, he was quick and smart enough to know that if Mr. J. C. "Just Cash" Freeman told the sergeant at the State Patrol Station to give him his license, he would get it. The only thing Po Boy had to do was promise Mr. Freeman he would go to work for him in the feed store as soon as he got his license, and he did. He loaded feed, Purina feed: hogena, fatena, layena, chicken scratch, chicken mash, mule feed, etc. He loaded fertilizer, which he and lots of the customer called guano. He waited on customers, sold them turnip seeds (eighty-five cents for one ounce), rat poison, yard rakes, tomato plants, cow manure, baby chicks, rabbits at Easter, insect dust, DDT, etc.

Po Boy was good with numbers. He was strong. He smiled a lot. He started driving two feed routes (one to the south end of the county on Tuesday and one to the north on Thursday). This started on the same day, a Tuesday, that he got his license. He was dependable. People liked Po Boy and Mr. J. C. knew it. When folks would run into Mr. J. C., they'd say something like, "Mr. J. C., how is Po Boy doing? He's a good ole boy." Mr. J. C. knew that meant money to him, and that's why he paid Po Boy forty dollars a week, although he held out sixty cents a week for the six Cokes Po Boy drank—one every work morning at 9:00, unless he was busy. Then he'd drink it when he got unbusy.

Po Boy, like I say, never gave Mr. J. C. trouble. Actually, I should say that he seldom caused trouble. But there was one time, in the spring of the year, that there was a problem. Let me tell you about it.

At Freeman's Supply Co., there were three employees, if you count Mr. J. C. In addition to Mr. J. C., there was the bookkeeper, Ida Green, and Po Boy. That is, until Mr. J. C. came in one morning in April and announced that they were so busy he had hired another employee, Bubba Ottwell, who had been recommended to him by his banker, Mr. Claude Worthington (Mr. J. C. was on the bank board), and that Bubba would be to work the next day. Mr. J. C. went ahead to explain that Bubba would help, generally, and would start doing the driving on the feed routes because he had a commercial driver's license. Well, that really made Po Boy mad, but he didn't let Mr. J. C. know, although Po Boy didn't know how long he could hold it. Hadn't he done a good job with the driving? He'd been driving and doing all the delivery work for almost a year, May 28 last year, and hadn't had a single problem unless you count sliding into the ditch getting stuck on Lighter Knot Road after the big rain this past January. Po Boy was mad.

What would he do if he quit? Could he find another job in the county if he quit—especially if Mr. J. C. got involved in it. If he had to leave the county, where would he find another mobile home to rent for thirty-five dollars a month? He couldn't, especially not one as good as the one he had and close enough to walk to work. He'd just have to see. But it really made him mad, Mr. J. C. taking the driving away from him as good as he'd done.

Monday morning came and Po Boy was there, on time, 7:00 as usual. Well, who was there waiting but a strong and good-lookin' boy about Po Boy's age, who Po Boy assumed was Bubba. Po Boy nodded and Bubba nodded and that was it. Po Boy had a key given to him by Mr. J. C. after he worked there six months, and he was proud of it. Sometimes when he got there at 7:00 A.M., customers were waiting to get in (Mr. J. C. got there about 8:30), and he'd let 'em in, sell, take their money, and give it to Miss Ida. So, Po Boy says to the young man he assumed was Bubba, as he opened the door, "What can I get for you?" to which Bubba responded, "I'm Bubba and I've come here to work." Po Boy responded, "What can you do?" Bubba, "I'll do anything. I really need a job and don't know what would've happened to me if Mr. J. C. hadn't given me this one. He told me you were mighty good, would teach me the business, and I'd like you. I'm looking forward to working with you. I had a job driving trucks, but lost it in the cutback. I've got a wife and baby and have to have this job."

Well, that seemed to be the end of Po Boy's mad. At least he said it was. I believe that he was just too good of a person to stay mad after what he had just heard. Exactly why he changed so fast, I don't know. He hadn't been raised in the church and wasn't particularly religious, but like I told you, he was a good person, and he and Bubba quickly became fast friends. And it didn't turn out at all like Mr. J. C. said. Bubba would drive on Tuesdays and Po Boy on Thursdays. And this was with Mr. J. C.'s approval. Po Boy, who didn't have a wife or a steady girlfriend, spent lots of hours at Bubba's place and ate lots of meals with Bubba, his wife, Trixi, and their little girl, Sara Elizabeth. Bubba's coming to Freeman's Supply was a good thing for Bubba, Mr. J. C., Po Boy, and probably Miss Ida.

Speaking of Miss Ida, and I do believe that was a "Miss" and not a "Mrs.," as to my knowledge she had never been married, I need to tell you a little about her. First, she always wore her hair in a bun and never wore any makeup. But she did wear strong perfume, and sometimes you could smell her before you saw or heard her. Really, she wasn't a bad looking woman, but she was pretty plain and I expect her "plainness" was on purpose, and that was the way she wanted it.

Actually, Miss Ida had worked for Mr. J. C. when he was in the shoe business. She went to work for him when she was eighteen years old and worked for him until she died, and I will get to that later. She was pretty protective of Mr. J. C., and I guess he liked that.

Once, I asked Miss Ida why Mr. J. C. didn't sell women's shoes when he had his shoe store. It seemed to me that he would have had a shot at twice as many customers. I will never forget her response: "I once asked him that same thing, and Mr. J. C. [she always called him that] told me that he didn't know anything about women's shoes, any more than he knew anything about women's dresses or underwear, and he wasn't going to get into the business of selling women's panties or braziers and he wasn't going to sell women's shoes," and that was the end of that.

Miss Ida, by the way she told it, seemed to agree with what she said Mr. J. C. had said, so I never raised the subject with her again. In other words, that was really the end of that.

I've told you most of what I know about Miss Ida except I will tell you again she was very loyal to Mr. J. C. and he knew it. Bubba and Po Boy knew it too, and when they were around the two of them together, they acted accordingly. I'm not saying that there was anything improper between Miss Ida and Mr. J. C., but they were close.

I don't want to belabor this next little story, but I think this is too good to pass. I think this story shows Mr. J. C.'s goodness and Po Boy's and Bubba's naivety. Now, in some ways, Po Boy and Bubba were very sophisticated, but in other ways, they were green as gourds. They could worm a dog or tell you when to and how deep to plant butterbeans and were great in dealing with Mr. J. C.'s customers. But in other ways, they didn't know much. I think this little story, which got widely known in our community, but was not used so as to hurt anyone's feelings, shows you what I mean.

It was late on a Thursday afternoon, and Mr. J. C., Po Boy, and Bubba were sitting on the horse feed behind a stack of Purina Hog Fatena, talking, when Mr. J. C. brought up church, and specifically the local Methodist church on Main Street. Po Boy and Bubba admitted that they'd never been to church before. Po Boy had gone to Vacation Bible School in Glenwood once as a child, and Bubba had been to his uncle's funeral at the Baptist church in Jesup, but that was it.

So Mr. J. C. set out to talk them into attending the service at the

Methodist church he attended on Sundays. Miraculously, and with persuasion from Mr. J. C., including a little money, they agreed to go together, and they did.

I won't get into what Bubba and Po Boy wore or where they sat (Mr. J. C. didn't sit with them, but the bookkeeper at the feed store did, as suggested to her by Mr. Freeman) because I've got something more important to tell you.

As fate would have it, Brother Billy Dews was preaching on Joshua and the Battle of Jericho, and after all the preliminaries, including the singing (congregational and choir) and the offering (the usher had to pry the plate out of Po Boy's hands), Brother Dews commenced. Although not like they do at the Pentecostal church or even the First Baptist church, it was pretty fiery for Methodist. Brother Dews talked very fast. Apparently, as Bubba and Po Boy had never heard preaching before, they listened and concentrated (they were both hard of hearing because of working around the feed mixer and the loud noise it made) and tried to take it all in. Now, I'm not saying they were saved, but they were greatly impressed and took it all to heart, and the next morning at the feed store, Bubba and Po Boy discussed what they'd heard.

Bubba: "What Brother Dews said was that a man named Joshway was in some kind of a big fight down at Elko." Po Boy added: "Yes, and the walls of some building fell down and lots of folks were killed. And that must have been that cotton warehouse that Mr. Frank and Mr. Billy Giles owned down there." They both agreed that was what was said, and they would check it out when they ran the feed route to the lower end of the county on Tuesday.

Tuesday was just the next day, and they couldn't wait to get the hogena, layena, and fatena delivered to Mr. J. C.'s customer so that they could slip over to Elko and see the warehouse on the ground and maybe some blood and body parts scattered around. So, they went, and much to their surprise, the building was standing and the only thing they saw was one big, green John Deere tractor going in front of the old Elko bank building pulling a wagon with a load of hay.

Just at that time, Po Boy said to Bubba, "I don't believe there's been no war down here." And Bubba replied, "No, the more I think about it, I've never seen more than four or five people at one time in Elko, and ain't enough going on in Elko to have a big ruckus about."

So, that was it. Bubba and Po Boy wouldn't go back to church, but Mr. J. C. did give each one five dollars for going that one time and promised to give them five dollars again if they'd ever go again. Even as tempting as it was, they wouldn't go back. Folks all over town remarked how strange it was that Mr. J. C. would give them money to go to church the way he loved money and given how he could hold on to it.

I've told you a good bit about Mr. J. C., but not too much personal stuff. The reason is that no one knew too much personal stuff about him. This is what I do know.

He was an average-sized man with a balding head. He always wore a hat to work, took it off and put it on top of the safe in his office when he got to work, and put it back on his head at 6:00 P.M. every day when he started home. A straw hat in summer and a wool hat when the weather cooled.

Mr. J. C. always wore black, cap-toed shoes, and they were always polished. He wore black dress pants, usually rumpled, and always, always a white shirt and tie. Best Po Boy could tell, he had three black ties that he rotated on weekdays, but on Saturday (the best business day of the week), he wore his white with red checkerboard tie that he got at the Ralston Purina Convention in St. Louis Missouri for being in the top ten dealers in his region for selling Purina feed.

Mr. J. C. got lots of comments about his "Saturday" tie, and he told folks exactly how he got it—in some detail.

One day at work, Mr. J. C. was going out of the front door with a Coke to his lips when his hand slipped off the door and he spilled the soft drink all over his tie. Well, Po Boy and Bubba had a one-dollar bet as to whether he would wear the tie the next Saturday. Po Boy said "no" and Bubba said "yes." The next Saturday, Mr. J. C. showed up with the rumpled Purina feed tie around his neck. The checkerboard red had turned to pink when Mrs. J. C. put the tie in the washing machine, but Mr. J. C. continued to wear it every Saturday, and the customers continued to ask about it, and Mr. J. C. continued to tell them exactly how many tons of Purina feed he had sold to win the tie.

It's time for me to end this story, if things ever end. People do. Not when they die, but when no one remembers or ever talks about them anymore. Most things don't end, but they do change, and so I'll end this by telling you about some changes.

Mr. J. C. lost his wife about two years after Po Boy went to work for him. She was almost a recluse, and most folks in town had never seen her, so when she died there was not a big "to do" about it, despite her being married to a prominent citizen.

Then something happened that caused tongues to wag. Mr. J. C. married his bookkeeper, Ida Green. I'll tell you nobody in the community saw that coming, and the big question by many was: "Why would Just Cash do anything like that?" But marry her he did. Then, after they'd been married about two years, Ida Green caught the pneumonia and was gone. And so Mr. J. C. buried two wives in three years, and since he had no children, he lived alone in the big, white colonial home on Hodges Circle. His health began to decline, as did the business at Freeman Supply, to some extent, although Po Boy's popularity kept lots of the locals coming and buying. In other words, Just Cash no longer had the only "game in town," but the business was still fairly good. I should add that Mr. J. C. did not come in every day, and Po Boy was generally handling everything but the money.

Oh, I almost forgot to tell you that Bubba left soon after Mr. J. C. married Ida Green. Bubba wasn't upset about anything, but through his wife's family he got a job driving trucks for a big company in south Mississippi. Po Boy hated to see Bubba leave, not because he couldn't handle all the work, he could, but because Bubba had gotten to be his best friend, and he knew he was going to miss him and he did.

And then on a beautiful spring morning in April, after he had opened the store and at about 8:00, the police came to Freeman's Supply and informed Po Boy that Mr. J. C. had been found dead in his bed, apparently as the result of a self-inflicted gunshot to the head. Po Boy was devastated, and despite all he could do, broke down and cried in front of the officers. Po Boy had come to love Mr. J. C. In fact, Mr. J. C. was the best friend he had in the world.

What I'm going to tell you next you're not going to believe. Po Boy didn't know what to do about Freeman Supply, but he kept opening up every morning, waiting on the customers and putting the day's receipts in the safe in "Miss Ida's office." And then the day after Mr. J. C.'s funeral, Bubba got a call from Chester Mixon, a prominent local lawyer, who asked Po Boy if he could come over to his office after he closed the store at 6:00. Nervous though he was about what he had possibly done wrong, he told him he would. He walked down the street and was there at 6:10.

Chester Mixon had been in Freeman Supply many times, and Po Boy waited on him every time. Po Boy liked Chester and thought Chester liked him, and at the store he had always been comfortable around Chester. But today he was nervous. He wasn't at all comfortable. What had he done? What was going to happen to him? Where was he going to get another job? Who was going to run the store?

And then Chester told him. He invited Po Boy back into his back office and told Po Boy that he wanted to read Mr. J. C.'s will to him. Po Boy said, "Okay," but he didn't know what business it was of his and was so nervous he could hardly breathe.

What Chester read was unbelievable to Po Boy. Mr. J. C.'s instructions were almost unbelievable. First, Mr. J. C. said he wanted all his debts paid, but Chester said there weren't any. Then he said he wanted a funeral at the Methodist church, which had already been done and with a very large crowd. Then he said he wanted the church to have $100,000. Po Boy had no idea Mr. J. C. had this much money. In fact, he couldn't imagine this much money. And then he said he wanted everything else to go to Po Boy and wanted Po Boy to be in charge, with Chester to help him as needed. Po Boy couldn't believe what he had just heard and thought he was going to have a heart attack, but he didn't. In time, he was resigned to what Mr. J. C. had done, but he never really got comfortable with it.

Well, I won't get into how much money and property there was, but I will tell you that it was enough that Po Boy sent Bubba a cashier's check for $25,000. Also, Po Boy kept running Freeman Supply, and he installed air conditioning and otherwise improved the store. Business also improved. So, Po Boy had to hire a helper and a bookkeeper, and he bought a new feed truck, took on several hardware items, and managed to compete quite well with Wal-Mart, Ace Hardware, and even Tractor Supply.

Some things stayed the same. Po Boy never changed the name of the store. It was Freeman Supply Co. It did well, improving in the amount of sales almost every month. Po Boy still went on the feed route twice a week. Po Boy drank a Coke around 9:00 every morning, and he put fifty cents each time in the cash box.

Some things changed. Po Boy joined the local Methodist church and was regular in attendance. He was generous to the church and all the local charities and in particular the schools. He bought ads in the football program and the yearbook and gave annually to the local FFA and 4-H hog and steer shows. He even endowed a scholarship at the University of Georgia in Mr. Freeman's name. It was to be for boys and girls of limited means from rural Georgia. Chester Mixon, a UGA law graduate, helped him get all of this set up.

Po Boy never forgot Mr. J. C. Freeman. He bought an office building downtown and named it the J. C. Freeman Building. He told folks what a good man Mr. J. C. was. And he never again referred to Mr. Freeman as "Just Cash, Just Cash."

But the biggest thing that ever happened to Po Boy was when Mr. Claude Worthington telephoned and asked him if he could come by the bank sometime that afternoon. They agreed on 4:00, and Po Boy was there, wondering what Mr. Worthington wanted. He knew that he was current on the two notes that he had with the bank and thought maybe Mr. Claude wanted to talk with him about the Angus cows he had just bought to put on his farm just outside of town. But that wasn't it.

What Mr. Worthington wanted was to ask Po Boy if he would agree to serve on the bank's board of directors "to take Mr. Freeman's place." Po Boy was astounded. Was he hearing Mr. Worthington right? But finally he said yes. It was the hardest thing he had ever agreed to.

Po Boy attended his first meeting on the first Tuesday in January, and his seat was just to Mr. Worthington's right at the head of the table. He knew it had been Mr. Freeman's chair because there was a little gold plaque on the table where he was sitting that read: "In Memory of our Great Friend, J. C. Freeman, 1918–1986." And when he sat down he saw his name plate in front of him, and it read "Junior (PO BOY) Pinkston Jr." with the Po Boy all capitalized.

Po Boy continued to work at Freeman Supply Co. He never married and had no children. The folks in town, almost all of them, liked Po Boy, and what they said about him the most was that the "smartest thing Mr. Worthington's bank ever did was to put Po Boy on its board because Po Boy was generous, kind, and was a mighty good man." And he was.

THE CONFEDERATE MONUMENT

THE BOY

The Boy was anxious. Being only twelve years old, he probably didn't know exactly what "anxious" meant, but that's what he was. He didn't say anything to his parents about it, but ever since Billy Bailey informed him that he had gotten his letter, or at least his parents had gotten it, he had been worried.

Billy Bailey was the Boy's best friend, and the letter to his parents told them that Billy's sixth grade teacher was going to be Miss Mattie Lee Hood. Billy told the Boy about his teacher assignment, and that made the Boy think that his parents would get a letter that day, or soon, telling them who the Boy's teacher would be.

The Boy wanted to be in the same room with Billy, but even more, he wanted to be in Miss Mattie Lee Hood's room. The Boy had heard the talk: "Miss Mattie Lee loves history and English and spends lots of her time and her pupils' time teaching English and history." Well, that was fine with the Boy because he loved English and reading and especially American history, and Miss Mattie Lee loved American history and especially the War between the States. The Boy did, too, so he really wanted to be in Miss Mattie Lee's room. He was anxious and didn't understand why his parents hadn't gotten the teacher assignment letter from Wesley Creek Middle School.

The next day it happened. His daddy came home from work about 6:00 P.M., as usual, and while the Boy, his younger brother, and mother and daddy were eating supper, his daddy surprised him when he said to the Boy: "By the way, I brought home the letter I got about a week ago from Mr. Cason at Wesley Creek Elementary. It's about your teacher for next year. It got buried under some insurance policies on my desk. Sorry that I didn't bring it home last week. You will be glad to know you are in Miss Mattie Lee Hood's class."

The Boy wanted to shout, but he didn't. Rather, in a calm voice, he said softly, "Good, I wanted to be in her class. And Billy told me about a week ago he was in her class. So, I'm glad."

That was it. With school starting in about two weeks, the Boy was happy. Miss Mattie Lee, Billy, the War between the States, things were good. The Boy was no longer anxious, although if he had to say how it was, it would have probably been something simple like: "I feel better. I'm glad to be in Miss Mattie Lee's room with Billy."

The Boy, when he had become a man and even an old man, remembered his first day of school with great clarity. It was in 1947. His mother had walked with him to school. Up the big road, paved Spring Street, back towards town, then left on dirt Third Street, and then after two blocks across the paved US Highway, with his mother holding his hand all the way from home to the first-grade classroom. When his mother left and turned him over to Miss Francine Coley, he cried and his mother cried. That, and how Miss Francine took his little hand and guided him to his little desk on the row next to the door and close to the front of the room. Also, how she seated him next to Billy Bailey, that being the first time he had ever seen Billy, even though Wesley Creek was a small town. Billy was a Baptist and the Boy was a Methodist. Billy had gone to kindergarten and the Boy hadn't. But the Boy had been taught to read by his mother. She told him just before she died, many years later, that the first word he ever said was "read" as he climbed into his daddy's lap and his daddy read the "funny papers" to him. Reading had always been a big part of his life.

Another day of school he remembered was also a first day, and he remembered it in some detail. It was in 1953, the sixth grade, and in Miss Mattie Lee Hood's class. He took the same route to school, by himself, as he would every school day from home to Wesley Creek Elementary. But then he was helped across the paved US Highway by one of the school boy patrols. The Boy thought that these young men, high schoolers at Wesley Creek High, were "cool," and he contemplated being a school boy patrol himself when he got a little older, but it never happened. In any event, the Boy had been walking to school by himself, or with other students, every day that he went to Wesley Creek Elementary since the first day in the first grade.

Actually, the Boy, even when he was an old man, could remember lots about the 1953 to 1954 school year and what was going on in Miss Mattie Lee Hood's sixth-grade class. And mostly they were good memories.

Miss Mattie Lee, on the first day, placed the Boy in the first chair in the third row, middle of the classroom and just in front of her desk. She put Billy Boyd Bailey, by then known as Billy Boy, directly behind him. Later, the Boy thought that his fifth-grade teacher, Mrs. Akin, had probably told Miss Mattie Lee how much he loved history and thus her reason for where she seated him.

Miss Mattie Lee probably knew that Billy Boy, who was much larger than the Boy, was also a good student and the best athlete (he had actually played on Wesley Creek's Junior High basketball team in the sixth grade). Probably, she also knew that the Boy and Billy Boy were great friends. Regardless, the Boy remembered that he was happy that Billy Boy was behind him. The Boy thought that Billy Boy liked it too.

The Boy, even when he was an old man, could tell you how Miss Mattie Lee started her class after all the boys and girls introduced themselves. (The Boy thought the introductions were odd given that there were only fifty-eight students in the two sixth-grade classes and that there was only one new student who was not there in '52 and '53.) Miss Mattie Lee introduced herself. She told the class that she had lived in Wesley Creek all of her life, that her father had come to Wesley Creek from Kentucky to be the manager at the local cement plant, that her mother had taught civics, English, and history at Wesley Creek High School for many years, and that neither of her parents were still living. Then she told her class that they would soon be young adults and that she intended for them to learn many new words and how to spell them, English grammar and literature, and government and American history. The Boy remembers how delighted he was with this and that he was ready for it all to begin.

Then Miss Mattie Lee told the class that Confederate general John Bell Hood, originally from Kentucky, was her grandfather. That he was born in 1831 and died in 1879, and that he was in charge of the Confederate Army in the Atlanta Campaign.

The Boy knew a good deal about the Battle of Atlanta and knew that the Confederates were soundly defeated there. Nonetheless, the Boy could hardly wait for the class to get to this.

Billy Boy, who preferred math and science, told the Boy that he was bored with history and wished that they would spend more time on other subjects. But Billy Boy was smart, and the Boy knew Billy Boy made good grades in everything, including history and English.

The Boy remembered Miss Mattie Lee telling them that when they finished the Revolutionary War she would take the War between the States out of order. It would be taken up after World War I, the Depression, and World War II, and she would end the year with the War between the States, beginning about the first of March, with a big assignment in connection with Confederate Memorial Day, which was on April 26. She also told the class that while slavery was an issue causing the War between the States, "states' rights" was the primary issue. The Boy didn't know what "states' rights" was, but he knew he was going to learn and could not wait to get to it.

The Boy's maternal grandparents, whom the Boy loved very much, lived right up the street from the Boy and his family. He loved both of them and particularly liked to visit with his grandfather, whom he called Papa. Papa had come to Wesley Creek from Arizona in the early 1900s and had been in the insurance business in Wesley Creek since 1927 and with the Boy's daddy for the past ten years or so.

Papa told the Boy about homesteading in Arizona in the early 1900s, branding the cattle, digging a well to get water, and many of the hardships that he and Granny endured during the five years that they were there. Also, how they decided to move to Wesley Creek when his half-brother contacted him and told him that there was a small, new insurance company in Wesley Creek for sale. He told the Boy about seeing Pancho Villa, a bandit chief who became a general of the Mexican Revolution and raided Tombstone, Arizona, during the time when Papa and Granny were there. The Boy thought Papa knew just about everything that had ever happened in our country and wanted to tell Papa what Miss Mattie Lee had said about what caused the War between the States.

It was a fast year, 1953 to 1954, in Miss Mattie Lee's sixth-grade at Wesley Creek Elementary. The Boy had made good grades in all subjects to and through the March report card: A's in history and English, B's in everything else. The Boy's parents and grandparents were satisfied, the Boy was happy, and the best was yet to come: a complete study of the

War between the States with a paper to be written towards the end. Still, the Boy didn't know what his subject would be: Robert E. Lee, the Atlanta Campaign, Jefferson Davis, the cause of the war, Georgia's War between the States, Georgia's Civil War, Governor Joseph E. Brown, or what? He thought about writing on General John Bell Hood, but Billy Boy told him he was going to write on General Hood with the comment, "I know Miss Mattie Lee will give me an A." With the exception of General Hood, the Boy had much to choose from; what would he write about? He knew it would not be about General Hood.

Almost every Saturday morning, at least when he and his family were in town, the Boy was in downtown Wesley Creek selling peanuts. In the late summer and fall, it was boiled peanuts, and in the spring and summer, it was parched peanuts. He got the peanuts from Mr. Hugh Thompson's farm, raw, and he and his daddy washed them, boiling them in the summer and early fall, and keeping the remainder and parching them for the spring and summer sales. The Boy sold 100 sacks of peanuts every Saturday for ten cents a sack. They were easy to sell and he enjoyed doing it. He especially liked the teasing he got from the adults, and the fact that they liked him and his product, and they knew his name. At twelve years of age, he was already developing business and political skills.

From Dale's Restaurant on the corner, he walked down Dogwood Street and then along Government Avenue in front of the Creek County Courthouse. It was a walk he'd probably made over a hundred times, and yet this was the first time he'd ever really done anything more than to notice, casually, the Confederate monument in front of the courthouse. It was between the large Magnolia tree and the table and benches where the men gathered in late afternoon to talk, chew tobacco, play checkers, and tell tales.

That was it. He'd write about Creek County's Confederate monument. He stopped and looked. For the first time, he really looked at the monument. Then he looked down at his box of peanuts. About thirty bags left to sell. He had plenty of time. Off the sidewalk and onto the courthouse grounds and to the monument, with his eyes focused on the erect soldier, rifle at his side, facing to the north. The Boy's first thought: "The soldier must have been carved in 1861 when the war was going well for the South, before it all went bad. The soldier was erect, handsome, and looked well-fed. This Boy knew the war started at Fort Sumter in South Carolina or Manassas in Virginia, which the north called Bull Run, in 1861, and he was probably the only student in Miss Mattie Lee's class who knew this, but know it he did. Despite how badly it pained him, he knew that the ending for the South was horrible. The Boy couldn't wait to write his paper about the Confederate monument and the pride that white Southerners had in their sons of the South, regardless of the cause of the war or the outcome. He turned to go back to the sidewalk but then noticed the writing on the statue, so he turned back and removed his little pad in which he ordinarily wrote a record of his deposits from peanut sales. He removed his number 2 lead pencil and wrote the words that were carved on the statue, ending it with "United Daughters of the Confederacy, 1907."

It was Sunday after Sunday school, church, and mother's Sunday dinner of roast beef, mashed potatoes with gravy, butter beans, squash, homemade biscuits, sweet ice tea, and banana pudding when the Boy asked his daddy if he could ride his bike downtown, look at the Confederate monument again, and be sure he had everything he needed for his paper.

The Boy's father seemed surprised but said, "Yes, provided you will come straight home after you get through doing it." The Boy was off on his red Rollfast bike for his ten-minute ride to the courthouse in the downtown. He spent more than thirty minutes looking at the statue and sculpted soldier and, again, the words on the monument. He knew he had selected the right theme to write about for Miss Mattie Lee.

The Boy wrote his paper using the words adopted by the Daughters of the Confederacy and entitled it "Our Monument, the Confederate Monument." And as Miss Mattie Lee said was permissible and preferred, he had it typed by his father's secretary, who bragged on his paper profusely. The Boy's father told the Boy that he should give Miss Rose a gift for typing the paper. The Boy went to the Wesley Creek Pharmacy and with some of his "peanut money" got her a bottle of perfume and a box of chocolate-covered cherries. She thanked him and gave him a little kiss on his forehead.

The Boy then took his paper to his grandfather, Papa, and watched until he had read all five pages. When he finished, Papa said to the Boy, "Very, very good. I am proud of you, but I do have one thing I would like to say to you. On page one, about half way down, you write, 'The War between the States was largely an effort by Southern states to claim what was the constitutional rights of the states. While there were other issues, "states' rights" was the primary issue.'" Then Papa said to the Boy, "I disagree: slavery was the primary cause. There were other issues such as states' rights, but slavery was the primary cause." The Boy was hurt and confused. He knew what Miss Mattie Lee had taught them, but he knew Papa was smart, knew about what he called the "Civil War," and wouldn't have said this to the Boy had he not felt strongly about it.

The Boy said, "Thanks, Papa," and Papa said, "Good job. I'll bet you get an A." When he got home, the Boy told his daddy what Papa had said, and his daddy responded, "I'd leave it like it is, you know Papa was originally from West Virginia, later lived in Arizona, and they think a little differently than we do." So the Boy did leave it like he had it, although it worried him considerably, and when he became a man, he realized that Papa was right all along. Miss Mattie Lee loved his paper and gave the Boy an A+. She read the paper aloud to the class and told them it was the only A+ she had ever given as long as she had been teaching and doubted she would ever give another. Of course, the Boy was a little embarrassed but proud and believed that Miss Mattie Lee, his teacher, was probably right all along about the states' rights issue.

THE MAN

The Boy graduated from Wesley Creek High School in 1960. He was president of his class and finished in the top third of the class. His friend, Billy Boyd Bailey, was the valedictorian of the class and was voted the best athlete in the class. The Boy applied to and was accepted at the University of Georgia. Billy Bailey got a football scholarship to Georgia Tech and went to Tech that summer, preparing for the fall quarter and his participation on the freshman team as a running back. After two serious shoulder injuries, the second one during the Thanksgiving Day game against the University of Georgia freshmen, Billy Boyd Bailey, at one time the most promising running back in Georgia, returned to Wesley Creek without a Georgia Tech diploma but with a new nickname given to him by the Georgia Tech coach, "Big Bull" Bailey.

That would remain his name for most of the rest of his life. Big Bull Bailey was hired by his uncle, the sheriff of Wesley Creek, at age nineteen to be a deputy sheriff in Creek County. Folks who knew the family were already saying that Big Bull would be sheriff himself one day.

Ironically, after two years in Vietnam as a marine and with a University of Georgia diploma in hand, the Boy returned to Wesley Creek and got a good job teaching at Wesley Creek High School. The Boy became the Man as he taught history, geography, and English. In his third year, he became an assistant coach. The Man learned a great deal about football from Coach Kuhlke, and in his second year he became the assistant head coach and the defensive coordinator. Coach Quentin handled the offense.

Coach Quentin had won the district in football eight times and the State Class B football title four times. He was Georgia's High School Coach of the Year twice, and he sent twelve football players to Division 1 colleges.

The Man was in his second year as assistant head coach to Coach Kuhlke (theoretically, a Wesley Creek Indian's assistant) when Coach Quentin, at age 61, dropped dead at football practice from a massive heart attack. The Man became the head coach immediately and continued as the coach for four years, compiling a record of thirty-eight wins and ten losses while winning three district titles but no state championships. Without pressure to leave, the Man gave notice and resigned as a teacher and coach and went into the insurance business with his daddy and grandfather in downtown Wesley Creek.

Wesley Creek, Georgia, is in Creek County, Georgia. As the old-timers in the community would tell you, "The creek, Creek Creek, was named after the Indians, and the county was named for the creek." They would also tell you the name Wesley came from John Wesley, the founder of the Methodist church in America, who, supposedly, in the mid-1700s, came up the Altamaha and Oconee Rivers, spreading Methodism and with a campsite at or close to where Wesley Creek is now located. Whether or not any or all of this was true, the Man did not know, but he liked it. He also liked, no, loved, Wesley Creek and Creek County, and it was evident to the people in the community that he felt this way. He was generous to the school, the churches, and the charities in the county. He was popular with the people in the community. The insurance agency prospered.

You should also know this: Creek County had a somewhat unique form of county government. Only eight out of Georgia's 159 counties had what Creek County had, which was a sole county commissioner form of government in place of a board of commissioners, usually five, which was the standard for the rest of the state. So when Creek's sole commissioner, Mr. Hubert Tucker, died unexpectedly in 1972, the leaders in the county started looking for someone to elect to take his place.

The Man got a telephone call from Wesley Creek's mayor, Jimmy Meeks, early on a Monday morning, after Mr. Tucker's burial service at the Wesley Creek First Baptist Church on the previous Sunday afternoon. The Man had no idea what they wanted as they requested that he meet with a group as soon as possible. The Man suggested 4:30 P.M. that day, and that's when they met. Their business: to get the Man to run in the special election as commissioner. He was flabbergasted and ended up telling them he would think about it, would talk it over with his wife and family, and would be back in touch with them. One thing he wanted to know, while they were there, was whether he could continue to help run the insurance agency that he owned with his father. Mayor Meeks told him that they anticipated this question, that the county attorney had researched it, and that he could continue his insurance business but that they expected him to give the county enough time to do the job. They also told him the salary was $75,000 a year plus a $500 a month expense account plus the use of a county car while attending to county business. He would also be on the county's insurance program, and if he kept the job for at least ten years, he would be vested in the Creek County retirement program. He didn't immediately respond, but all of a sudden he was very interested in the job.

The Man decided to run. Just as promised, all in the group offered their full support and let it be known in the county. Several more prominent citizens came forth with offers of support and campaign contributions. He qualified in the nonpartisan election and had no opposition. Two months later, the Man was the sole commissioner of Creek County with a nice office on the top floor of the beautiful courthouse.

The Man's first day on the job was January 2, 1973, and it was largely uneventful except for putting several meetings on his calendar for the next few weeks, helping to cut a ribbon for a new county road that was opening, and which he had nothing to do with bringing to pass, and listening to a group of citizens complain about dogs running loose in the county. He greatly enjoyed all of it. His state representative lawyer friend, who had been in office for many years, came by to see him late on his first day and told him that "the three worst things to deal with in politics were, in order, people's children, dogs, and garbage," and he reminded him that he "had all three with a county recreation department, garbage pickup, and animal control." They both had a good laugh, although the Man would find out it was true and remembered the old saying, "Many truths are spoken in jest." And yet it continued to go well, and he was proud of how good Creek County and its county seat town, Wesley Creek, were doing. That's the way it was for many years. He loved his job. But then, after he had been in office a long, long time, he developed an uneasiness about things, and he knew, or thought he knew, the source of his concerns.

THE OLD MAN

It started prior to the 2008 election. He did have a primary opponent in 2008 and, for the first time since he had been Creek County's sole commissioner, it was a tough race. He knew he would run well in the black community. He always got a good vote there, even when he didn't have an opponent. In 2004, he had a worthy opponent, but he still got 63 percent of the vote, with 87 percent of the black vote. African Americans comprised 46 percent of Creek County's population but voted less often than its white constituents, although in the 2008 election they turned out a strong showing, with 65 percent of the eligible black citizens voting. Without this exceptionally strong vote, he would have lost in a close race. He was proud of this, yet he was troubled.

His political problems, if you could call them that, started in 2007. Actually, they started sooner, and he knew there were potential political problems, but they surfaced in 2007. Like many issues in politics, it involved money, it involved his closeness with the black community, and it involved Creek County's most visible and active politician, Sheriff Big Bull Bailey. Some additional history is in order. The sheriff was having the "word" put out by some of his deputies and supporters that the Old Man intended to move the Confederate monument to the Confederate Soldiers' graves in the Wesley Creek Cemetery. The Old Man had never considered such a thing, although it suddenly became a big and controversial issue. But the real issue was the sheriff's budget, with the "monument" issue a diversion and yet a very potent political challenge for the Old Man.

Billy Boyd Bailey, formerly known as Billy Boy Bailey, was now officially Sheriff Big Bull Bailey. It was official because the second time he ran for sheriff, in 1976, he qualified using the "Big Bull" name and got a challenge from his opponent. After a much publicized hearing before Superior Court Judge Culpepper Aultman, the ruling was that since most people called Billy Boyd "Big Bull," he could use this name. Not only did the incumbent prevail in court, but he also overwhelmingly defeated his opponent, and, like the Old Man, had run unopposed except for one time, and Big Bull won that contested race with more than 70 percent of the vote.

The Old Man thought that Billy Boy, later Big Bull, would always be his best friend. Billy Boy was in the Man's wedding, and the Man was in Billy Boy's first wedding. Big Bull left his first wife in 1996 and about six months later married his young secretary. There were "raised eyebrows," but Big Bull's popularity continued. He was popular with the voters, especially the white voters. At least, everyone thought he was, because, after all, he'd not had but one opponent since 1976. By and large, he was a good sheriff.

Of course, the sheriff and the commissioner both had offices in the courthouse and visited each other periodically. In fact, at least two or three times a month, they would cross the street to Dale's Restaurant and drink coffee with the locals. It was where most of the problems in Wesley Creek, Creek County, and the United States were solved, at least temporarily. Both the commissioner and the sheriff thought it was good for their politics to be seen with each other, although this was never discussed by them. In all truthfulness, the Old Man didn't feel as close to the sheriff as in the past. Truth be told, the Old Man suspected the sheriff was behind his having an opponent in 2008, although he was not absolutely certain about it.

And then it happened. The first thing, as you might expect, involved money. It started in the fall of 2007 when he was trying to put a budget together for the next year. The years 2007 and 2008 were not good ones for the Old Man. His job wasn't fun. The economy was "in the tank." Some called it a recession, but it seemed like a depression to the commissioner. The property-tax income remained about the same, but the sales tax and the SPLOST tax declined appreciably. So, the commissioner had to adopt a budget for fiscal year 2008 with 28 percent less money than the county had in 2007. Every department head took at least a twenty-percent cut except the sheriff, who was cut 13 percent. All of the department heads were upset except the sheriff. He was livid. And so there was a tremendous strain on the commissioner's and the sheriff's diminished friendship, although both managed to keep their differences out of the media. But the rift was deep and real. And it would get worse.

The next rift would be even greater. It was the worst thing that ever happened to the Old Man, and it happened three months after the Old Man was elected in 2008. This time, the commissioner knew that the sheriff was involved.

THE MONUMENT DECISION

One more term is what the Old Man wanted, and it had been delivered to him by a majority of the Creek County voters in the August 2008 primary election. He had no general election opposition. His final term would be from January 1, 2009, to December 31, 2012. That's what the Old Man wanted, and then he would be glad to give up the office, for, after all, he would have had forty years of public service, and he would be seventy years old when he left. But now he knew it would not end this way. It would not end well.

The first Tuesday in November started cool and breezy, at least that was the way it was when the Old Man got up, around 5:30 A.M., as was his custom. Uncharacteristically, the Old Man didn't feel well. He was a little faint and dizzy, but after two cups of hot black coffee and an aspirin, he felt better. He blamed his discomforts on what he had facing him at his upcoming commissioner's meeting that day. It was going to be

119

unpopular with lots of his friends and supporters, but he thought he would feel better after his decision was made, and as most of the citizens in the county, and really, many people all over the state knew, Creek County was going to decide, today, about the fate and future of the monument. The decision, as written and typed by the Old Man's secretary, was in his inner coat pocket, and he would read his decision around 10:15 A.M., shortly after the meeting started at 10:00. He anticipated that there would be protesters regardless of what he decided, including possible demonstrations. Ironically, crowd control was in the hands of Sheriff Big Bull Bailey and his deputies. The Old Man thought: *"Talk about the fox guarding the hen house."*

As usual, for "meeting days," the Old Man had on a dark blue suit, white shirt, and tie. Today, his tie was red, white, and blue. He also had an American flag pin in the lapel of his suit coat. He knew he looked the part, but as to whether he would handle things well, he did not know. He did know, at least he thought he did, that this meeting today would be different from any of the thousands of meetings he had held in the past thirty-six years. Regardless, he was ready to announce his decision and suffer the consequences. At least he thought he was.

The easy way out for the Old Man was to have a referendum. He knew that the issue, if voted on, would favor non-removal, and probably by a sizeable majority. But he had no intention of calling for a popular vote. He thought it was part of his job to make this decision, and he intended to do his job to the best of his ability, as long as he was in office. There would be no referendum. He would make the decision, with all of its ramifications.

After his coffee and two pieces of cheese toast, the Old Man was in his pickup truck, down his driveway, stopping at the paper box at the road to take the *The Wesley Creek Signal* from the paper tube. The headlines read: "Commissioner to Make Confederate Monument Decision Today." Then the articles rehashed previous stories about what had gone on in the community concerning the "moving the monument controversy" with quotes from seven local citizens giving their views next to a picture of each one. The four white citizens were adamantly opposed to removal, two African Americans favored removal, and one African American said he thought it should be moved but didn't think "we needed to fight another Civil War over it." That was about it, and the

Old Man thought, "And that's about the way Creek County is split over the issue."

The Old Man knew they didn't know what he was going to do about it but figured those against removal thought he was going to favor removal, thanks to Sheriff Big Bull and his minions, and those for removal thought it wasn't going to happen, because that's the way it had always come out in Creek County, Georgia.

The meeting started at 10:00 A.M., but it was just 7:30, and he had some things to do. For one, he was still thinking about his decision, which he thought of as a "monumental" decision. The people were expecting a decision, and they were going to get it. What they didn't expect was that the first thing he planned to do, after the pledge to the American flag and prayer and thanking the people of Creek County for reelecting him for four more years to the commissioner's office, was resign, effective January 31, 2009. This would give the election officials enough time for a special election to elect someone to take his place by February 1.

The Old Man couldn't help but think that the events of the morning were going to be quite a show, and that he would be the main actor. He managed a wry smile and then, sadly, thought about Elizabeth and that in December, December 20, exactly, she would have been gone eleven years. He wished she were here. He thought she would be proud of him and what he was doing, but he knew Elizabeth would never be here again.

His usual eight-minute drive to the courthouse took ten minutes this morning and would have ordinarily been unnoticed, but today he knew why it was taking a little longer. "Do I know why? They are coming to see the show." Then when he got to the courthouse, someone in a white Ford SUV had parked in his place. This had not happened in years. Was this Big Bull's wife's car? Slowly, he drove through the already crowded parking lot and then up Government Avenue, parking almost adjacent to the Confederate monument.

As he left his car, he walked slowly along the street and then across the courthouse lawn. He stopped at the base of the monument. Just like he had done fifty-four years ago, he reached into his coat pocket and removed his little pad on which he had written in 1954, with his lead pencil, the words from this very monument. He read them aloud to be sure he had gotten it right back then: "In Honor of the Men of Creek County Who Served in the Army of the Confederate States of America, Those Who Fought and Lived, and Those Who Fought and Died. Erected by the Daughters of the Confederacy. 1907."

Well, he wrote it right in 1954, and it was still right. He thought: I'll read this right from this little paper I wrote back in 1954, that is, if they'll let me be heard on anything.

Just as he turned from the monument, he looked across Dogwood Street and saw Shot Brown watching him. Shot was an African American business and property owner in downtown Wesley Creek. He was also a part-time Baptist preacher. His business was a prosperous shoe and leather repair business. His third job was befriending the Old Man and seeing to it that he got reelected every four years, and he had been good at it. Shot was a close friend and confidant of the Old Man. The Old Man liked, no, loved, Shot very much.

As he walked away, the Old Man threw up his hand, waved, and shouted to Shot, "Say a little prayer for me today." Shot hollered back: "Good luck. I'll be at the meeting if I can get in." The Old Man thought, "I'm glad Shot is not closer, I'd have to tell him I still don't know what I'm going to do."

The Old Man's time in office, all but the last few weeks, had been good, very good. He worked hard and the county prospered and made great progress during his long tenure. Creek County was the envy of the other counties in the area. The sole-commissioner form of county government was an aberration in the area, but probably because of how well things were working in Creek County, there was talk in several of the surrounding counties of going to this form of government. But nothing substantive had been done by any of the other counties. The talk was that several of the counties had discussed it, but according to what the Old Man heard, there was resistance from other county officials, saying it made the sole commissioner too powerful. Most, if not all, of the sheriffs, clerks of court, probate judges, and tax commissioners seemed to be opposed to changing the way their individual counties were governed. So, it was not going to happen in the any of these other counties.

The Old Man watched all of this with interest. He didn't feel that he was "powerful" and felt that if anyone in the county had political power, it was Big Bull.

Then it happened. The commissioner in Creek County was approached at the August meeting by a group of citizens, around seventy-five in all, and led by the commissioner's friend, Shot Brown, asking that he consider renaming the "big county road" just north of the Wesley Creek Road, which was really, often, Wesley Creek's perimeter road, from "Wesley Way" to "Dr. Martin Luther King Jr. Drive." Of the seventy-five present, about forty were black ministers and local black business people. About ten or twelve were high school students, and the remainder were unknown or unidentifiable to the Commissioner.

These citizens were some of Creek County's best citizens. After hearing them out, he told them he would put this on the September agenda and would take action on their request then. All of this started around the first of the year and was still going on just before the 2008 primary election, but it hadn't stirred up a formidable opponent and most of the white citizens with whom he discussed it, and admittedly they were largely friends of his, seemed to either support it or were resigned to the fact that it was going to happen. The most common response he got was, "It's happened everywhere else, and I guess you'd better go ahead and do it here."

Then the talk started. The Old Man heard it, and while he was not certain, he again thought Big Bull was encouraging it. He got two letters, unsigned, in opposition. One accused him of selling out to the blacks, "your friends," and another said, "I guess our Confederate monument will be next." At the first September meeting, there were only the usual attendees, department heads, and a couple of old timers who attended all meetings. The Old Man approved the road name change and that was that. But the talk continued and intensified. The Old Man heard it directly and through his friends and supporters, and the Old Man knew then that Big Bull was behind it. And so now was the hour, or it would be in a short while, when alliances and friendships would be broken or severely strained by what the Old Man felt he had to do.

Always, there was paperwork. So, after taking another close look at the monument, and with long thoughts about Miss Mattie Lee Hood, the Old Man took the elevator to his office on the top third floor of the courthouse. The county attorney, Mike Short, was waiting on him, a cup of coffee in hand, when he opened the door, and his secretary, Mary

---

Brooke, gave him the same greeting she had given him for the last thirty-six years, "Good morning, Mr. Commissioner." And he responded as he had likewise done for thirty-six years, "Good morning, Miss Mary."

Condemnation cases for the new road in the north end of the county were Mike Short's business. The Old Man tried to pay attention, but his mind was on the upcoming meeting. Fortunately for the Old Man, Mike Short was updating him on the twenty-three cases—about the ones that had been settled and the ones where condemnations would apparently have to be filed and the ones he thought could be settled even after the cases were filed. Then the Old Man looked at his letters, faxes, and even a few emails, returned several calls, and before he knew it, Miss Mary was at the door reminding him it was 9:45 and time to go downstairs.

The Old Man was astounded by what he saw as he exited the elevator on the second floor. There must have been 300 people in the halls and meeting room. News media showed up from all over the state, including at least four television stations from Atlanta. Randy Branch, the local reporter from *The Wesley Creek Signal*, was in his usual seat in the front row.

The Old Man, who never got nervous at a meeting, was. He could feel his heart rate increase, and his mouth was all of a sudden very dry. He had difficulty getting through the crowd but finally got to his assigned place at the front of the room. When he sat down and looked, he was again astounded. So many people, and so many he did not know. And so much media. Big Bull had seen what he had seen, and there were eighteen deputies with bulletproof vests in the crowd. The Old Man thought: Is this for protection and control or intimidation, but he gave the Sheriff the benefit of the doubt. I'm glad they are here, he thought.

The Old Man was having trouble thinking and deciding what he needed to do first. "It's a good thing I'm resigning. I've never been like this before. I guess I'm getting old," he thought. But he managed to call on the Boy Scout from the local Boy Scout troop to lead the pledge to the flag to be followed by prayer from Rev. Lee Ragan from the First Holiness Baptist Church. That went off as planned, and then the Old Man rose to speak. The order, flag first and prayer next, had been changed because the Old Man wanted the prayer as close to his decision as possible.

"Welcome, all, to the second meeting in September of the commissioner of Creek County. Obviously, there is something on our agenda in which many of you have an interest. I cannot imagine what it is!"

There were a few snickers, but most in the audience sat in silence, with no expression changes on their faces.

Then: "Before we get to the matter that brings you to this meeting, I have a brief announcement. I will resign as commissioner of Creek County effective February 1, 2009. That will give our election officials time for a special election to have someone in place for this job on February 1, 2009. I have already signed and filed a letter to this effect. And the election is already being scheduled. Qualifying opens next Monday and closes on next Friday."

There was some clapping and a little cheering, though not much, and a few shouted, "No, no," but it, too, was limited and in short duration.

Then the Old Man reached into the inner pocket of his coat and pulled out the papers he had prepared for the Confederate monument issue. But before he could unfold his papers, he made a noise gasping for air, turned an ashen color, grabbed his left arm with his right, and fell face down on the floor.

The first person to the Old Man was Creek County's sheriff, who turned the Old Man over, started mouth-to-mouth resuscitation, and alternated with pressing on the Old Man's chest. Obviously, the sheriff had been trained and knew what he was doing. The crowd sat in total silence. Some watched and some, with eyes closed, prayed.

Within about five minutes, one of Sheriff Bailey's deputies was in the room with the Sheriff Department's defibrillator, and efforts with electric shock continued for some ten to fifteen minutes until EMTs from the Creek County Hospital arrived and took over, along with the assistance of two local doctors. Sheriff Bailey watched in total silence. After about thirty minutes from the time of the heart attack, the Old Man was put on a stretcher and taken to the ambulance. As the EMTs exited the room, one of them whispered in Sheriff Bailey's ear, "He's dead." Several saw tears run down the sheriff's face.

And then Sheriff Bailey did something that astounded many in the room. He turned to Shot Brown and said, in a shaky voice, "Shot, please lead us all in prayer, praying for this good man, my long-time friend, who has done so much for all of us in the room." And while Shot was praying, Sheriff Bailey picked up the Old Man's speech from the floor, and to his surprise discovered that there were actually two speeches folded together.

Both of the speeches were typed. But at the top of one of the speeches, at the top of the first page, written in red ink by the Old Man were the words "Miss Mattie Lee Hood. In Honor of the Men of Creek County Who Served in the Army of the Confederate States of America, Those Who Fought and Lived and Those Who Fought and Died. Erected by the Daughters of the Confederacy. 1907."

On the other speech, also written in red ink at the top of the first page by the Old Man, were the words: "Shot Brown and his people. Without their support, I would not be here today. For everything there is an appointed time, and an appropriate time for every activity on earth: A time to be born, and a time to die; a time to plant, and a time to uproot what was planted; a time to kill, and a time to heal; a time to break down, and a time to build up; a time to weep, and a time to laugh; a time to mourn, and a time to dance. A time to throw away stones, and a time to gather stones; a time to embrace, and a time to refrain from embracing; a time to search, and a time to give something up as lost; a time to keep, and a time to throw away; a time to rip, and a time to sew; a time to keep silent, and a time to speak. A time to love, and a time to hate; a time for war, and a time for peace." Ecclesiastes 3:1–8.

Then Sheriff Bailey saw a small piece of paper fall to the floor. There was printing by someone, obviously a youngster, with a lead pencil. On the little piece of blue-lined paper were the same words from the Confederate monument that were written at the top of one of the Old Man's speeches. The only man who knew where this old piece of paper came from was gone.

CONCLUSIONS

The Old Man died that day, the second Tuesday in September 2008. His funeral service, reported to be one of the largest ever in Creek County, was attended by whites, blacks, rich and poor. The most common thing heard among those at the burial was, "He was a good man. Creek County will miss him very much."

The Wesley Creek Signal published both of the Old Man's speeches in full. The conjecture was that the Old Man hadn't made up his mind as to what he was going to do, and that if he'd made a speech, he would have made up his mind at that time. Some said he was going to move it, and some said not.

Sheriff Bailey seemed to change after the Old Man died. Lots of the folks said his changing "was just politics," but others felt like he was really hurt when the Old Man was gone. In any event, Sheriff Bailey ran one more time in 2012, and much to the surprise of many, he ran as "Billy Boyd Bailey." He had no opposition, and when he retired at the end of his term in 2016, he was the longest serving sheriff in the history of Georgia. Sheriff Bailey, as he was now known, died two years after he was no longer sheriff.

Lastly, the Confederate monument is still on the front lawn of the Wesley Creek Courthouse, and the Confederate soldier still faces north with his rifle at his side. Shot Brown's son, Benjamin Scott Brown, a graduate of the University of Georgia School of Law, is now the commissioner of Creek County. Folks say, "Mr. Brown is doing a very good job. Nobody will ever be as good as the Old Man, but he's doing good." Mr. Brown agrees and thinks of the Old Man every morning as he looks at the Confederate monument out the window of his beautiful office on the third floor.

Indeed, for everything there is an appointed time.

IV

THE WAY WE ARE

DIXIE, MOLLY, AND KATE.
AMOS AND SOLOMON.

Dixie, Molly, and Kate. No, they are not the latest singing sensations out of Nashville, Tennessee. Nor are these the names of Jason Moore's hound dogs or Paul Hartman's beagles. And these are not the latest birth names at the Perry Hospital. These are the names of three of Papa's mules, long since gone but forever etched in my memory. There were other mules, but these are the ones I remember. Molly was a black mule with a surly disposition and a stubborn streak. Kate was a brownish-yellow mule, gentle, and Papa's favorite. And of Dixie, I can remember little except his/her colorful and appropriate name. But I do remember the sympathy I had for these beasts of burden. One of my jobs when I visited my Walker grandparents was to water and feed the mules. Instructions were "five ears of corn each." I always gave them six or seven. I felt sorry for them.

And then there were Amos and Solomon. Amos Brown and Solomon Brown. The sons of Ruth Brown. There were other Brown children, but to my knowledge, no Mr. Brown. Just a remarkable woman and her children. Amos and Solomon. Four or five years older than me. Plow hands. Strong. Handsome. Able to plow a mule all day long in the hot Georgia sun. Just enough older than me that I watched and admired everything they did.

And there was the system. The "tenant farmer" system. The mule and the tenant farmer. Notice that the mule is almost always mentioned first. Unfortunately, to many, the mule was more important. You could get some more tenants to live in the tar-paper shacks (and these were the better houses), but a good mule was something to treasure. A wretched system. One that grew out of the institution of slavery and was inherited by the Southern farmers. And so it went to and through the 1950s until the mule and the plow hand were replaced by the tractor.

Amos Brown and Solomon Brown are now both deceased. Thanks

for your kindness to a little white Southern boy who the system said was your superior, but which the three of us knew was a lie. And to Molly and Kate and Dixie, thanks for the memories of you and your kind and for your contributions to the survival of so many.

And so, on October 4, 2003, at 4:00 P.M. at the Georgia National Fair, the people of Georgia dedicated a bronze statute to the memory of the tenant and the mule. Important enough that a former president of the United States and a Nobel Peace Prize winner, Jimmy Carter, unveiled the statue and made a speech. All of this is not to extol the system but is an effort to say thank you from so many for so much that was so difficult and was done for so long and for so little. Thank you to Dixie and Molly and Kate. But more importantly, thank you to Amos and Solomon.

A PORCH OR A KITCHEN?

I guessed it started in the late fifties and has continued until now. It was a mistake then, and it is a mistake now. What I am talking about is building houses without porches. By porches, I do not mean those narrow little ledges that will barely hold a chair. I mean wide, wooded verandas that separate the home from the world. Aside from what I learned at the meal table, I probably had more information imparted to me on porches than at any other one place. Especially was this true about family, relationships, and kinfolks. Since families no longer gather at meal times, and since very few houses have real porches, it is no wonder that there is very little "family teaching" going on. Perhaps this is why the country is in such a mess.

I wrote a story some time back lamenting the demise of dirt roads. The loss of porches was even more critical. I guess that air conditioning and spiraling construction costs were the culprits. In retrospect, you don't learn much of any good in an air-conditioned room with a blaring television, and the importance of porches as a social institution and teaching facility were such that other rooms should have been sacrificed, if cost cutting was necessary.

My Walker grandparents, in an otherwise very modest home, had a wonderful front porch with great rockers and metal furniture. In the warm times, that is where we gathered to play rook (the only allowable card game) or Monopoly or simply listen to the adults talk and teach. When we visited the relatives in rural Washington County, we would sit on the visited kin's porch and the elders would converse. The children, like me, would listen. On these porches is where I learned who I was and where I came from and what was expected of me.

The W. W. Grays lived in Perry across the street from us on the corner of Swift and Third. Their house had a wonderful front porch that was in constant use. The Gray family gathered there at night and some of the men smoked cigars. It was an exciting sight to see the glow of the cigar ash in the black of the night. Often, my curiosity at what was being said on the front porch got the best of me, and I would wander over for a visit. It seemed to me that I was always welcomed, and soon I would be engrossed in listening to talk of farming and rain (or lack thereof) and politics. But the most exciting talk was of fishing. The Grays were great fishermen, often going to Florida, and their verbal reports of their exploits only served to stoke my vivid imagination. I learned much about much on the Grays' front porch.

Porches were great social institutions—gathering places and places for friends to stop and visit. Porches were wonderful learning places, especially for the young to learn from the "old heads." We made a bad mistake when we stopped building porches. I made an error when I built a house thirty years ago without a porch. I vowed not to make that mistake again. So when we built another house in 2007, we had a porch on the front and back, and we are enjoying both immensely. Although, truthfully, folks don't come by to visit like I thought they would. I hope it's the time and not the folks that live in our house.

I WISH I HAD SAID THAT

I recently read an amazing and fascinating book: *Jerry Lee Lewis—His Own Story* by Rick Bragg. I was mesmerized, and the only thing that prevented my reading it faster was eye fatigue. What a story! I'll write more about the book before the year is up.

Today, though, I want to write about Rick Bragg and his God-given and finely honed way with words. I've read lots of books, but no one writes better than Mr. Bragg. For example, even in his acknowledgements, as he writes about Lewis, he is unique in the way he puts it:

"Writing about a long life is easy, next to living it.... He was not, in hot spells, a man to be admired, but I liked him when it was all over.... He broke my heart a hundred times, and made me laugh a thousand or more."

With this introduction, I come to my subject. I call it, "I Wish I Had Said That," and I do! Here it is.

Several years ago, some friends gave me a book for my birthday titled *Great Quotes from Great Leaders*. When I read the book, I was fascinated by some of the quotes—most of which I had never heard or read. I knew the leaders but not the words. Let me share a few of the "quotes" with you.

One of my heroes was Sir Winston Churchill. This is one of his: *"The greatest lesson in life is to know that even fools are right sometimes."*

And so it is. Even the dull and ignorant can teach you if you will only listen and pay some attention. Another of his is: *"He has all the virtues I dislike and none of the vices I admire."*

Amen. I know some people just like that. The word "pious" comes to mind.

Abraham Lincoln said: *"What kills a skunk is the publicity it gives itself."*

I think of some of our national politicians who shall remain nameless by me, but probably you know those of whom I speak.

Another of Mr. Lincoln's: "*It has been my experience that folks who have no vices have very few virtues.*"

And another of Mr. Lincoln's: "*No man has a good enough memory to make a successful liar.*"

On the same subject, Thomas Jefferson said this: "*He who permits himself to tell a lie once, finds it much easier to do it a second time.*"

And this: "*Honesty is the first chapter of the book of wisdom.*"

I love what Benjamin Franklin had to say about neighbors, as it is so true: "*Love your neighbor—but don't pull down your hedge.*"

Another great truth spoken by Mr. Franklin: "*Creditors have better memories than debtors.*"

And yet another: "*Love your enemies, for they tell you your faults.*"

Confucius said this: "*To put the world right in order, we must first put the nation in order; to put the nation in order, we must first put the family in order; to put the family in order, we must first cultivate our personal life; we must first set our hearts right.*"

I love Harry Truman. Here are three of his: "*I always considered statesmen to be more expendable than soldiers.*"

"*A politician is a man who understands government, and it takes a politician to run a government. A statesman is a politician who's been dead for fifteen years.*"

"*Some of the Presidents were great and some of them weren't. I can say that because I wasn't one of the great Presidents, but I had a good time trying to be one, I can tell you that.*"

I believe Mr. Truman was in error in his last quote. I believe he was one of our great presidents.

Another great president, Theodore Roosevelt, said this: "*In any moment of decision, the best thing you can do is the right thing, the next best thing is the wrong thing, and the worst thing you can do is nothing.*"

When I read each of these quotes, I thought, how true! I wish I had been smart enough to think, say, or write some of these things.

SMACK DAB IN DOG DAYS

I think of myself as a realist tending towards optimism. Maybe others don't see me this way, but that's the way I think I am. I hope I'm right about myself, but I must quickly add it's hard to be even a little optimistic about anything when you are smack dab in dog days. Yes, if you didn't know, they start in mid-July and go through September.

Frankly, my view is that July doesn't have much to commend it. I can really think of only two things. It does have Independence Day and the Walker Family Reunion (which doesn't help you non-Walker readers, leaving you with only July 4th, which has already past). Come to think of it, so has the Walker Family Reunion, "already past." But we will have both next year, so I will go ahead and write about them.

Independence Day. It's the day we celebrate our independence and honor our veterans (we should do that every day) and is by far the biggest positive about July. But with the Independence Day celebration also come the fireworks, which, once again, are legal—and, once again, are causing controversy. Let's take a cursory look at this problem.

Truth be told, I think it was better when fireworks were illegal and folks that cared enough slipped into South Carolina, or some other more enlightened place, and bought their wares. When the cherry bombs, bottle rockets, and the like were illegal, at least the pyro-poppers stopped their show at a reasonable hour. You know, you have to be a little nervous when you're doing something illegal and you're making a big ruckus about it. It appears to me that we didn't have as many problems under the old firecracker system as we've had the first year under the new or reconstituted system. Just an observation.

Another thing July has going for it, at least for the members of the John F. Walker family, is the Walker Family Reunion. It's on the first Sunday in July in rural Washington County. Well, at least it has been for the last eighty-one consecutive first Sundays. And most of the time, it's hot as a firecracker. But in the balance, at least for us, it's a plus for July, which needs all the pluses it can get.

Lordy, Lordy, after July comes August. And with August, you are in the middle of dog days. As I said, I believe I tend towards optimism and am a positive person, so I want to say something good about August, but the bottom-line truth is that it's miserable. Let's see.

August. Well, it's named in honor of the Roman emperor Augustus. This is how the naming came about: during Mr. Augustus's reign, the Roman Senate lengthened the month to thirty-one days, taking a day from February, and they named the eighth month for Mr. Augustus, who must have been a popular or effective (or both) senator, or he must have had something on some of the other senators, so they named the eighth month for him. (Frankly, I don't think they did him any great favor.)

I wish the Roman Senate had left the additional day in February (usually a pretty nice month with basketball, hunting, improving weather, etc.) and not added it to August. I see that either this was a joke played on Mr. Augustus or the Roman Senate was making mistakes back then, just like our United States Senate is today.

Well, we do have September after August. Think football, cooler weather (we have hope), school is back in session, life is in a routine, and there is some return to normalcy.

Let me add a cautionary note about dog days. Do not cut your hand peeling tomatoes or peaches, get your finger caught in a car door, or step on a nail during dog days lest it, the injury, immediately become infected. But if you do, tie a rag (or medical gauze) around the injury and soak the cloth in kerosene (you can get kerosene at Ace Hardware—I know, I bought some there) and it will get well quickly, and usually with no swelling or pain.

I have learned one thing from this and that is you can subtract and add days to months. With that in mind, I'm going to request that our two US senators, Isakson and Perdue, take five days from July and add to October and take ten days from August and add to April. I don't think naming the expanded months for either of them will be necessary.

TIME TO STOP CHANGING OUR TIME

This column is not about ducks. But this little story involves some ducks that used to stay at our pond, and it is absolutely true. We had a fish feeder on the pond that came on automatically every day. I want to write that it came on at the same time every day, but I will leave it to you to decide, after you read this article, as to whether or not it did so. Well, about three or four minutes before the feeder threw the pellets across the water, the ducks would gather to eat the feed. They did this every day. You could see them coming from all points in the pond. By the time the feeder went off, all of the ducks (about forty or fifty) were there, and they ate most of the feed.

Several questions. How did the ducks know? Did they look at the sun? What about when it was cloudy? Did my feeder come on at the "same time" every day? You know, our government changes "our time" on November 2. My feeder on November 1 disbursed at 6:00 P.M. Now, according to the government, it disperses at 5:00 P.M. In fact, was it feeding at the "same time"? Did my ducks move their watches "one hour backwards" so as to not miss supper? Does our government say they were eating an hour later and are now an hour earlier? I think they were eating at the same time.

I don't let many things bother me. But I do not like all of this "spring forward" and "fall back" with our time. It makes no sense to me. Oh, I have heard the arguments. "Saves fuel," "School children in the dark," etc. Split the difference. Make 6:00 P.M. 6:30 P.M. or keep it the same year-round, and it will "average out." Would that work? Reckon how many man-hours are spent changing clocks and watches back and forth. How many man-hours are lost or are ineffective and sluggish because their biological clock (is this what my ducks had?) has not changed?

In this article, I've called it "our time." It is "our time." It's not Congress's time. It is our time. If you agree, rise up. Write your senators and congressmen. Tell 'em you're like my ducks. You want to eat at the same time every day and get up and go to bed and do other things that your biological clock tells you to do. Let's unite and retake our time and stop all of this foolishness. We can do it. I believe that the reason Congress doesn't change it is that they don't understand it (of course, that can go for lots of what they do or don't do).

Another true story. It involves a local farmer, now deceased, whose name will not be used because he has family in and around Perry. Seems that years ago when "the government" imposed Daylight Savings Time, he was incensed. Refused to change his clocks and watches, and was heard to say: "The government can go to **** [you know where]. They are not going to tell me what time it is. I know what time it is!" Well, don't laugh too loudly. If you were dealing with cows and hogs and chickens and ducks and other animals that are on a biological time, you might feel the same way. I guess he was afraid that the extra hour of sunlight would burn up his crop!

I used to ask my friend Jerry Wilson what time it was. His response: "In Perry, Georgia, the Greenwich Village, Naval Observatory, Ocmulgee River, Fannie Gresham Branch time is 2:45 P.M." Now, there was a man who knew his time!

A few years ago, Janice and I were in Italy. It took me a few days to adjust to the six-hour time difference. I was wondering. Now that we've moved "our time" one hour backwards, are we now five hours or seven hours different from Rome? Glad it didn't happen while we were over there. I never would have gotten straightened out.

I should have stopped with the above paragraph, but I have one other true story that I must share with you. A farmer told me about a blind mule he had. Used the mule to plow his fenced-in garden; said the mule would plow to the end of the row and stop before running into the fence. I asked him how the mule knew. "Simple," said my farmer friend, "he was counting his steps." Well, he said it was true! And, by the way, what is time to a mule?

Now I know it's time to stop.

TEN THINGS I DIDN'T WANT TO DO

For no good reason, I want to tell you of some things I did as a child and young man that I didn't like to do. They say doing this "stuff" builds character. I'll leave it to you who know me to decide on that. One through ten, and one was the worst.

10. Delivered feed on the feed truck with Joe Hodges. Daddy had a one-half interest in a Purina feed store. In the summers, I worked with Joe Hodges, and twice a week we loaded feed to deliver to chicken farmers and others. Have you ever been in a chicken house in July when it was 100 degrees? Couple the odor with the burden (I weighed about 135 pounds, the sacks of feed 100 pounds), and you will begin to understand.

9. Mowed grass for the public. I was about thirteen or fourteen. I had four or five customers. I did have a Briggs and Stratton power mower (not self-propelled) and frequently it did not work properly. You cut it off by pressing a little metal strip on the spark plug. I got shocked a lot. My customers let their grass get very high before they engaged me (saving money, you know). I got paid three to five dollars a yard.

8. Picked up trash in the front yard. We lived at the corner of Swift and Third streets in Perry. People walked to town along Swift Street, and some threw their trash in our yard. Daddy told me to pick up the trash. I didn't want to, so I picked it up and hid it under some leaves in the flowerbed. Daddy found it. I got a good spanking. I deserved a spanking. I was probably about twelve years old.

7. Assisted the oiler at Texas Steel Company in 1963. I was twenty-one years old. I had never been in a steel mill (or hardly any kind of a factory) before. The first Saturday I worked there, I had to go up on one of those overhead cranes that picked up the cradles of molten steel and help the "oiler" oil the crane. I was petrified. I can still hear him saying, "Don't touch that, it's 100,000 volts." I survived, but I do believe

this stunted my growth!

6. Math, Chemistry, Calculus, Physics. If you happen to be left-brained (or right-brained) to be good in science, technology, engineering, and math, I am the opposite. I can do arithmetic in my head, but beyond that I was, and am, generally lost in these other subjects. That's one reason I am a lawyer.

5. Took piano lessons from Miss Willie Ryals. The only thing I ever learned was "Here we go, up a row, to a birthday party." I must have been ten years old or so when I finally was allowed to give it up. We didn't have a piano. It's hard to practice on the kitchen table. I do distinctly remember the sweet smell of the cherry cough drops that Miss Willie sucked.

4. Busted out a concrete floor with Bobby Jones. Let's go back to Texas Steel. By then, I may have weighed 145 pounds. Jones weighed less. They gave us a fifty-pound jackhammer and told us to "bust out" a four-inch thick concrete floor and haul off the pieces. Have you ever used a jackhammer? This was one of the longest days in my life. We probably finished about one-fourth of a 1,200-square-foot floor.

3. Daddy decided I needed to work in the parts department at Gray-Walker Tractor Company. The farmers would come in and say something like this: "I need that little grease fitting that goes on the back axel of my WD 45 Allis-Chalmers tractor. 1961, I think." I would look in the book of drawings that some engineers drew. I don't think I ever found one part!

2. Removed a dead dog out from under our house on Swift Street. The odor solved the riddle of where the dog was. I had to crawl under the house with a rake or a hoe and get him out. It was awful. I still vividly remember it, and it was probably more than sixty-five years ago.

1. Picked cotton. I tried, but I never could pick much. On a good day, when I worked at it, I could get about ninety-five pounds; some of my cotton-picking comrades could gather 200-plus pounds. But it was hot work. I was thirsty. One day I picked twenty-seven pounds (I went to the bullis vines), and I got my rear end branded that night. One good thing, though, I learned lots from listening intently to the others who picked with me as they talked and sang. I won't write about what I learned, but it was very beneficial. Very.

Well, let me close. There is no better way than to use the last line in my lament about picking cotton. All of this "stuff" that I disliked so much taught me a great deal and has been helpful as I have gone through this wonderful thing called life.

A SOUTHERN TRADITION:
PRACTICAL JOKES

Years ago, in small towns, and before there were hundreds of television channels and you could keep up with most everyone's business through social media, people actually visited with each other. The men gathered in a local café and solved the country's problems. They also thought up practical jokes and implemented them. Here are four good examples. I could give many more.

1. Two to the Room in New Orleans. In Perry, James Moore may have been the king of the practical jokesters. He could fool even his closest friends on the telephone with his voice, and often did.

James was friends with Frank and Billy Giles of Unadilla and their families. Frank made the mistake of telling James that the two families were going to New Orleans for the Sugar Bowl and that both families were going to stay in one room.

Several of Foster and Martha Ann Rhodes's friends, including James and Nellwin and Jance and me, watched the game at the Rhodes's home. About an hour after the game, without saying anything to anyone, James went to the phone, telephoned the motel where the Giles were staying, was put through to their room, and said: "Mr. 'Gillis' [he always mispronounced your name to throw you off], this is the management. We've been told there is more than one family in this room. We've got laws to cover this in New Orleans, and you had better come to the front desk and pay what you owe." Frank told the caller that they were in bed but that he would come down in the morning and settle up. The "manager" told him to come down immediately. "We've put folks in jail for this." I believe Frank got up, dressed, and went to the front desk!

2. Christmas Tree Revenge Is Sweet. Foster Rhodes and I put this together. This was after what James Moore did to the Giles but certainly was not full payment for all he had done. It was still sweet.

About a week before Christmas, I ran an ad in the classifieds that went something like this: "I need your Christmas trees when Christmas is over to put in my catfish pond. Just leave them on my front lawn or telephone me and I'll come pick them up." Then I gave James and Nellwin's address and telephone number. It was a tremendous success. They got lots of trees and many calls. Several of James's friends who were in on the joke also contributed. I don't know where he took the trees, but it was not to a catfish pond!

3. Beware Mongoose. Do Not Touch. I'll bet you felt sorry for the Giles families that loaded up in that motel room in New Orleans. Hear this.

At their Giles and Hodge Warehouse in Unadilla, they had a prominently placed wooden box with a screen-covered end displaying a protruding animal tail (probably a fox tail) with a sign that said "Beware of Mongoose. Danger. Do Not Touch." There was a stick in a hole that fed into the enclosed part of the box.

When you inquired about the "mongoose" they would tell you to "push the stick in the hole and it will probably come out," and when you did, the tail would fly up in your face and you would almost have a heart attack. I almost tore out the side of the brick warehouse. Still feel sorry for the Billy and Frank Giles families?

4. Just Taking a Little Right of Way. This Foster Rhodes joke on Riley and Sandra Hunt is my nomination for the best that was ever played on anyone in Perry.

A little background. Several years ago, Riley and Sandra Hunt built a beautiful home on a dirt road on the outskirts of Perry. The house was set back a couple hundred feet from the road. A decision was made to pave the road with an understanding that a "little property" would have to be taken by DOT to straighten out the curve.

Now, Foster Rhodes, friend of the Hunts (who knew they were out of town), enters the picture. Foster was riding by the Hunt's new home, and as he says, "It hit me what I was going to do." I went to Tolleson Supply and got them to cut me what look like right-of-way stakes. Then I took a marker and I wrote on the stakes "R/W 180, R/W 190," etc. Then I took the stakes and started driving them up in Elmo Meadow's property and on down through Riley and Sandra's to about twenty feet from their front door. Then I waited.

The Hunts came home, discovered the stakes, and all, well,

"confusion" broke loose. Riley called me, his representative in the state House. He called county commissioners and the local DOT man, who told Riley, "We're just taking a little property." Riley, son of a Primitive Baptist preacher and one of Perry's finest, responded, "a little ****!" (see "confusion" above).

Life was good in small towns. Fun, too!

LIKES AND DISLIKES

I'll start with some of my "likes," since there are many, and then go to "dislikes," which are but few. Then I will confess and "correct."

Likes: I like chocolate milkshakes. I do not want them to be too thick or too "chocolatey." If they are so thick you can hardly suck them through a straw or are dark brown with chocolate, the shakes move from "likes" to "tolerates." By the way, I think Mike at Twila Faye's in Bolingbroke makes the best shakes I've had since Mozelle Sutton's at Houston Drug Company, Perry, in the fifties and sixties. I've, of course, not tried all the shake places in Middle Georgia, but I'm working on it!

I like quail hunting. It's the only hunting I now do. It's the dogs, first and foremost, and the dog handlers, the out-of-doors, your companions, the birds, and, invariably, a wonderful host. I experienced all of this just last week. Everything was superb. Note that I've said nothing about how many you kill. It's the hunt and the fellowship and not the number of birds killed.

I like a dark suit, perhaps with a small pinstripe. A white shirt with a modest matching tie and polished shoes. Go to see the movie *Race*, which is about Jesse Owens and the Berlin Olympics, and observe how sharply folks dressed in the 1930s. This movie should have won an Oscar for its costumes.

And I like speakers, including preachers and politicians (especially politicians), who know when to use humor and know when to quit. I never heard anyone leave a church service or any kind of a meeting and say, "That speaker did not talk long enough." Have you?

Dislikes: Most televisions commercials. Some are way too explicit to suit me. Also, their creators have gotten so "creative" that it is often difficult to tell what they are trying to sell.

There are a few things I've eaten, or when young had to eat, that I don't particularly like. This goes from just don't enjoy to can't hardly get it down. Let's talk about "can't stand." First, I do not like liver of any kind. I do not want to ever eat any more liver. I do not believe I could get any calves' liver down.

On the other hand, there's Brussels sprouts. I can eat them, but I do not particularly like this vegetable. George H. W. Bush (my favorite Bush) and I 100 percent agree on this. I feel about English peas like I do Brussels sprouts.

I've eaten all kinds of wild game. I've eaten rabbit, squirrel, dove, antelope, rattlesnake, buffalo, quail, and more. Some was delicious and some was fair. I've never eaten any goose, pheasant, or much duck that I thought was very good.

Believe it or not, I once tried dirt. I saw some folks eating dirt (kaolin?) and asked Papa if I could try it. He gave me permission, and I took a bite. It tasted like, well, dirt. I spit it out.

I don't like rude shop clerks or rude fast-food clerks. I don't like rude television talk-show hosts. I don't like Judge Judy. I think that clerks—store and fast food—are better as a group than they were when everyone had a job and employers were looking for help. I think that politicians have gotten worse. Judge Judy has always been harsh and ugly to people (I know it's only a show) and gives the legitimate, real judiciary a bad name.

I talked about people who talk too much—preachers, politicians, etc. Let me add that I don't like gossipers and tale totters. "They say" and "I heard" are the two biggest liars in America. But social media users—many of them—are giving "They say" and "I heard" a run for their money.

NO PLACE TO GO

For me, I believe it started at Papa's country store in very rural Washington County, Georgia. This small, white, tinned-roof store stood at the intersection of two dirt roads, Centralia Rachels and Sparta Davisboro. I was intrigued by lots of things about the store and what took place in the store, but none more than the conversations that took place.

One example: Mr. Hubert Hawkins would come up, overalls-clad and often with nothing underneath, from down Sparta Davisboro, either walking in his dusty brogans or riding one of his mules. When I saw him, I wanted to be there, listening, because I knew it would be interesting. I made it my business to be there.

This is part of what really drew me and at the same time confused me. I'd heard my grandparents talk about Mr. Hubert and how he had gone off for a while for making illegal, untaxed liquor. To me that meant he was a bad man. Yet Grandma and Papa seemed to like and respect him. So, when he came, I wanted to hang around and listen, and I did.

Mr. Hubert usually sat by squatting down on his haunches, and Papa usually set up an upturned wooden Coca-Cola crate. Both could do this for long periods of time. They would talk about the weather, cotton, and how their crops were, how many squirrels Mr. Hubert had killed lately, and people who lived in the area, north Washington County. If there were local or national elections going on, they might briefly talk about politics. And they kept up with who died and when their funeral would be.

I learned to love the talk, the talkers, the tales, and the lessons. I was hooked. The better the talkers and the better they were at the talk, the more I was drawn to them. And it has lasted a lifetime.

Let me move to the sixth grade, Perry Elementary School, and my teacher, Jean Pierce Bledsoe. Periodically, she would let me tell a story to the whole class, and I would. I'd include every classmate, by name, in the story. This great teacher and this opportunity are probably seminal reasons for my writing today. And why I'm pretty good at politics. I ran sixteen times and had an opponent twice.

Law school at UGA was a hotbed of talkers and tale-tellers. I think lots of lawyers are inclined this way. And while in Athens, lunch at the Snack Shack around a long table in the back room with other law students, talking and eating, further fed my desire to be there, listen, and participate.

Then I was back in Perry practicing law, but some part of most every day was spent by me listening and talking with other men in the community. There were plenty of good places to go for this fun and learning experience.

There was the Coffee Cup in downtown Perry. Our country's problems were solved there every morning, only to be resolved the next. Probably twenty-five or thirty men, usually the same crowd, in about three shifts, drank coffee, talked, and listened, sometime between 6:30 and 9:00 A.M., five days a week. It was politics, sports, economics, weather, and just plain gossip from Monday through Friday.

The Swank Shop, where the Perfect Pear is today, was another of my learning and hopefully teaching places. Billy Bledsoe, proprietor, was a world-class quipster with hundreds of appropriate and funny sayings. Lots of days after work, and sometimes during lunch, I refueled my tales tank at Billy's.

Then there was the feed store, Walker Thompson Supply. I'd worked there as a youngster and had great affection for Ed Thompson, Mr. Glea Gray, and Joe Hodges. So, periodically, I would go by to learn more and be reminded of "stuff" I already knew. And I must say, Mr. Glea Gray knew and told more funny stories than anyone I ever knew.

Then there was the tractor place, Gray-Walker and later Walker-Rhodes. Whether it was Daddy and Mr. F. L. "Doc" Hammock discussing farming, Marvin Dorsett and Daddy, two school board members, discussing farming, or Daddy and Foster on a wide variety of other subjects, there was much to be learned from wise, smart, savvy, articulate people.

And, so now, after over fifty-two years of practicing law and previously having a wide variety of places to go after work or even during the day to learn and contribute, I find that there are no longer any such places. If there are, I don't know where.

Oh, there are stores and restaurants and good and smart people, but no atmosphere for visiting and talking. Why? Television. Too busy. No interest. I don't know. But I do know that it was good, to me, while it lasted. And I do know that it is a part of what I am today. And I do know I miss it. I'm sad that there's no place for me to go. I think our culture is being changed because of these lost opportunities. Also, by those little hand-held devices. How do people learn about their family, friends, and the community's history? I don't think they will or do.

WALKER PERSONALITY PROFILE TEST

This is a test. My test. Call it the Walker Personality Profile Test. I first wrote this test about ten years ago. I thought that by now some great university, such as the University of Georgia, would have picked it up, gotten a research grant, and built a senior-level course out of it. I continue to wait, but in the meantime, it will have to be my test—strong on questions and short on answers.

1) You have two light bulbs in your garage ceiling. Both were installed at the same time. Replacement requires a ladder and a screwdriver to remove the cover. After about 500 hours, one of the bulbs burns out. Question: when replacing the burned-out bulb, would you also replace the still functioning bulb?

2) Your shower can be adjusted so that the water comes out sharp and focused or softer and in larger rivulets. How do you adjust your shower?

3) Steaks for dinner. T-bones. Do you save the tenderest part (rib eye) for last, or do you eat the tenderest part first? My wife, Janice, eats hers first and I eat mine last. What does this say about us?

4) How do you install the toilet paper on the roller: so that the paper comes off the back side or over the top and front? Or do you care?

5) Dark-meat chicken or white-meat chicken? Note: a majority of Americans prefer white, although, as I understand it, this is not true with most of the rest of the world.

6) Dogs or cats? When I was a child, I thought dogs were males and cats were females. I recently learned better.

7) This one is related to number 3 above. Cereal and banana. Do you cut up the banana and put it in the bowl first or do you put the banana on top of the cereal?

8) Panama City, Florida, or Highlands, North Carolina? St. Simons or Sea Island? Idle Hour Country Club or yard sales on Saturday morning? This might have to do with money, or lack thereof.

9) Money or looks? This might have to do with your age and experience.

10) The Atlanta Symphony Orchestra or Jerry Lee Lewis? What if you like them both? I do, but I prefer Jerry Lee.

11) You win a contest and are given the choice of spending a week with Dolly Parton or some of the Duck Dynasty crowd. Who do you choose? (Or is it "whom" do you choose?)

12) You lose a contest and are given a choice of spending a week with Donald Trump or Kim Kardashian? Which one?

13) Sweet tea or unsweet? Grits or hash browns? Beef or pork?

14) Men, do you shower and then shave or do you shave and then shower? Women can answer if you shave your legs.

15) Your young daughter gets a toy stove set from ole Santa. Do you read the plans before starting the assemblage or do you plunge forward and read the plans as a last resort?

16) You drive to your local grocery store. Do you take the first parking spot you see or do you keeping riding around trying to get a space closer to the store? How long do you persist in trying to get a "better" space?

Well, here are the questions. Answer them truthfully and a psychiatrist can probably tell a good deal about you and your personality. As for me, I'd replace both light bulbs, let the toilet paper come over the top, and I'd spend my week with Dolly! Beyond that, I'm not telling. If I did, I might have to go off for a while.

THE TIMES THEY ARE A CHANGIN'

"The Times They Are a Changin'"—Bob Dylan, 1964

I was born in 1942, March 9, to be exact, at the Middle Georgia Hospital. Mother and I stayed in Macon for over a week, and then she and I were taken by ambulance to our home in Perry and, according to Mother, "past the beautiful blooming peach trees." It wouldn't happen that way today, as times have changed. And it wouldn't have happened that way when Mother was born at her home on Hay Road in Perry twenty-two years earlier. Times had slowly changed between 1920 and 1942.

I was born into a hot world—at least it would be hot in Georgia by the time I made it to June, and being able to do something about the Georgia heat and diaper rash was nearly impossible until Mr. Carrier gave us air conditioning, which we got in the late 1950s. It would have been a window unit cooling one or two rooms. Still, we Southerners were ever so slowly winning our battle with the heat.

It was a tightly segregated society by race that I entered in 1942. Lincoln issued the Emancipation Proclamation on January 1, 1863, and the US Supreme Court issued its school decision, *Brown vs. Board of Education*, in 1954, but it would be about twenty years before there was much racial integration in the South. There were no African American students at Perry High School when I graduated in 1960 and only one African American, a male, Chester C. Davenport, in the class behind me when I graduated from UGA law in 1965. Social changes of almost all kinds were very slow.

I remember our first television. The set was big and bulky. We got one or two stations. Reception was black, white, and very fuzzy. It came on at 10 or 11 o'clock in the morning, and prior to that time I had to watch the test pattern, which I was excited to do. The stations went off the air at sunset with the playing of the "Star-Spangled Banner" (the

American flag was depicted on the screen). Then we eventually got more stations, longer hours, color, remote control, and cable, but those improvements probably covered forty years or so.

Automobiles improved dramatically between 1958 (I was sixteen) and the 1990s. Tires would last 50,000 miles! We got car air conditioning, but Daddy restricted its use, as "running the air conditioning lowered the gas mileage." Still, over those forty years or so, there was a good deal of change. Couple the improvements with birth-control pills, better roads, more places to go, an "entitlement" to an automobile by many of those sixteen years of age, and this was a pretty major societal change, but again, it happened over many years. Come to think about it, air conditioning in autos probably helped to accelerate more promiscuous activities!

I've gone from a world where no person with any class would say words like "panties," "breast," "pregnant," "condoms," "constipation," and many others in public to a world where you can see more on television today than was available for viewing at tent shows at the old county fairs—and I'm just thinking about the commercials! Compare what can be shown and said today on television with what could be said, shown, and advertised twenty years ago, and it's dramatic. It was a slow change, but it got here about twenty years ago, and it's changing ever so rapidly today.

And what do we have now? Telephone/cameras/games that astound and become obsolete within months, video recordings by something or someone of most everything that happens. Loss of privacy. Medical miracles. Driverless autos. Trips to planets? Drugs—legal and illegal. Many that think they know everything. Difficulty of elected leaders to lead those who know everything. Loss of social mores. Churches and religious beliefs under attack, etc., etc.

The times have changed. From 1942 to the 1990s, changes were slow, understandable, but significant, and most people could absorb and keep up. And then it, "change," increased faster and faster and many fell behind. It is as they say, apparently: "You ain't seen nothing yet." Where will all of this take us—or take some? Indeed, Bob Dylan, the times they are a changin'.

THESE THINGS I BELIEVE

Let me confess up front that I stole the idea for this column from my friend Billy Chism, editor/publisher of the *White County News*. In fact, I am using Billy's column name. But I have not read a word of Billy's column. I will read his after I finish mine.

These Things I Believe:

Our Founding Fathers Were Geniuses: They gave us the Constitution of the United States. This document establishes the form of our national government and defines the rights and liberties of the American people.

Washington, Franklin, Madison, Hamilton, and the thirty-five others were signers. William Few and Abraham Baldwin from Georgia signed the Constitution.

We Americans have drifted away from some of the Constitution's principles. We can lose our democracy and country if we don't adhere to the Constitution, the supreme law of our land.

Churches Hold Our Country Together: The church, by whatever name called, mosque, temple, house of worship, etc., and what is taught and practiced there is what holds our society together.

If we lose our religious rituals, we lose our codes of conduct, and then we lose our country. Perhaps even our world.

Our churches need our support because we need our churches.

Friends and Family: The most important thing is family. The American family has eroded rapidly in the past fifty years. Divorce is rampant. Many, many families, immediate and more extended, are scattered across the face of the earth. The mores of society, as taught to me at the University of Georgia in 1960, don't work with scattered families like they did with the mostly close families of an earlier time.

Next to family are friends. Friends accept us as we are. Friends listen to our problems. Friends don't judge. Friends tell us their innermost secrets, including their aspirations, goals, worries, and fears.

Friends keep our secrets. Friends are there when you most need them.

Live a long life and you will conclude that friends and family are the most important.

Lots of Good in the Worst. Lots of Bad in the Best: No one is perfect. No one is without hope. Maybe they just need a good friend, or the church, or God. The best make mistakes. The best lose control of their temper. Sometimes the best become the worst. Sometimes the worst become the best. Don't give up on anyone. Don't put anyone on a pedestal.

We've Lived in the Best of Times: Most of us are cool in summer, warm in winter, seldom hungry, do not do without things we need, including medicine, vehicles, food, some discretionary money to spend, entertainment, time off, a good job, a fine family, friends, a good bed, clean water to drink, a hot shower, a chocolate milk shake when we want one, and several televisions with lots of channels.

Alexander the Great, Henry Ford, King David, and George Washington didn't have it as good as we do.

Dogs Are Smarter Than I Thought They Were: As I've gotten older, and they've gotten older, I've watched them more closely.

Hershey is thirteen years old. Like her master, she's hard of hearing. Unlike her master, she's feeble. Some would say, "You should put her down." I don't think so. She guards (lays nearby and watches) as Janice works in the yard. She still likes to go to the back side of the place, so we help her into and out of the four-wheeler. Sometimes I pick her up, put her in the back of the four-wheeler, and pick her up, and put her on the ground when we get back.

Chloe, our "put-out dog," still likes to fish, but seldom catches them like she used to. But when the feeder goes off, she's there trying to catch a fish. She's a little crippled in one leg as a result of an accident, but she still runs in front of the four-wheeler when we go to the back side of our place, which is about a mile. Then she walks back. She refuses to ride with us.

These two dogs watch us closely and love us very much. We love them very much. They are polite to us and to each other. They eat out of the same bowl and at the same time and are considerate of each other, even when eating.

Our two dogs could teach our politicians and office-holders a few things about politeness and manners and the importance of family and friends. Indeed, our dogs are like family and are our friends. We'll miss them when they're gone, or, if we go first, I know they'll miss us.

These are a few of the things I believe. Now, I'll read Billy Chism's column.

REMEMBERING MUHAMMAD ALI

I think it was in the early nineties, because I think Zell Miller was governor, although it could've been somewhat earlier, when Joe Frank Harris had the job, but exactly when it was is not important to what I am trying to impart. What is important to this report is my remembrance of the three times I met Muhammad Ali.

During many years of my legislative tenure, I kept a room year-round at what was then Atlanta's Downtown Marriott, now the Downtown Sheraton. It's at Courtland and Andrew Young International.

It was during a legislative session. I know this because I visited, on several occasions, and on more than one day, the huge bottom floor of the hotel where fighters were in training for soon-to-be fights in Atlanta, which included a world heavyweight championship match that, of course, was the top fight on the card. There was lots of interesting activity on the first floor.

Guess who was at the training sessions with his boxing shorts, shoes, and protective headgear? You've got it! Muhammad Ali! Not only was Ali properly attired, but "the Greatest" would get in the ring and spar with the other fighters. Obviously, he was not in fighting condition or physically well, but he would lumber around and all of a sudden release a flurry of punches at his opponent, with a huge grin on his face. It was quite a show!

Sometime during the same time period, he came to the governor's office in the Capitol and I happened to be there. While he and I both waited to see the governor (guess who the governor saw first—it wasn't me!), we had a nice visit. Ali was very approachable, had a great smile, and as he left to go into the governor's office, he gave me a card with his name and religious information on it. I suspect I have this card somewhere or it could be with my papers in the Richard Russell Special Collections Library at the University of Georgia.

Just before I left the lobby of the governor's office, the camera lady took our picture, and it now hangs in our barn. We both had on suits and both were smiling. He was much bigger and much better looking. I didn't have to tell you that, did I?

Assuming I had a brief visit with the champ at the Downtown Marriott (I can't remember any of the particulars), that's two memorable visits or one visit and one up-close observation. My impression was that Ali was a kind and nice man. I didn't think I'd ever see him again.

Several years later, the Hortons, Jerry and Carol, the Wilsons, Jerry and Faye, and Janice and I made a Christmas trip to New York City. During our trip, and while the six of us waited outside the hotel for a cab, guess who walked out of the hotel? You've got it, Muhammad Ali.

Again, he was affable, approachable, polite, and impressive. It was quite exciting, though brief. And, disappointingly, he didn't mention our two prior meetings!

In addition to what I wrote above, Ali and I had something else in common. We were both born in the same year and were the same age.

Many years ago, when Marcus Tripp was the pastor at the Perry United Methodist Church, he preached a sermon I'll never forget. His sermon was entitled "Jesus, Elvis, and Coca-Cola." Marcus said that these were the three best-known names in the world. It was a great sermon. But I'd say that for the twenty or thirty years of Ali's prime, he was the most recognizable person in the world. Literally, hundreds of millions knew Muhammad Ali if they saw him or his picture. Why?

I don't think Ali was the best-known man in the world because he could "float like a butterfly and sting like a bee" or because he was self-proclaimed "the Greatest" or even because he was the heavyweight champion of the world.

My opinion: he was the best known because he was all of the things mentioned above, but also because of the things I mentioned in the paragraphs earlier. He was friendly, approachable, kind. And, of course, he was uncommonly handsome and quite a man. I guess in lots of ways he was what he said he was: "the Greatest." He'd say, "I am the Greatest," and then he'd smile.

NAMING THINGS

"SoHo," as in Walker's SoHo Farm. Originally located on the lower end of the county on Highway 26, it was SoHo for South Houston. Just like the street in New York City, SoHo means the neighbor or district south of Houston ("Howston" and not "Hewston") Street. Then we bought another place in the west part of Houston County. It's loaded with big oaks, so we kept the name SoHo, and it stands for Southern Oaks of Houston. We didn't have to change bank accounts and charge accounts and that type of thing. It's still Walker's SoHo Farm. And, by the way, it could still stand for South Houston (it's more south than north) or even Southern Hospitality in South Houston.

We like to name things. We have an old, blue Ford pickup truck named, of course, "Little Blue." We used to have a white one that we called "Casper." Casper, the ghost, was white, wasn't he (she)? You get the picture, we like to name things.

What if I had the right to name a professional sports team? Well, it might depend on what type team and where it was located, but I like the name "Bats." Like, if I inherited the Atlanta Braves, I might change the name to Atlanta Bats. Yes, there is a double entendre. See the next paragraph.

Let me confess. Sometime back, I read an excellent book, *Bacardi and the Long Fight for Cuba*. Bacardi Rum's label is a black bat inscribed in a red circle. The family says these are the reasons this symbol was used: "As creatures, bats exemplified the ideal of brotherhood, lived and flew together, symbolized self-confidence, could fly in the dark without hitting anything, stood for discretion, kept silent, represented faithfulness, and they always returned home." Yeah, Atlanta Bats. I like that.

What if I could name a singing group—a good one capable of top-ten music? Well, I tend to like the older names such as "The Spinners," "Classics IV," "The O'Jays," or "Gladys Knight and the Pips." I like the name of the band Russell and John Gray were involved with—"Gypsy

Train." And my grandson Wade's band is "Design Company." But the question is, what I would name a singing group. What about "Countdown to Zero," "Phoolish Fonics," or "Modern Blacksmiths"? Kinda dated for 2018, I'd say.

I've had the privilege of naming lots of corporations and limited liability companies. Clients would come in wanting a new legal entity and would say to me, "You come up with a name," and I would. I've named lots of companies with which I was personally involved: Royal Union Productions, Main and Ball USA, Jancel Corp., Make Your Day, Atlanta Import Export, 1211 Company, and 1007 Jernigan come to mind. These names seemed to have worked pretty well.

What if I wrote a book? It would have to have a name, wouldn't it? Of course, the subject matter would have lots to do with the name, but I've thought about *Characters with Character* and *A Flash of Joy in the Pan of Life*. Connell Stafford told me one night in the jungles of Costa Rica that I was a "flash of joy in the pan of life." I thought it was one of the best compliments I was ever paid. So, I might call my book this.

A new car—"Sleek" or "Potent." An incorporated city—"Bountiful." Political party—"American." A bank—"Foundation National." A restaurant on General Courtney Hodges Blvd.—"General's Restaurant" (and I would fill it with pictures of generals from Robert E. Lee and U. S. Grant to General Hodges himself). Construction company—"Grand Builders." River in Georgia—"Cherokee Red." Clothing company—"Joseph's Threads." Beauty salon—"Heads Up" or "On Top of Things" (both Janice's ideas). And an oil company—"T D Oil" for "Thanks, dinosaurs."

Well, this is getting a little silly, so I'll stop. But if you need help in naming something, call me. I'll help you for free, which is pretty good when you consider that those big ad agencies in New York get millions to do the same thing.

I'm reading a little book, *Slide Mountain or the Folly of Owning Nature* by Theodore Steinberg, given to me by my friend Abby Sue Hunt Ginn. I'm really enjoying it and will end this with two quotes from the book: "To represent or to say a thing is already to bring it into existence" and "To name is to know, but it is also to own." Pretty heavy, but it makes me know that my proclivity for naming things doesn't mean I'm crazy.

CHRISTMAS '56 AND CHRISTMAS '16

Let's see, it's sixty years from Christmas in 1956 to Christmas in 2016. And yet for some inexplicable reason(s), I've had these two Christmases on my mind lately. In 1956, I was fourteen years old and not too far removed from the wonder of Santa Claus and from having my years defined by Christmas. You know, or some of you do, that you lived from one year to the next waiting on Santa Claus to come.

When I was fourteen there was a lot going on with me. I don't think age fourteen was a great time in my little life. My body was changing, and I didn't know why. And my interests were changing, at least some of them, and I didn't know why. Girls were becoming much more important, and I had given up on getting a pony and I didn't really care. And I wanted someone to tell me what was causing those bumps on my face and nose and how could I get rid of them, but no one did.

1956. I think we had a 1952 or 1953 Chevrolet in 1956. I know that we got a 1958 Chevy either in '58 or late '57, and Daddy let me pick out the colors—black and white. But back to 1956 in Mayberry or Mayperry.

This was our Christmas day routine. We'd get up at 1211 Swift Street in Perry just like I did all my life. David was five years younger, so he was nine. Did Santa come to see him in 1956? I don't know, and I'm too embarrassed to ask him because I know he still came to see me when I was nine. Lynda and Charles, twins, were six. Santa came to see them.

After seeing what Santa brought, and to whom, we made our way up Swift Street three houses to my Gray grandparent's where the "Gray family" had a great breakfast by Granny Gray. After opening a few gifts, we were off in our little Chevy to rural Washington County.

Get the picture. Daddy, Mother, my three siblings and me, in our 1952 Chevrolet, on our way, ninety miles or so, to rural Washington County with gifts and clothing for a two or three day visit. If it was cold, Papa would have the wood cut and the stove warm. And he had oranges ready to be "holed" and sucked. Then there was the sugarcane he cut to chew.

The presents were modest (Papa, when asked what he got, usually said "a pretty little new nothing"), and the house could be very cold. No television or poor television in 1956. One bathroom, about six feet by eight feet, that also served as a hall or passageway, with the necessity to save the limited water so that sometimes more than one child, even a fourteen-year-old, had to use someone else's previously used water.

We had a wonderful time in Washington County. And maybe, with luck, Uncle Jim and I would get to go squirrel hunting with Hubert Hawkins and his six or eight squirrel dogs. I loved it. Wish I could do it again. Intertwined with all of this, in Perry and Washington County, was a strong and deep emphasis on the baby Jesus and his birth and what caused us to have Christmas and what it was "really" all about.

And now it's 2016 and Santa still comes, bringing much more to most than he did to most in 1956. To many, Christ and his birth are still the center of it all, but, sadly, I say, in increasing numbers it's Santa or something else or nothing, and the real reason no longer matters.

Janice has been trying to get me to make a list of "what you want for Christmas this year." Finally, last Sunday, I made one. I had seven or eight items, including Pantene Classic Clean shampoo and conditioner, Kiwi black shoe polish, a gift certificate from the Sports Center and one from Barnes and Noble, and some Doctor's Brushpicks (toothpicks). It's not that I'm that modest in my wants, it's just that I already have most everything that I want or need.

I'm not mad at Santa, but I thought he was going to bring me a pony one year and a car when I was sixteen, and then eighteen, but it didn't happen. I don't know what you think about Santa Claus, but I know he had lots more sense than I did, especially when I was fourteen or sixteen or eighteen. I really wish I could be fourteen again and go back just like it was at the Walker homeplace in Washington County, Christmas in 1956. But after Christmas, I wouldn't want to be fourteen, because it's not a good age. Then again, it might beat being seventy-four.

GOODBYE, LITTLE COWBOY

She was five or six years old, our granddaughter, Haley Way, and she would come to visit for an overnight stay. Janice and I thought Haley was about the cutest little girl in the world, and we were anxious to have her, with our enthusiasm being somewhat dampened when she would tell us, "I want to go see that little cowboy." That's the way he was. Children, animals, and everyone who knew him wanted to be around the "little cowboy."

We laid him to rest last Saturday, across the road from where he grew up—assuming he ever did "grow up"—and in one of the fields, now Perry Memorial Gardens, where he used to rabbit hunt. They came in great numbers to the Friday visitation at Watson-Hunt Funeral Home (Draper Watson said it was one of the largest visitations he had ever seen) and to the Perry United Methodist Church and his funeral, a cross-section of our society, rich, poor, black and white, all to say "goodbye." Goodbye to Jerry, to Horton, to Do-Tricks, to Tricks, to that wonderful little cowboy.

We'll not see his like again. His death was our loss and not to be filled by others, ever, for he was one of a kind, unique, a character, a sport, tender-hearted, kind, stubborn, exasperating, and "good as gold."

He was audacious. Until Jerry died, I had never thought of "audacious" to describe him, but it does. As defined, he was unrestrained by convention or propriety. He had verve and a vitality and liveliness for life.

I won't attempt to mislead or gloss over, for those who knew Do-Tricks know better. So here it is: he smoked too much, as if smoking any is not too much. He occasionally "cut up" too much. He sometimes gave too much. And he loved too much, if that's possible. He wasn't perfect, but he was lots more perfect than those people who think they are perfect. Jerry did much of what Jesus told us to do, and he did it for the right reasons. Truly, he was a good man. Yes, we won't see his like again.

You can tell a lot about a person as to how little children react to them. I've told you about how Haley responded to him, and then there's his next-door neighbor, Beck Beckham, age seven. Just ask Beck about "Mr. Jerry" or any of our children or grandchildren or Jerry and Faye Wilson's kids or grandkids or Bobby and Laurie Jones's or Derry and Janie Watson's and a world of others. These children, many now adults, loved and love Mr. Jerry. They knew good and kind when they saw it.

Then there were his animals: Eugene, his cockatiel, who would sit on his shoulder and sing; Mildred, his pet squirrel, who would eat nuts out of his hand; and Mick, his dog, who would lick him "to death." Animals know good and kind when they see it.

I knew Jerry Horton for more than sixty years—we were friends and buddies that long. But everybody at his memorial service last Saturday knew him, loved him, and had "Jerry Horton stories." So, rather than tell my stories, which are wonderful to me, let me just mention, reminisce, remind, and let you think of yours.

• Man, how he and Carol could dance! Ever see them jitterbug?

• He was strong as a mule. I've never known a man, pound for pound, as strong as the young Do-Tricks. I saw him stand off (for about five minutes) a man, a state weightlifting champion, almost twice Jerry's size, in an arm wrestling match one night. The big man eventually won the match, but the little man won the crowd.

• He could play guitar and sing "Ring of Fire" better than Johnny Cash.

• Where did the nickname Do-Tricks come from? Ask Ed Beckham (the older), who gave him this name, or Bobby Horton, his brother, but I will tell you it had to do with rabbits. No man ever had a more appropriate nickname. Yeah, Do-Tricks!

• Jerry was the first employee at the Ag-Center and just retired last December. The Ag-Center never had a better ambassador. I'll bet they miss his riding around the grounds on his golf cart decked out in his cowboy hat, cowboy boots, and Wrangler jeans. As the Ag-Center folks put on their marquee after he died, he was "Employee #1."

• Jerry was neat in dress and appearance and as a youngster was quite dapper.

• He could fix anything and would, too, if you asked him to.

• He could out hunt you, out shoot you, and out fish you. He had a great knife collection and a great gun collection and knew lots about both.

• Jerry was a "soft touch" with a tender heart and always wanted to, and did, help the downtrodden and less fortunate.

• He still holds the record (90-plus yards) for the longest kick-off return at Perry High School, and he got a college letter for pole-vaulting at ABAC.

• He did so many bodacious things, you could write a book about 'em. I don't have the time or space for even just a few of 'em, but will give you one example. After attending a Saturday afternoon cowboy movie as a youngster, he jumped out of his grandmother's barn loft onto his saddled Shetland pony below. Just like the movie cowboys. The results were not good! Incidentally, if you don't know what "bodacious" means, you weren't around Do-Tricks nearly enough.

• He had and rode a Harley-Davidson motorcycle. He looked good and natural on his bike. My one ride with him almost scared me to death, and I promised God if he got me off, I would never get on a motorcycle again. God came through, and I've kept my promise!

• Jerry had a "ball hat" (a painted army helmet liner) and convict overalls that he wore to the ABAC basketball games. What a sight! What a sport!

• There are too many frog gigging, rabbit hunting, and skinny dipping stories to tell.

• Our Bobby Jones, along with others, played lots of golf with Do-Tricks. Ask Bobby Jones about it. He says, "I never had as much fun golfing as I did with Do-Tricks."

• Jerry and Carol, weren't those Georgia-Florida games and weekends wonderful?

• Bobby Jones, Do-Tricks, Jerry Wilson, and I went to Fort Worth, Texas, in the summer of '63 to work at Texas Steel Company. We came home as a band of brothers.

• The best thing Jerry ever did was to marry Carol. She's been his rock. And their progeny, Jennifer, Cindy, and "Little" Jerry, are almost as popular as their parents. That's saying a lot. God bless them all. We love you ("we" meaning tons of people).

I'll never listen to Frank Sinatra's "My Way" again without thinking of Jerry. Truly, he did it his way. And so we say goodbye to this stubborn, hard-headed, exasperating, wonderful, unique, bodacious, and audacious little man, Jerry Eugene Horton. Do-Tricks. That Little Cowboy.

I think Haley had it right. He was a cowboy—that is, if you are talking about the kind of cowboy that he used to watch on Saturday afternoons at the Muse Theater in Perry. The kind who talked straight and simple, loved his horse, worked hard, stood for justice and doing right and good, could ride, fight, rope, and shoot, all for the right causes, and would jump out of a barn loft onto his horse below to ride off and rescue the damsel in distress.

I have this in my desk drawer. I don't know where I got it or how long I've had it, but I think it applies to Do-Tricks, because this is what he did. Here it is:

Dance
As though no one is watching you,
Love
As though you have never been hurt before,
Sing
As though no one can hear you,
Live
As though heaven is on earth.
—Unknown

Jerry, you bless God up there in heaven, just like you've blessed us. See you soon.

V

DOGS AND OTHER OF GOD'S
ANIMAL CREATIONS

JUST ANOTHER FISH STORY

This is a story. A fish story. No, it won't rival *Moby Dick* or *The Old Man and the Sea*. In fact, it won't even rival some of my other fish stories. But I do think it good enough to go from memory to story, and by reducing it to writing, that's what I'm doing.

Interesting how fishermen are so taken with outwitting fish. Man's brain is about the size of a softball, and a fish's brain is about the size of a black-eyed pea. Actually, I've never seen a fish's brain, although I've cleaned thousands of them. I made up that "black-eyed pea" part. Also, most fishermen have hundreds, and in some cases thousands of dollars of equipment, including electronic equipment to help find fish. Bottom line: it's an unfair contest, but fishermen continue to brag about how they caught and what they caught, including me, with this story.

I was fishing with a Heddon Super Spook signed right there on the plug by Jimmy Houston. This top water lure has been my favorite since the latter part of last year. As all fishermen know, favorites change like women's fashions. I've had as favorites plastic worms, plastic lizards, Pop 'R Rebels, broken-back Rapalas, rubber shad, and others too numerous to list.

Late on Sunday afternoon last, Janice and I went to the pond to fertilize it. When getting my bucket to hold the fertilizer and the scoop to spread it, I noticed my open-faced spinner with the large Super Spook attached. It looked ready to go! The Super Spook was about as big around as those Tampa Nugget cigars Mr. Hilt Gray used to smoke (and later chew) and about two-thirds as long. It is mostly green with a little red and yellow under the head end. It had three sharp, deadly treble hooks—two underneath and one on the end.

We were at the pond doing the fertilizer job. Janice was helping, driving the old pickup truck, Blue Kate, and I was diligent to the task— off and on the tailgate, scooping and throwing. I did not want to lose my driver. We were both tired, having driven to Dothan and back to see

Janice's sick uncle, who was in the hospital. But I'm at a place in the pond where I've caught lots of bass before, so I threw out two scoops of fish pond fertilizer and then say, "Let me cast three or four times to see what they're doing." No resistance, so I do it.

The first cast or two, nothing. On the third cast, a small to medium bass rolls the Super Spook, but I can't get it hooked. Next, I cast further to the right, close to the dam, and it hits and I set the hooks. I judge it to be about two pounds, and the youngster is putting up a good fight, but I'm winning the contest. I'm bringing it to the shore, but about where I got the first strike, the "reeling in" gets more difficult. I think: The bass must've wrapped around a limb or some other trash. I continue to reel, and when I lift the Super Spook from the water, I see something I've never seen before—two large-mouth bass, about two pounds each, firmly hooked to the Super Spook. Amazing, and best of all, Janice has seen it all and takes several pictures.

I love to fish. I've been doing it since I was eight or nine years old, and I get great satisfaction out of it. I've got lots of great fishing stories, at least I think they are: a 115-pound tarpon caught at Boca Grande, Florida; the 27-pound king mackerel caught when I was fishing with Allan Stalvey about two miles from downtown Miami in the Intracoastal Waterway; the 130 speckled trout (all legal) Billy Bledsoe and I caught fishing out of Shell Island or Shell Point (I can't remember which) on Florida's Gulf Coast; the bass, bream, and catfish my cousin James Maddox and I caught out at Uncle Eugene's pond in Washington County when we were about twelve years old; the two times I got a treble hook embedded in a finger, which necessitated emergency room visits, etc.

Now I have a new story: two bass on one cast and one plug. It was a Jimmy Houston, Heddon Super Spook. I hope I can remember all about the plug. It makes it a better story. And I don't want to forget about the comparison to Mr. Hilt's cigar. Not many of the readers will remember Mr. Hilt, but I always will. I used to fish with him.

By the way, did I ever tell you about Mr. Hilt, Seabie Hickson, Billy Bledsoe, and I fishing at Steinhatchee, Florida, when it was so cold we had to scrape ice off the boat? Well, this is what happened... It's a good story.

DOGS I HAVE KNOWN
(PART ONE)

She was an illegitimate, out of Peach County, Georgia—a "put-out" dog, she followed our son, Russell, who was riding his bike on Clopine Lake Road over to our place in Houston County. All it took to seal the deal was one supper and Cloie was ours, or we were hers, when shortly after the first night, Russell moved into town, buying a house, taking a wife, but leaving Cloie behind.

I'd say Cloie was less than a year old when she came, joining Hershey, our Lab-Golden Retriever cross. Cloie was solid black, like a Lab, but with a pointer bird-dog look and an eagerness to hunt, catch, fish, and eat.

Hershey, the sweetest dog in America, and Cloie, one of the most interesting—but let's stop here on these two and let me talk about other dogs I have known, and then next week, we will come back to Hershey and Cloie.

My first dog, when I was about six or seven years old, was a Chow, Blackie. Blackie was black, and despite the general reputation of Chows, was a gentle and sweet dog. As is common to the breed, Blackie had a blue-black tongue and a black-lined mouth. I was taken with the color of Blackie's tongue and mouth and was familiar with it as she licked me often. Blackie started off in Perry, Georgia, but was soon removed to rural Washington County and to the home of my Walker grandparents. Blackie seemed content there, and we played together during my many visits and until her death, which was a sad occasion for me. Yes, I know that "Blackie" was a pretty simple name, but as you will see, we got better at naming as time went on.

Before I get to other dogs owned by our family or me, let me mention Papa's feist—a small dog. His name was Fritzie. I don't remember much about Fritzie except his unique name and his always following Papa, right at his heels, wherever he went. Still, Fritzie made enough of an impression on this little boy that I feel compelled to mention his name.

We had a dog when we lived on Swift Street in Perry named Beau Winkle. At least, I thought it was Beau Winkle. Janice thought it was Bo Winkle. I guess it depends on whether your inspiration for the name came from Charles Dickens and London, England, or Columbia, Alabama. Given Beau's conduct, I believe Janice was right. She was right. It was Bo. Bo was always acting like he would bite someone—the mailman, garbage folks, friends, strangers, etc. We didn't get many issues of the *Watchtower* when we had Bo. He would bark loudly as he raced by, nipping at heels. It was embarrassing. It was scary. Definitely, it was "Bo" Winkle. We got rid of this "redneck" dog.

One of the best dogs we ever had was named Governor. Alan Stone named this beautiful Golden Retriever and gave him to us. We loved Governor. Governor loved us. Unfortunately, Governor also loved to chase the UPS truck. Governor got too close to the truck. That was the end of Governor. It kinda reminded me of my one-time fleeting aspiration to be a governor.

After Governor was killed, Mrs. Jean Nation gave us a black dog named Georgia. Georgia was a great dog. We still missed Governor, but Georgia took away some of the pain of losing him. Georgia died of old age.

Then there was Tux (mostly black with white on her neck, thus Tux). As a puppy, Tux was another "put-out"; she was left on the side of the road and left to starve. It's a really sorry human that will do this! Lucky for Tux (and she was definitely a female, as was evidenced by several litters of puppies), we were at the farm that day. We fed her. Our neighbor across the road, Keith Felder, also fed her when we were not there. She had two homes and two masters, but, psychologically, this didn't seem to affect her. Tux stayed with us when we were at the farm on Saturday and Sunday and stayed across the road with Mr. Felder during the remainder of the week.

I wrote an article about this once, opining that it was better to own a two-sevenths interest in a good dog than a full interest in a sorry dog. I think that was true then and now. Tux was one smart, cunning dog—a survivor. We loved Tux. Unfortunately, she crossed the road once too often and was killed by a vehicle. We were sad. Tux was one of the best dogs we ever had, especially considering it was only a minority interest.

Next week, "Dogs I Have Known, Part Two," focusing on Hershey and Cloie.

DOGS I HAVE KNOWN
(PART TWO)

Now, Janice and I have Hershey and Cloie. I'll get to Cloie in more detail momentarily, but first let's give Hershey her due. Hershey is the sweetest dog in America, or at least we think so. She is the polar opposite of Bo Winkle. I have never seen Hershey growl at anyone—not even another dog. I take Hershey to ride in the back of the pickup several days a week. She loves to get in the pond. She also likes treats and great leftovers such as Domino's pizza. Hershey is a great dog and much loved.

Now, I want to tell you more about this interesting dog, Cloie. Let's start when she first took up residence with us. We'd feed her every day. But just because she gets fed doesn't mean she's given up her old ways. Example: she still likes to run through the fields making grasshoppers hop-up into the air (grasshoppers do "hop-up," don't they?) so that she can snap them up as a supplement to her Purina Dog Chow dining. And woe unto the lizard or mouse that strays into her path. Survival instincts, you know. And then there's fishing—and catching fish.

Cloie also catches turtles, turns them on their back, and spends hours playing with them. Then they disappear. Do they get back in the water or does she eat them? It wouldn't surprise me if she does eat them. I know that she steals pecans out of the buckets under our carport, cracks and eats them. So why not a turtle?

We have a small pond behind our house, and Cloie spends about one half of every spring and summer day fishing—and, yes, catching two or three a week. This fishing dog stalks the fish. She stands stone still on the side of the pond until an unwary fish (bass or bream) swims into her range. Quick as lighting, she snaps them up and then runs around the pond with the catch in her mouth looking like Bill Dance displaying a twelve-pound bass! One difference in Dance and Cloie, though, is that Cloie doesn't believe in "catch and release." Cloie is a "catch and eat" dog.

Actually, we have four fishing ponds on our place, and I spend lots of time fishing for and catching bass. Cloie, who always goes fishing with me, knows that one of the small bass will be a treat for her, and she's right! If I catch one of two pounds or less, it goes to Cloie, who immediately runs off with the bass, about fifty yards or so, and proceeds to eat the entire fish—always head first. And woe to you if you try to retrieve the bass—or, should I say, good luck in your trying, you'll never get it back!

One other thing that I saw Cloie do that I could hardly believe. She dived off the platform that holds the feeder, head first, with her head down like a human (rather than up like a dog holds its head when they jump into the water), and came out with a fish! Unbelievable. What a dog!

I shouldn't conclude without sharing with you the best dog story I ever heard. It was told to me by Buster Byrd and in the presence of his younger brother, Chuck, who for many years was a law partner of mine. Here it is, as told by Garland T. Byrd Jr. (Buster):

"Daddy wasn't much on any animals that you couldn't ride or couldn't pull something or ones that you couldn't eat. But he finally consented for Chuck and me to get a dog, a beagle hound named Sam. He told us that we each owned a half-interest in the dog. I was about ten years old and Chuck was about five. We were specifically instructed not to bring the dog into our brand-new house, which we had lived in for about three or four months and which had new wall-to-wall carpet. Daddy and Mother went off and we took the dog inside. At just about the time Daddy returned home and came in the door, the dog made a big deposit in the middle of the new carpet. Immediately, five-year-old Chuck said to Daddy, 'Look what Buster's half of the dog did to the carpet.' That's when I realized that Chuck was going to be a lawyer!"

I can't top Buster's story, so I'll stop with a final salute to some good dogs I have known, dogs who have enriched my life. Blackie, Fritzie, Governor, Tux, Georgia, Hershey, and even Bo Winkle. And then there is Cloie, irrepressible, irresistible, irreplaceable, Cloie. Go, you hairy dogs!

MY AFFILIATIONS WITH CHICKENS

I like Warner Robins mayor Randy Toms very much, and I am supportive of the Warner Robins City Council, as they effectively govern one of the most dynamic cities in the South. But I must admit some disappointment in their recent action, or should I say failure to act, as they make decisions concerning fowls in the International City.

Obviously, and is often the case, I had an exalted idea as to my reputation in dealing with, and solving, over a long period of time, problems involving chickens. It is now apparent to me that Mayor Toms did not know of my expertise. Let me put it simply: I have history with those pecking, clucking, scratching, crowing birds with that piece of red flesh on the top of their heads—those producers of eggs and meat. Why didn't the officials call on me for advice?

Barred Plymouth Rocks (gray and white), White Leghorns (white), White Plymouth Rocks (white), Rhode Island Reds (red), exotic fowl, and cross-bred birds of a wide variety of colors—I've seen them all. At least, it seems as if I've seen 'em all.

Grandma had chickens. Funny thing, in retrospect, the hogs, mules, and cows seemed to belong to Papa, but the chickens seemed to fall under Grandma's control and ownership. Also, the eggs produced and the "egg money" were apparently Grandma's. That's where I came in: I took my orders and duties relative to the chickens directly from Grandma.

"Larry, go up under the barn and see if there is a setting hen, and if so, count the eggs." Exactly how you "go *up* under" a barn, I don't know. But I do know it meant to "climb" (another interesting word) under the barn and find the eggs. I did it, and let me tell you, if I had found the Confederate gold under the barn, I wouldn't have been any more thrilled. "Grandma, the red hen is under the barn, and she has twelve eggs," I would dutifully report. And before long, mother red hen would proudly march out from under the barn with her little brood of yellow chicks in tow. My report was authenticated.

To be honest, I'm not exactly sure how all of this chicken and biddies thing comes about. Oh, I know that the big chicken that struts about, the rooster, is a male, and that the little hens pecking and scratching, tending to their business, are females. And I know that you can get eggs without roosters, but you can't get biddies without roosters. But exactly how you get from eggs to chicks, I don't know. I was especially confused with how the roosters were always jumping on the hens, and despite my best efforts to stop this tawdry behavior, I was largely unsuccessful. I felt sorry for the hens and considered the larger roosters as big, feathered bullies. Frankly, the roosters' behavior seemed to bother me lots more than it did the hens.

Another thing that Grandma felt strongly about was hawks. She didn't appreciate these birds, and her instructions to me were that if I saw a hawk, to get Papa's shotgun and "shoot 'em." I don't think she was impressed with how the Department of Natural Resources or the federal authorities or anyone else felt about this. Hawks tried to get chickens and biddies, and Grandma was protecting "her brood" and her "egg money." I never saw a hawk get a chicken—maybe it was because I did such a good job in defending the flock. I never hit a hawk, but I did scare two or three, at least that's my recollection from more than fifty years ago.

I could go on and on about moving from this early stage of "chicken relationships" to grading eggs at Gray-Walker Supply with Mr. Glea Gray and Ed Thompson, to delivering eggs to Perry Super Foods, and then to taking chicken feed with Joe Hodges to Mr. Henry Cullen Talton's store at Bonaire and G. W. Hicks's chicken house south of Perry. Space won't permit. So, let me simply say that I have had a long and pleasant relationship with chickens, and it has been a learning experience as to exactly how little I really know.

You know, the more I write, the less I seem to know. So I guess I'd best stay out of the "Warner Robins Chicken Controversy." But that's okay. I know the Warner Robins mayor and council will "do the right thing."

CHICKEN STUFF

At the same time I send my weekly article to *The Telegraph*, it gets emailed to a long list of interested readers. At least, I hope they are "interested," and I know that many of them are very interesting. There are judges, lawyers, lobbyists, a nationally known gospel singer in Dallas, Texas, legislators, family members, and just friends. It's a good group, and I get good responses from them.

To my mind, none of the readers are more interesting than Jim Minter, former sports writer for the *Atlanta Journal* and later editor of the *Atlanta Journal-Constitution*.

Jim, who Dink NeSmith says "was our Google before there was Google," often responds to my articles. His responses are always good, but the one I received last week after my article having to do with carrying chicken feed into hot, smelly chicken houses was, to my mind, a classic. I must share it with you, and here it is: "Chicken Stuff."

"The only thing between our house and our neighbor, Frank Reeves, was a one-acre cotton patch. (Frank's son, Walter, is a garden-advice guru on Atlanta radio, TV, and in the *Journal-Constitution*.)

"Frank raised chickens, or rather hens, in three long houses. He sold eggs for a living. You might not know this, but hens at some stage quit laying eggs, or maybe take a vacation from laying. I don't know exactly how this works, but a chicken expert can stick his hand up a hen's rear-end and deduce whether or not the hen has quit laying. That's when you do the culling, taking out the hens who have quit doing their egg duty.

"The problem, at least the one for me, was that you have to do the culling when the hens go to roost.

"On too many nights, just as I was finishing eating and looking forward to listening to 'The Lone Ranger,' I'd see Frank Reeves making his way through the cotton patch to our back door. I knew what he wanted.

"'Can you get Jimmy to help me cull hens?'

"The way you cull hens is in total darkness. Frank plucks one off the roost, sticks his hand up the rear-end, passes the hen to me with instructions to put it into either the 'keeper' pen or the 'culled out' pen. As he hands the hens to me in the dark, the hen arrives flapping in my face. I'm talking 100 to 200 hens on any given night. About half of them mess on you when Frank passes them back.

"Sometimes, Frank would give me a quarter.

"My chicken culling ended in 1944 when Frank was called into the Army. Before leaving, he made one more after-supper walk through the cotton patch to our back door. This time he was carrying his prized 12-gauge double-barrel shotgun. He wanted to leave it in my custody for the duration, or forever if he didn't get back. It was a nice reward for hazardous duty.

"These days, organic vegetables are the rage among a generation who don't know chicken doodle about chickens.

"I prefer my tomatoes fertilized by 10-10-10 rather than chicken manure.

"Culling hens tops my list of things I'd rather not do."

Grandma and Papa had chickens which, at that time, would have been called "yard chickens." Today, in an attempt by restaurants to command exorbitant prices, they're called "free range chickens."

What I learned from my grandparents' chickens were two things. First, these fowl probably were the examples used by my grandfather—though unwittingly on his part—to introduce me to information about procreation. You know, "the facts of life." On this subject, I was as dull as the chickens about which I write. Papa, in a limited way, explained the differences in the rooster and the hen. And he told me that you could not have "biddies" (baby chicks to you Yankees) without roosters. Also, he smiled ever so slightly when I attempted to break up "fights" between roosters and hens. Slowly, I began to sense that there was something going on about which I needed to know more.

All my memories aside, if you think Jim Minter's writing is as good as I do, I hope you will help spread it all over Middle Georgia. It will tickle lots of folks and should improve the productivity of our farmer's fields. Chicken stuff, you know!

WILD HOG TALK

I did not start off to be against 'em. I really didn't. I guess when I first noticed 'em, like most folks, it was an "olfactory thing," which means "of or contributing to the sense of smell," which Papa's hogs certainly did.

I was probably less than ten years old, but close to it, when I began to take notice of the hogs and how important they were to Papa and Grandma's well-being. Oh, I didn't one day say, "These hogs contribute to my grandparent's lifestyle and survival," but I began to realize that the hogs mattered. I don't quite remember when I related the country ham, with its red-eye gravy, syrup, and biscuits, directly to the hogs, but at this time I began to develop a growing awareness of their worth.

Grandma and Papa "killed hogs" every year (it was cold but not freezing, lest the meat would freeze), and I watched all of this with great interest. I watched the men shave the killed hogs (the knives had to be razor sharp and the water had to be hot, but not too hot or it would "set the hair"). Some of our politicians today "set the hair."

Out of the hog killings came sausage (packed into the cleaned intestines), tenderloin, salt-cured hams, ribs, "chitlings," barbeque, etc. What do they say? "They ate everything but the squeals." Hogs were important to the David Walker family.

What I'm getting to is my strong dislike of Papa's hog's descendants, which I will call "wild hogs" and which have become a scourge on this country. If you have a little land and a lot of wild pigs, which many of you do, then you know what I mean. Let me vent.

A little explanation is in order. I was in Athens at the University of Georgia this past weekend, and my friend Toby Carr, who works with UGA, gave me a manual by Michael Foster and Michael T. Mengak from the university's Warnell School of Forestry and Natural Resources. The following mostly comes from their work.

Swine were first introduced to North America by Spanish explorers in the sixteenth century, and settlers raised pigs with free-range practices for centuries. Eurasian species of boars for sports hunting resulted in interbreeding with free-ranging domestic pigs. The pig population exploded.

Wild pigs are the most fertile large mammals in existence. They have a gestation period of about sixteen weeks, start reproducing at six months, and a typical sow will give birth to two litters per year of four to six piglets. Lots and lots of pigs and hogs!

These pigs are mostly found in moist areas but are highly mobile and nomadic. They are now colonized in more than forty of the fifty states.

These pigs will consume almost anything, from agriculture crops and mast crops, such as acorns and fruits, to grub worms and dead animals. They will also consume fawns, livestock, and eggs of wildlife. I seldom see a snake on our place. I think the hogs are eating the snake eggs and the snakes!

Wild pigs travel in groups called sounders, which consist of two or three related adult females and their offspring. Males, especially larger boars, are often solitary. Members of a sounder often suckle from one sow while the other stands watch for predators. This contributes to low mortality rates of the wild pigs.

Some statistics from UGA: 90 percent of people do not like having wild hogs on their land, and 81 percent report that they hunt or allow hunting of the pigs on their land. Eighty percent believe wild pigs negatively affect deer and quail, and 70 percent believe they have a negative effect on wild turkeys.

Wild pigs cause substantial damage to fencing, food plots, and can quickly destroy a newly planted pine stand. They can tear up a tract of land at night that will take you years to get smoothed back to usability.

The most effective means of control is trapping, which, of course, is difficult, if done properly. But it can be quite successful. Shooting is another attempt at control, but it is apparently not very effective.

Back to Washington County around 1952 or so. I had a pet pig that followed me around my grandparent's farm. Sometimes, he (or she?) would lie down in the warm sun and I would lie down and put my head on its side. Both of us would take a nap. Little did I realize all the problems the descendants of my pillow were going to cause. But I did know that these pigs were important to Grandma and Papa and to me, too. Important can be positive or negative.

MEMORIES FROM FISHING ON THE FLATS

It was cold, really cold, on Saturday morning, 7 o'clock, March 18, as Connell Stafford, our guide, Travis Harper, and I motored in an open boat out the mouth of the Altamaha River at Two Way Fish Camp into the ocean flats, surrounded by many of Georgia's treasures, its fields of marsh grass, its historic islands, and its earliest history.

I had on lots of clothes, lots of clothes, but with the wind whipping me in the face and with the temperature in the upper 30s or low 40s, it was cold. As I sat in the bottom of the boat with my back to the wind and with my eyes closed, my thoughts were not of discomfort, but warm memories of fishing trips past and the people who made these parts of my life so unforgettable.

I never go to the flats that I don't think of Cedar Key, Florida, and one of my favorite people of all times, Edgar "Yellow Legs" Campbell. He guided my fishing companions and me many times. Sometimes we caught fish and sometimes we didn't, but we always had fun. "Yellow" saw to it with his keen wit, sharp mind, and constant chatter and showing us that catching fish was just a bonus to the trip.

Funny, but I thought of Charlie Howell from Macon, now deceased, with whom I never went on a fishing trip but one time. Charlie took Mr. Hilt Gray's place. Mr. Hilt was a late cancellation, so I called Charlie and he went with us. Billy Bledsoe, Seabie Hickson, Charlie Howell, and me.

This is true and a good story, but space limitations require brevity. The bottom line: Billy and I, with our guide, caught 130 speckled trout, all legal, and Seabie and Charlie, with their guide, caught 90, all legal, out of Shell Island in Florida. It's the most we ever caught in one day. But thirty-five or forty years later, it was Charlie Howell about whom I was thinking on that recent cold Saturday morning.

I also thought about Mr. Alan Branch, gentleman and guide extraordinaire, his wonderful son, Bobby, and his kind and gentle wife,

Kitty, and the fun we had fishing out of the Yellow Bluff on the Georgia coast. This was in the same part of the ocean where we were fishing this past cold Saturday. There were others, Glen Bryant and Charlie Jones, Hinesville folks who helped provide the hospitality and coolers of beautiful Georgia shrimp as we turned from the coast back towards Middle Georgia with our memory-making trip ended.

Ben Porter, another Southern gentlemen and someone who was easy to be around, was also on my mind as we motored towards Little St. Simons last week. Ben had money and many material things, but he also had the common touch and too many real friends to count. Lots of folks have style, but not nearly as many have class. Ben Porter had class. I wish I could go spend one more night at Ben's place on the Georgia coast and go fishing with him in his big, fine boat one more time. Unfortunately, it can't happen.

Time marches on, and as Daddy used to say, "The days get longer and the years get shorter." And so it is. And with far too many days gone by, memories of them are all we have. Perhaps it was the cold weather and the waters in which we were fishing, but that wonderful, blistering cold morning that I spent with Tom Murphy in a small boat in a "creek" at high tide on St. Catherine's Island fishing for and catching many, many red fish was another memory that made me both happy and sad, and all of this as Travis, Connell, and I motored to where Travis thought we could catch fish (and we did).

Billy Bledsoe. Seabie Hickson. Hilt Gray. Glea Gray. James Moore. Bryant Culpepper. Daddy. Grandbuddy. Alan Branch. Bobby Branch. Kitty Branch. Charlie Jones. Glen Bryant. Jerry Horton. Jerry Wilson. Horace Evans. Charlie Howell. Felton Jenkins. Larry III. Wendy Walker Way. Russell Walker. John Gray Walker. Janice Walker. Connell Stafford. Buddy DeLoach. Foster Rhodes. Yellow. Travis Harper. And for all those who have enriched my life while fishing on the flats, I'll try to remember you next time, just like I hope some will remember me.

By the way, we caught about twenty-five specs, eight were keepers, but we kept just four. When we got back to the fish camp, Travis cleaned four and the local restaurant, Mudcat Charlie's, cooked them, furnished "2 sides" in addition to hush puppies and a drink, all for eight dollars a plate. It was delicious and we made more memories.

I can't believe I've finished this and haven't even mentioned Suwannee, Horseshoe Point, and Steinhatchee, three other great fishing villages. Also, St. Marys, another good place on the Georgia coast. Lots of good memories of these great places.

VI

POLITICS

SELMA: ANOTHER PERSPECTIVE

Janice and I saw the movie *Selma*. I think it was the first day it came out down here in the South.

I have read what many have written as a result of the movie. Some have written about the movie and some have written about the events as depicted in the movie. The movie and the writings have stirred lots of memories.

The February/March edition of my favorite magazine, *Garden & Gun*, came out last week. Congressman John Lewis was featured, and his gracious remarks began on page 23. This is part of what he had to say: "I always felt growing up that in the South there was evil but also good—so much good.... I travel all the time, but when I come back to the South, I see such progress. In a real sense a great deal of the South has been redeemed."

Charles Richardson's "Sadness about Selma" in last Sunday's *The Telegraph* was excellent. It was not about being sad about Selma (although I know he was), it was about being sad that so many young people have not taken advantage of opportunities won, often bought with loss of life, at Selma and other places in the South during those times years ago.

I think most everyone would agree with Charles about opportunities surrendered. However, we only have to look at these Georgians—Andrew Young, congressman, mayor, and UN Ambassador; Congressman Sanford Bishop; Crawford County sheriff Lewis Walker; State Representative Calvin Smyre; Atlanta mayor Kasim Reed; Central Georgia Technical College president Ivan Allen; television personality and journalist Charlayne Hunter-Gault, and so many others—to see that positive and unimagined progress has been made since 1965.

Let me go back to Selma, Alabama, but further back than 1965. It was June 11, 1963, and four Perry white boys had stopped at a drugstore in downtown Selma to eat lunch. I was one of the four boys. This was the day that George Wallace "stood in the schoolhouse door" in Tuscaloosa, Alabama. The boys were on their way to Fort Worth, Texas, to work in a steel mill for the summer.

We made it to Meridian, Mississippi, and spent the night. Byron De La Beckwith Jr. shot and killed Medgar Evers in Jackson that night shortly after midnight on Thursday, June 12. The next morning we drove through downtown Jackson (there was no interstate in 1963). There was rioting in the streets, and we were frightened.

The four of us lived in a garage apartment next to the Texas Christian University campus while we worked at Texas Steel Company. Apparently, we lived very close to Lee Harvey Oswald and his family. We left Fort Worth in August 1963, and Oswald killed President Kennedy three months later on November 22, 1963.

I read the Pulitzer Prize-winning book *All the King's Men*, by Robert Penn Warren, that 1963 summer. Also, I followed with great interest Senator Richard Russell's leading the Southern senators in fighting the Civil Rights Bill.

I wrote above that four "boys" went to work in Texas at a steel mill, and we did. When the summer ended, four "men," Jerry "Do-Tricks" Horton, Bobby Jones, Jerry Wilson, and I, returned to Perry. Now, the other three are gone, and I am left to keep the memories.

I didn't have an epiphany that summer of 1963, but I did have an awakening. I'm different today than I was then, and so is everyone, black and white, who lived in those times. I believe my change started in the summer of '63. And like Charles Richardson wrote last week, "even with all the sadness, I'm hopeful."

I returned to Selma with Janice in the summer of 2013, fifty years after my first trip there. I tried to find the drugstore where the four boys from Perry ate lunch, and I think I found it. Janice and I rode over the Edmund Pettus Bridge three or four times, but none of it was like it was in '63, and it will never be that way again. And like life, some of that is good and some of that is sad.

TIME HAS CURED THE LOVE OF POLITICS

That orotund, sage, enigmatic raconteur from Enigma, Bobby Rowan, says it this way: "The only cure for the love of politics is embalming fluid."

"The love of politics." What a quaint phrase. It's in the same category as "mash the foot feed," or "it's time for our school prayer," or "get the milk off the porch." You just don't hear folks talking about getting into politics much anymore.

It was July 1962, a typical hot, summer Saturday. They came from all over Georgia in motorcades with signs identifying counties on the sides of their cars, over the gnat line and up from the wire-grass country, down from the mountains and over from the coast. Those signs, removed from their cars to be held high at the orchestrated time, and to be accompanied by shouts and whoops as "Dooly, Washington, Ben Hill, Peach, Jones" and more were called out by the master of ceremonies.

According to my favorite, unofficial Georgia historian, George Hooks, "There were at least 17,000, because that's how many plates of barbeque we served that day at the Americus ball field—9,000 pounds of hams and shoulders." They came to eat, but they also came for the show. And if raw, racial Georgia politics was what they wanted, they got it.

The invocation was given by Methodist bishop Arthur J. Moore, the master of ceremonies was Wingate Dykes, and the fiery, young, pugnacious George Wallace, who had just been elected governor of Alabama, introduced Marvin Griffin, who was trying to become Georgia's governor for the second time. Wallace's introduction wouldn't be acceptable in today's political world.

Yes, it was quite a show. But the people of Georgia, while liking their politics fiery and hot, opted to send a smooth, urbane, handsome young Carl Sanders to the governor's office. This 1962 campaign gave rise to two enduring phrases: As to Sanders, "the New South"; and as to Griffin, "They ate my barbeque, but they didn't vote for me."

The shifting in Georgia politics, with the 1962 governor's race being an apt precursor for this now dramatic change, probably started at the ball field in Americus on that hot July 1962 Saturday. Georgians still liked the show, but they wanted Georgia to do better, be better, and not embarrassed, and they showed it with their votes. Georgians opted for the New South, not the Old.

Who could have seen in 1962 just how extensive the change would be? And is it all for the good? Gone are the personal contacts, the gatherings, free food, huge outdoor meetings, country and gospel music, political signs on every power and telephone pole from Macon to St. Simons—gone is the soul of the quest. Gone is the fun.

Also gone are the great stump speeches. Oh, to hear Garland Byrd, Denny Groover, and Peter Zack Geer one more time. Or to hear Richard Russell eviscerate his opponent with great effectiveness: "If you'll quit telling lies on me, I'll quit telling the truth on you." And, too, to hear Herman Talmadge say anything—just to hear it roll out as if words were escaping a mouth full of marbles.

With what did we replace the old? PACs—huge amounts of personal-interest money (much of it from out of the state) buying what should belong to the Georgia people, outside advisers who do not really understand Georgia and its people, high-tech money solicitations, punctilious campaigning, mostly north of I-285, and the lack of fervor of our people for their candidate(s).

Bobby, it might still be true that "the only cure for the love of politics is embalming fluid." Sadly, however, most of the love for politics is gone. So, we just really don't need nearly as much fluid as we used to.

LARRY'S LEARNED POLITICAL LESSONS

So, you want to be in politics, or maybe you are already in it. Either way, if politics interests you, and assuming your interest is at the state legislative or local level, let me talk to you about some lessons I learned from long years of political involvement.

First, realize that success in politics is like success in most any endeavor that is worth pursuing. It takes lots of hard work to get elected, and it takes lots of hard work to do a good job if elected. The public is harder to please than ever before. Also, know that running for office is kinda like running in a minefield—you never know when there is going to be an explosion. It's more this way today than ever before.

Likability is the number one asset of a candidate or an official. If folks like you, they'll probably vote for you and will even "cut you some slack" when you do something as an elected official that they don't like—and you will. I call it the "going fishing test." You know, the one you'd most like to be with fishing.

Be yourself. Don't try to be something or someone you're not. If you are arrogant (or shy and it comes across like arrogance), you probably should pick something else to do. As I like to say, incompetence will beat arrogance every time. And it will.

Say what you think, even if it is not what the voters or your constituents want to hear. Voters appreciate candor even if they disagree. And voters can see through false or patronizing answers or statements. In the long run, honesty, candor, and conviction will win out.

Learn the most important two words in politics—the other person's name. And call their name a lot. Learn the most important four words: "What do you think?" Then listen. First, you'll learn something. Next, you'd be surprised at how smart that person will think you are when the conversation ends.

As to constituent service, know that you will spend 90 percent of your time with 10 percent of your constituents and 10 percent of your time with 90 percent of your constituents. You will be amazed by what some folks ask you to do for them, and your success in helping encourages them to request additional help. And some of them will—again and again. Get 'em a job and some will be back in six months asking you to help them get a promotion. Really!

Most of your fellow elected colleagues are conscientious and want to do a good job—yes, from your party and the other party. Talk to folks on "both sides of the aisle." Learn something about them, their families, and where they are coming from. They might turn out to be a good friend and might be unexpected help when needed. You don't have to agree with them to like 'em and respect 'em.

Know that the job you are elected to do is probably not as important as you think it is, and learn that you, as the officer holder, are not nearly as important. In other words, don't take yourself too seriously. Take the job seriously, but not yourself.

This lesson (truth) is closely related to the one above. With regard to political positions, Thomas Jefferson said something like this: "Very few die, and none retire." In other words, all office holders eventually get defeated. Prove Jefferson wrong and retire when you need to and before the voters retire you. Believe it or not, when you leave, someone will take your place and will do the job—perhaps better than you did it.

All of these lessons can be combined into this great proverb, which goes something like this: "The sun doesn't shine on the same dog all the time." Or, to put it another way, if you are in politics and it's going well, you better get ready for the bad; and if it's going bad, do not despair, you might be on the top of the political heap in a year or two.

These are just a few of the lessons. There are lots more. Good luck!

NAWLEANS AS REMEMBERED BY JIM MINTER

This is absolutely too good to pass up. It's by Jim Minter, former sports writer and later editor of the *Atlanta Journal-Constitution* and still a great storyteller and writer, as you will see.

According to Jim, all of this was precipitated by a book, *The Earl of Louisiana* (about Earl Long, governor of Louisiana) by A. J. Liebling, which I sent to him (more on this great book in my 2014 Books Report—upcoming). In fact, in a later email, Jim wrote: "The book made me want to go back to New Orleans, one more time, even if Kolb's German restaurant and the Poboy place on the Canal is gone.... Can't see a UGA trip back to the Sugar Bowl in my lifetime, and Tulane is not on the schedule."

Enough. Let's see what Jim wrote on November 14.

> Larry,
> I can't tell you how much I enjoyed the Long-Liebling book!
> Early in my checkered sports-writing career I went to New Orleans five or six times in the fall. In those days we got into a town on Thursday afternoon. Tulane played on Friday night. We'd go to Thursday afternoon practice in the old Sugar Bowl and back to downtown for the rest of the evening. On Saturday, I got a ride with one of the writers for the Picayune or States-Item up to Baton Rouge for LSU on Saturday night.
> My first trip to New Orleans I happened up on John Rauch, who was scouting for Georgia. John and I went to Pat O'Brian's for dinner. I remember John eating four dozen oysters on the half shell while I ate two. Just as we finished, about twenty cops crashed in and rounded up a bunch of kids, the bartender and waiters for serving drinks to under-aged kids. John and I were upset but our waiter told us not to bother. It was all for show. The cops did that about once every two or three months to make it look like they were enforcing the law.

We always stayed at the Roosevelt except when traveling with the Atlanta Crackers, who stayed at the St. Charles. When we checked into the Roosevelt there would be a bottle of whiskey and a vase of roses in our room. When I asked some of my older colleagues about it, they explained: The Roosevelt manager (I can't remember his name) was a former Huey Long operative who had spent time in the Atlanta pen. While in Atlanta, the Journal had written several stories about him which he apparently appreciated. So anyone from the Atlanta Journal got special treatment, even during Sugar Bowl week.

I also got to go bet on the horses and spent many an afternoon watching fighters train in the gyms that Liebling mentions. If I had not been there, I'd have suspected Liebling made up some of the stuff people told him. But I know how people in New Orleans like to talk. On the two-hour ride up to Baton Rogue on Saturday morning, Pie DuFour, a columnist from the Picayune, would fill you in on everything.

Saturday night in Baton Rouge was something else. Once, Coach Dodd invited me to run onto the field with him to experience how it felt. When Coach Dodd and I ran out of the tunnel leading Tech onto the field, they hit that tiger with the electric cattle prod. His screams and those of nearly a hundred thousand half drunk Cajuns made the hair on your neck stand up.

I was there for Billy Cannon's Halloween run, made with five minutes to spare on my deadline. After the game, everybody who was anybody went to Bob and Jerry's for steaks. What a gathering! Another world.

I stayed in the Capitol Hotel on the river. I remember getting up at 4 on a Sunday morning with Sterling Dupree, who was scouting for Georgia, to watch for Sputnik on the Capitol Roof. We didn't see it.

I did get to climb up the State Capitol stairway and see all the bullet marks where the troopers shot the doctor who shot Huey.

I ate my first Poboy in New Orleans. Roast beef and gravy. Never tasted anything so good. Those weekends are among my best memories and they all came back reading the book. Thank you again.

jm

Thank you, Jim Minter, for letting me use your email and for bringing back so many great memories for so many people.

SWILLING THE PLANTERS WITH BUMBO

Jim Minter, former editor of the *Atlanta Journal-Constitution*, sent me the book about ten months ago, and there it lay on Janice's coffee table, in front of Janice's sofa, where I sit, read, write, and often nap.

James Madison, A Life Reconsidered by Lynne Cheney. Really, how good could a book by a politician's wife be (especially a serious work on what I supposed to be a rather dry subject)? Washington, Jefferson, Lincoln, Teddy Roosevelt—yes. But James Madison by Cheney? Really, just how interesting and compelling could it be?

Then one rainy, dull day about a month ago, I picked up Cheney's 465-page tome and started reading and underlining and reading and underlining. Wow! What a book. At the rate I'm underlining, I'll use up two EnerGel Liquid Gel Ink pens before I'm through. And I'll know more about the US Constitution, the Bill of Rights, and how the pattern for our government was made than ever before. It's knowledge that I should've gained in the eleventh grade of high school. I would've been a better lawyer, legislator, and citizen if Cheney's book had been available to me and required reading around September of 1958.

The Articles of Confederation, the Federalist Papers, Notes on the State of Virginia, Marbury versus Madison, North versus South, Nullification, Hamilton versus Jefferson, Hamilton versus Madison, Adams versus Jefferson, Madison and Jefferson, Federalist versus Republicans, the War of 1812, the Louisiana Purchase, Alien and Sedition Acts, and more. All are important, and it is great to know something or something more about these subjects. But then on page 68 I read words that bolstered a long-held belief, but which I could not verify. Let me explain.

In discussions with Janice and others, including sometimes the media, I have often opined that the way political business is done in our country is not new, and that it had probably been done similarly in Williamsburg, Virginia, pubs, with lobbyists buying food and drink for

Washington, Jefferson, Madison, and other politicians who were running the country or destined to run the country. (Lobbyists can spot 'em, you know!) And there it was on page 68 of Cheney's book:

> For Madison, however, the early years of the war had even more peaks and valleys than they did for his fellow countrymen. No sooner were there signs that the American effort might succeed than he suffered an ignominious political defeat. "Swilling the planters with bumbo," as providing food and drink for voters was called, was a long-established practice among Virginia politicians. Madison's great-uncle Thomas Chew had gained a measure of fame in 1741, when as a candidate for the House of Burgesses he brought a punch bowl into the courthouse itself. Believing that the spirit of the Revolution demanded a more sober approach, Madison choose not to treat freeholders as they arrived to vote, a decision that caused him to lose the election to Charles Porter, a barkeep who offered an ample supply of spirits.

I'm not saying or even implying that the current practice of providing politicians with food and drink is the way it should be. But I am saying that, apparently, it's the way it has been done since our country's birth, and it's probably the way it will be done in the future. And at least today it's not done in the polling place itself, so maybe we're making some progress.

Swilling: to drink or eat greedily. *Planters:* those who plant; early settlers or colonists. *Bumbo:* I couldn't find a definition for bumbo, but I've got a pretty good idea as to what bumbo is, don't you?

Another thing that the author does so well with her book is to show the humanity of our Founding Fathers. I have concluded that the politics of the late 1700s has more in common with twentieth-century USA politics than there are differences. It was a rough game then, and it's a rough game now. Amazing, this swilling the planters with bumbo in the courthouse. And amazing, this book by Lynne Cheney.

I'll probably write more about this book at the end of 2015, but in the meantime, why don't you get the book (or read it on your Kindle) and see if you think as highly of it as I do?

Thanks, Lynne Cheney, you've done a good job with this book.

WHO RUNS GEORGIA?

Several times in the past I've had someone, usually a younger person, ask me what they should read to learn about politics in Georgia. My answer is always the same: "Start with the book *Who Runs Georgia?*, written by Calvin Kytle and James A. Mackay—it's an account of the 1947 three-governor crisis that set the stage for Georgia's political transformation."

Really, Larry, how can a book about events in the 1940s tell me anything about modern-day Georgia politics? Good question. Let me quote from Mackay's preface and you decide whether this old book is instructive and helpful:

> The name-calling, the negative campaigning, the unregulated solicitation and misuse of campaign funds, the crushing weight of corporate power, the civic passivity and low voter turnout—all have come to typify our national political behavior. It's as if the gallous-snapping, shirt-sleeved demagogues of Georgia's yesterday have merely moved north, acquired Armani suits and new accents, and gone on network television.

It's almost as if I can see Donald Trump and Hillary Clinton inhaling deeply and coughing slightly as Mackay's words from years ago escape from this old, cracked-open book into the modern Georgia political air.

Indeed, who does run Georgia? With my recommended book as a guide, here's what I'd say, starting with a name from the past.

Former governor Marvin Griffin is reported to have once said (and this sounds just like him) "that regardless of who Georgia's governor is, it's a big potato." And Governor Griffin was and is right, it is a "big potato," so I'd put Governor Nathan Deal at the top of the pile as to who is running Georgia. As an aside, I'd say that he's doing a good job of it.

Then you've got the corporate people: banks, gas and electric utilities, news media, railroads, trucking companies, highway contractors,

LARRY WALKER

alcohol beverage folks, and insurance companies, etc.

These folks don't go en masse to Atlanta. They send their representatives in the form of lobbyists who have a big hand in influencing elected officials at all levels of government. The state legislature and its members await them with open arms.

And let's not forget that the government itself, in an in-house, incestuous sort of way, influences the government of which it is a part with lobbyists and "spokespersons" as to how things should be run. Think: judges, Department of Education, Department of Transportation, Board of Regents, Technical College System of Georgia, Georgia Association of Educators, Professional Association of Georgia Educators, Georgia Farm Bureau, county and city associations. They all have their people at the Capitol.

The Georgia Chamber of Commerce (its board of "big mules") is another potent force in the group who runs Georgia. And it's probably true that when the people who make up the Georgia Chamber do good, Georgia does good. So, not a bad group to have influence.

My terse look at who runs Georgia is not a criticism, just observations. And I do believe it's true that mainly the same interests who are running Georgia today are the folks who were running it in the 1940s, were running it when I was in the state House, and will be running it twenty years from now.

As mentioned, all of the groups have lobbyists. They had them when I was in the legislature and they have them today. Now the lobbyists are probably younger today, and there are more females, but their work is the same. It is their job to press on the elected officials their employers' views as to how it could be—how it should be run.

When I was there, I found lobbyists to be informed and helpful. Those who didn't tell you the truth didn't have any influence and didn't last long. They were, generally, people of integrity. As to anything of controversy, there was almost always a lobbyist on both sides, so you could get a quick education, which helped me to make my decisions as to how I should vote.

Before I filed this article, I asked my long-time friend Connell Stafford, formerly a lobbyist with Coca-Cola (now that's a "big mule"), to look this over. His response: "Larry, I can't think of any group you've left out. Like a big circus under one tent, the ringmaster runs the show, but it won't work at all without the lions, the tigers, the elephants, and last, but not least, the clowns."

Fortunately, the lack of clowns under the Georgia government big tent is one thing about which we've not had to worry in Georgia!

ADVICE TO LARRY WALKER III

Larry, first let me say how proud your mother and I are of your recent election to the Georgia State Senate. You ran a good, clean race and defeated some good people. You know how it feels to lose, and now you know how it is to win. Winning makes you feel better, but your earlier loss probably taught more and prepared you to win this time.

Someone once said, "Don't give advice. The wise don't need it and the dull won't heed it." Nonetheless, I plunge forward with my advice, for, after all, you are ours and often I think of you as just a youngster (that's natural for a parent, I think). Sometimes, in my mind's eye, I see you as that little first-grader with your eyeglasses, learning to read and soon to be "working" with Papa at Gray-Walker Tractor Company.

So, here I go, bolstered in my trepidation in giving this advice by my long service in the Georgia House and with the certain knowledge that these ten things, in reverse order of importance, need to be considered by you.

1. *Take the Capitol Steps and Not the Elevator.* You will be offered lots of "free" food and drink. If you eat and drink everything you are offered, you will gain weight during the legislative session. Exercise every day is important. Take the steps and not the elevators. My memory is that there are seventy-four steps from the sidewalk on the Capitol side of Martin Luther King Jr. Drive to the fourth floor of the Capitol. Walk 'em, count 'em, and let me know if I'm right—about the exercise and the number of steps.

2. *Don't Eat All of the "Free" Food and Drink You Are Offered.* As I said, if you are not careful, you will gain a great deal of weight during the legislative session. Watch your calories. Exercise when you can (see number 1 above).

3. *The Free Food and Drink Aren't Free.* Lobbyists and special interests feed the elected. It's the American way. It's how the governed

get focused time with elected officials. Thomas Jefferson and George Washington were being wined and dined in the Williamsburg cafés and pubs when the Republic was being formed. There is nothing wrong with this as long as you keep exercising your independent judgment.

4. *Be Likeable.* Be friendly. Smile. Be courteous. This applies to your constituents and your fellow legislators (on both sides of the aisle). Don't think you are too important, even though the office you hold might be. Use words like "please," "I'm sorry," "please forgive me," "that's a good idea," etc.

5. *Develop a Thick Skin.* You are going to need it. Everything imaginable will be said to you. Generally, you just need to smile and take it. During your legislative tenure, you will lose some so-called friends over votes and positions on issues. This just goes with the job. If you don't develop a thick skin, you will be miserable and probably don't need to be in politics.

6. *Be Yourself.* Most folks like you or you wouldn't have been elected. People in the public eye who try to be something they aren't are spotted immediately. Be yourself, and as I said above, don't take yourself too seriously.

7. *Be Willing to Compromise When Compromise Is in Order.* Politics is the art of compromise—or, at least it used to be. Listen to the other person's point of view. Try to reach consensus. Don't compromise your principles, but sometimes you ultimately get what you want by initially starting with something less or different than you preferred.

8. *Treat All of Your Colleagues with Dignity and Respect.* You might not agree with them. In fact, on many issues, you may seldom agree or vote with them. That doesn't mean you can't like and respect them. Nor does it mean you can't understand where they are "coming from" and why. There can be friendship in disagreement.

9. *Don't Lose Your Family and Business Over the Legislature.* Keep things in perspective. Yours is a part-time job. You have to make a living for you and your family while giving "part-time" to the state Senate. Give both jobs and your family their entitlements. This might be the most important advice I have for you.

10. Know When to Quit. You might say, "This is strange advice to be giving when I am just starting." But the time will come, and there will be life after politics. Knowing when to quit is more important than

deciding to run.

Good luck, Larry. We are glad you are our son—and our senator. And, by the way, please let me know how many steps there are to the fourth floor from the sidewalk. Daddy

IS "LOBBYIST" A DIRTY WORD?

I've been around politics all of my life. At age twenty-three, I was Perry's municipal court judge and then I was the city attorney. I was elected to the state legislature as a young thirty-year-old and left thirty-two years later, in 2004, as a seasoned (that's a good word) sixty-two-year-old.

After the legislature, I ran for and was elected by legislators, Republicans and Democrats, as a member of the Department of Transportation board from the 8th Congressional District and served two and a half years (being on the DOT board was kinda like being a statewide county commissioner). I was rescued from the DOT board by Governor Perdue when he appointed me to the Board of Regents, where I served for six years until Governor Deal reappointed me for another term. I continue to be a member.

I've pretty much seen it all. By "all," I mean what goes on during the session, after the session, in the open meetings, in executive sessions, when two friends and supporters are running for the same office at the same time, when an elected colleague gets in trouble, in-house politics, etc.

I've seen elected officials vilified. I've seen elected officials "cut lots of slack." I've seen elected officials, sometimes icons, stay too long, not ending up well, and I've seen friends, generally good folks, go to prison because of something inappropriate they did while in office. I've seen good people lose their families and businesses over politics. I think I've seen it all.

My view is that those in and around the governing process who get the worst rap are the lobbyists. It's the way that some folks say the word "lobbyists" with a little hiss and with their face all screwed up. They say "lobbyist" like they have hemorrhoids or an upset stomach. Nothing good about it.

So, knowing lots of lobbyists, and having dealt with many lobbyists, and actually considering some as good friends, I decided to do something, in my old-fashion way, and look up the word "lobbyist" in my dictionary.

I went to my *Merriam-Webster's Collegiate Dictionary*, and on page 683 there it was: "Lobbyist: one who conducts activities aimed at influencing public officials and especially members of a legislative body on legislation."

Well, that could have been the finest man I ever knew, and that was my daddy. He was in the farm-equipment business and he talked to me lots about what was good for the farmers (if they did well, he did well) or about taking the tax off farm equipment. The less it cost, the more he sold. You get the picture.

Teachers talked to me every year about pay raises. Doctors wanted to make it harder for them to get sued (I don't blame 'em). Dentists didn't want denturists making false teeth. Local gas distributors didn't want the big boys (Shell, Texaco, etc.) to be able to sell gas in their stores cheaper than they sold it to the distributors. Farmers wanted the tax off equipment. Car dealers, too. Large property owners wanted changes in the ad-valorem tax laws.

Let's see: "Trying to influence legislators." Well, it looks like Daddy—it's hard for me to write this—might have been a lobbyist. Surely not. Then, again, isn't most everyone? Preachers, back in the day, didn't want alcohol sales on Sunday, and back even further, didn't want most stores to be open on Sunday. They lobbied. Every major agency of state government has lobbyists. The National Rifle Association lobbies. So does the National Organization for Women, the Georgia Association of Educators, the Professional Association of Georgia Educators, and most every other interest group in Georgia.

Our newspaper folks, those guardians of right and wrong, wanted the costs of legal ads raised and lobbied accordingly. The media (television, radio, papers, etc.) fought against four-year terms for legislators. Surely, those revenues for political ads every two years rather than four had nothing to do with it. Lobbyists?

Let's see. Daddy, school teachers, dentists, doctors, gasoline jobbers, car dealers, farmers, preachers, and media folks. Bedrocks of most communities. How can it be that they were lobbyists?

Mr. Wilton Hill was one of my favorite lobbyists when I was in the legislature. He didn't have a credit card, or if he did, he never let me see it. But he did pay a few legislators that he really liked. At the end of the session, at the same time he asked you to come over to the FFA and FHA camp at Lake Jackson to eat in the lunchroom with some of the school bus drivers, he would give you a silver dollar. One silver dollar to eight or ten people and lunch for the same eight or ten in the lunchroom.

Wilton Hill was State Senator Jack Hill's dad. Cohen Walker was Larry Walker III's granddad. Two lobbyists and two of the finest folks I ever knew. No, "lobbyist" is not a dirty word.

POLITICS, NOT FUN ANYMORE?

It was the talk of old men. Not only the subject, at least for this early time, but the way in which it developed and flowed. It was as casual as if it was the weather and yet it was of a brutal game in which strong and capable contestants have already vowed to participate, with the probability of more to come. Many are called. Few are chosen.

Last week, Foster Rhodes and me. Foster: "Who is going to win the governor's race?" My response: "You've got to think Casey, but it's too early to tell. We don't even know who will actually make the race." Good discussion (at least we thought so) as we rode along between Fort Valley and Roberta, but no conclusion. Impossible to conclude.

And then I think I started it: "Politics is not much fun anymore. It used to be fun. It's not like it used to be." Foster agreed. It was unanimous.

Irony, based on agreed-to lamentations of the sordid state of politics as compared to the "good ole days." Within ten minutes of "not like it used to be," we turned off US 341, drove less than 300 feet, parked by T. F. Hayes General Merchandise store (open continually since 1900), dropped our campaign contribution checks in the offering plate-type basket placed for that purpose, and entered Dickey Farms Packing House, which, despite the fact that we beat the announced 6:00 P.M. starting time, was already full of people with more to come.

"Not like it used to be? Not fun anymore?" It could've been a Marvin Griffin August 1962 rally ("They ate my barbeque, but they didn't vote for me") or even a 1956 Telfair County gathering to help anoint Herman Talmadge on his way to the United States Senate. This was going to be fun. All of a sudden, this "Peaches and Politics" summer rally for State Rep. Robert Dickey, seventh annual, at Dickey Farms Packing House in Musella, Crawford County, Georgia. It was fun. On this Foster and I correctly agreed. We'd gone from 2017 whining to 1960 fun.

What a crowd! Republicans in the majority, but with a good scattering of Democrats who liked and supported the Republican honoree. Why? He treats them with dignity and respect and tries to help them when he can—like politics should be. Former and long-time senator George Hooks; Bob Hatcher of Macon; Gary Black, commissioner of agriculture; Senator Larry Walker and his wife, Adrienne; Senator John Kennedy; Mr. Robert Dickey Sr., age 89, and his wife and Robert's mother, Jane; State Insurance Commissioner Ralph Hudgens and his wife, Suzanne; Bob Ray, Flint EMC; Judge Tripp Self, Macon, and Judge Mac Crawford, Zebulon; Rabbi Larry Schlesinger, Bibb County commissioner; Buddy Hayes; Maurice Raines; Lorenzo Wilder; Rep. Matt Hatchett; Rep. Patty Bentley; Jack Causey, age 92; Glenn Lee Chase; Ellen Chase and Donald Chase; Martin Mosely; Peach County Commissioner Bill Stembridge; and about 350 more.

Did they come for the food? No. But it was delicious. Fried chicken, pimento cheese sandwiches, real Coca-Colas in those small bottles, pecans, peaches, peach cobbler, peach ice cream, peach ice cream on peach cobbler, etc.

Did they come because of the candidate, Robert Dickey? Yes. Robert is what all politicians should be. Perhaps he is a throwback to an earlier time. He smiles, he's pleasant, he treats everyone like the Bible tells us to do, he has time to talk and listen, and he will listen to your point of view. He'd be "nigh on to impossible to beat," especially if he keeps on being the Robert Dickey we know today, and if he keeps on having the annual "Peaches and Politics" at the 1936 Dickey Farms Packing House.

I'll bet they'll never eat Robert's peaches and not vote for him. Like I said, he'll be there as long as he wants to be. And I hope I get to go to the eighth annual "Peaches and Politics." By the way, Foster, I'll take my pickup and drive next year if you'll provide the conversation subjects; just don't let it be about how politics is not as fun as it used to be.

VII

MISCELLANY—INCLUDING THINGS YOU DON'T KNOW AND PROBABLY DON'T UNDERSTAND ABOUT THE SOUTH

THINGS I KNOW BUT DON'T UNDERSTAND

I don't know why I wanted to write about some things I know but don't understand, but I do know that there are lots of things I know and yet don't really understand. Here are a few:

* I know that if you are making meringue from egg whites, it will not jell, coagulate, or get thick (firm up) if there is even a speck of egg yolk in the white.

* I know that sometimes when you dig a hole and attempt to refill it with the same dirt you dug out, you can't get the hole full, while at other times you have a substantial amount of dirt left over. Does the phase of the moon have anything to do with it? I don't know.

* I know that you can be fishing, getting lots of bites and catching many fish, and the wind will get up out of the east and the fish will stop biting. Completely stop!

* I know that water revolves counterclockwise when emptying north of the equator and clockwise when emptying south of the equator. Is this true? I really don't know.

* I know that even with mountains of evidence that the nicotine in tobacco can cause cancer, many people still take up the habit.

* I know that religion is the glue that helps to hold our society together and that religion has also been used to justify slavery, war, and making women and some minorities second-class citizens.

* I know that the Bible clearly teaches that the love of money is a sin, yes, the "root of all evil," and yet we are told that the streets of heaven are paved with gold.

* I know that gnats are below the fall line, also known in political circles as the "gnat line," but are not above it. Why, I don't know, but I suspect that if gnats were in Washington, DC, or even Atlanta, they would be eradicated.

* I know that certain words are considered profane or vulgar or bad and yet there is nothing in the Bible or other ancient writings that tell us

this.

* I know that big drops usually mean little rain.

* I know that "no" and "know" are spelled differently but pronounced the same and that "read" and "read" are spelled the same and pronounced differently and that the English language can be baffling.

* I know that the vast majority of American citizens are disgusted with the performance of Congress of the United States but most of them, like and support their own congressmen and senators.

* I know that, oftentimes, small things were more fun when you couldn't afford them than are big things when you can.

* I know that life is like a train ride, with most of us thinking about the destination rather than enjoying the trip.

* I know that people who say "money doesn't make you happy" always seem to have plenty of it.

* I know that more "crazies" contact and come to our law office and that fish bite better on days when the moon is full.

* I know that the word "affect" can be a verb or a noun and the word "effect" can be a verb or noun and that there is a proper place to use "effect" and a proper place to use "affect," and that sometimes you affect to effect.

* I know that '57 Chevys are more popular today than they were in 1957 and that Harry Truman is better thought of today than he was when he was president.

* I know that lots of folks say "concrete" when they mean "cement" and "sewer" when they mean "sewerage."

* I know that words like "yes, sir" and "no, ma'am" are considered passé and unsophisticated and even "rural" in many parts of our country.

* I know that some of the finest people in the world have the worst fortune and some of the most roguish people have the best luck.

* I know that lots of things I used to know I no longer know and that lots of things I used to think I understood I no longer understand, and I know I don't understand this.

BLINDING FAST CHANGES KEEP COMING

My father, Cohen Walker, was born in Washington County, Georgia, on January 26, 1917. His father, my grandfather, David F. Walker, was born on June 4, 1883, in Washington County, and Papa's father, John Freeman (Flournoy) Walker, was born on February 20, 1854, in the same county. Papa's grandfather, Freeman F. Walker, was born on December 16, 1828, in Washington County. Freeman F. Walker died of erysipelas (an acute disease of the skin marked by spreading inflammation) as a Confederate soldier on June 22, 1863. He is buried in Thornrose Cemetery, Staunton, Virginia. He probably walked from Washington County to Staunton, Virginia, to die.

From the birth of my great-great-grandfather (1828) to the birth of my father (1917) is eighty-nine years. But the number of years belies the small life changes from the time of Freeman F. Walker's birth to Daddy's birth.

My grandparents traveled in 1917, and probably into the 1940s, primarily by mule and wagon. They never had air conditioning—never. They finally had a black-and-white television (one or two stations, with *The Lewis Family* and *The Lawrence Welk Show* being two shows I remember Grandma watching). The television was almost as big as Papa's safe in his small, one-room country store.

At some point in their marriage, Grandma and Papa got running water and an inside bathroom. The Romans had "running water" and "inside bathrooms" thousands of years prior to Grandma and Papa getting it. Papa had an old shotgun and a little "lemon squeezer" .32 pistol. Shotguns and pistols had been around for many, many years by the time Daddy was born in 1917. They had a crank telephone—and they were very reluctant to spend the money to make a long-distance call. Change was slow, very slow.

Daddy graduated from the ag school at the University of Georgia in 1937. I doubt that he ever had a car while in college. I know that he rode the bus some and hitchhiked a lot. Several times he told me about the time he was stranded in Bishop, Georgia, and had to spend the night on a bench in front of a service station. Yes, there were things called "service stations" in the 1930s. They actually gave needed service to your vehicle.

What would I say were the biggest changes in Daddy's life from 1917 until his death on March 25, 2002? First, electricity. Second, the automobile. Third, the television. Fourth, air conditioning. Fifth, medical advances. Sixth, telephone.

These are six of the things that I think affected Daddy and his lifestyle. Others might name different things, but I believe these affected Daddy the most.

Then things began to speed up. The interstate highway system in the 1960s had subtle but dramatic effects. We are still feeling them. It put lots of people out of business (mom-and-pop stores, motels, hotels, restaurants, "service stations," etc.) and made lots of folks rich (Wal-Mart, motels, hotels, restaurants, "gas stations," etc.)

Then it sped up more. Bag phones (yes, I had one, and it must've weighed five pounds or more), computers, cable TV (you could get more than 100 stations), satellite TV (you could get more than 200 stations), cell phones, iPhones, iPads, the internet, Facebook, Twitter, etc., etc. It's so fast it's hard (and impossible for many) to keep up.

My former law partner, Chuck Byrd, used to say that he knew every pay phone between Perry and Atlanta. How quaint. What a different, recent time ago. And, by the way, are there still workable pay phones by the roadside between Perry and Atlanta? I doubt it.

The federal government couldn't have the size budget and the huge deficits we have today without the computer. "So what," some would say. "Too bad," others would say. Everybody can know everything about you, and can make up things that are not true—and ruin you. So what? Cameras are everywhere. Satellites, drones, hacking. Do you care?

Dean William Tate, dean of men at the University of Georgia, told me this when I was a freshman at UGA in 1960: "If Jesus Christ had come to my grandparent's home in the mountains, he would have understood everything in their cabin except the flintlock rifle over the fireplace and the matches to light the fire." If my great-great-grandfather Freeman Walker came to little Perry, Georgia, today, he would not understand much of anything.

Notice that my father, his father, his grandfather, and his great-grandfather were all born in Washington County. Not much changed from 1828 to 1917. Four generations birthed in the same rural county is unlikely to happen today.

The changes keep coming—and we haven't seen anything yet. Hold on, if you can!

PLACES ON MY MIND

Let me start with a confession. I got the idea for this column from the excellent writing by Susan Percy in the April 2015 edition of *Georgia Trend*. Her article was called "Georgia Places on My Mind," and while I agreed with her selections, she and I have no selections in common. With this confession and justification, here are my ten, with a little about each.

10) Fort Worth, Texas: Could it be as good as I thought it was when I worked at Texas Steel Company on Hemphill Street in 1963? Then it was just a big country town with lots of character and characters. I like cows and cowboys (cowgirls, too), and that's a large part of what Fort Worth is (was) about. Yep, partner, Fort Worth is number ten!

9) St. Simons Island, Georgia: Lots of history of the State of Georgia in and around St. Simons. Great shops and interesting restaurants that serve great food. The King and Prince for middle-class folks (that's us) and the Cloister, just down the road, for those who have done well. It's a Georgia gem and could be higher than a nine.

8) Oxford, Mississippi: Ole Miss is the prettiest campus in the SEC (Sorry, UGA—I have to put you number two). Square Books on the square is the best bookstore in America (admittedly, I haven't seen them all, but I'm working on it). Really great restaurants such as Big Bad Breakfast and City Grocery. John Grisham went to law school at Ole Miss. William Faulkner lived just outside town at Rowan Oaks. Larry Brown was a fireman in Oxford until he started writing great novels such as *Big Bad Love*. I could go on and on, but if I did, Oxford, would have to be higher than just number eight!

7) Madison, Georgia: A nineteen-room hotel, the James Madison, with Ritz quality, anchors the town. Madison has some of the best antique shops in Georgia, beautiful and stately colonial homes that William T. Sherman spared, a grand courthouse, good restaurants, etc. It's a strong number seven.

6) Cedar Key, Florida: Do any of you remember Edgar "Yellow Legs" Campbell, who guided out of Cedar Key? He's gone, but he is not forgotten. A great, old hotel that goes back into the 1800s. Excellent fishing. Excellent seafood. Good shops. Go out on the peninsula about forty-five miles to Cedar Key and fish the Gulf. You'll have fun and will be engulfed with history in this quaint little town.

5) Fairhope, Alabama: I've been there five or six times. It has what I like. By now, you know that's nice hotels, good restaurants, great bookstores, and lots of history. Perry, Forsyth, Dublin, and other towns in Middle Georgia that are trying to improve the quality of life for its citizens, go look closely at Fairhope. "They say" that Fairhope has the highest per capita of artist and authors in the USA. Go there and you'll probably believe that this is one time that "they say" is right.

4) Sanford Stadium: (If you don't know this is in Athens at UGA, you probably won't understand any of this article). Join 95,000 of your friends on a crisp Saturday afternoon. Watch the Dawgs come out of the tunnel and through the smoke (or whatever it is) and onto the field. Listen to the bugler play "The Battle Hymn of the Republic" and then join the singing of the National Anthem. Stand for the kickoff. If you don't get chill bumps, you are probably so near death that you should have stayed at home in bed rather than going to the game!

3) Charleston, South Carolina: I love Atlanta, or most of the time I do. I think Savannah is great. Augusta has the Masters and so many other things, as does Columbus. Macon is beautiful and is "getting there." But to me, it's Charleston, South Carolina—and probably for the same reasons that I gave for Fort Worth, St. Simon's, Oxford, Madison, Cedar Key, and Fairhope. Charleston exudes the things I like about towns and cities.

2) Pinehill Methodist Church: It's where Grandma and Papa, as well as Aunt Lillian and Uncle Jim, are buried. Also, Daddy's older brother, Clyde, who at age fifteen died in a hunting accident. I went to Sunday school and church there and heard gospel singing at homecoming after the preaching and dinner on the grounds. When I can't sleep at night, I think about this little Methodist church in rural Washington County. Number two is a fair rating from me for Pinehill Methodist.

1) Perry: It's always been good and getting better. As I wrote once

before, it's where I want to be. You take Charleston or Fort Worth or some other great place, and I'll take Perry.

This is my list. It might change some, but not much. I don't have enough time.

TEN CONVERSATIONS I REMEMBER

John Kerry. It was at the 2000 Democratic National Convention in Los Angeles. I was not a delegate, but a visitor to one of the suites overlooking the convention hall. Senator Kerry was also in the suite. I attempted to strike up a conversation with him by telling him I was from Sam Nunn's hometown of Perry, Georgia. Kerry had served with Nunn in the United States Senate for many years. Actually, his arrogant response was more like a non-conversation than a conversation. Guess he didn't like my Southern accent. I vividly remembered the encounter and repeated my recollection many times when Kerry was a presidential candidate. Incidentally, I have said, often, "In politics, incompetence will defeat arrogance every time."

Mickey Mantle. Janice and I were at the Polo Park over in Greene County, Georgia, several years ago. My all-time favorite major league baseball player, Mickey Mantle, was also there, and I had a thrilling opportunity to visit with him. Remembering 1956 and Mantle's winning baseball's triple crown, .353 batting average, 52 HR, and 130 RBI, I said to him: "Champ, 1956 was really a good year for you, wasn't it? What I remember was how you could drag that bunt and move down to first base." Almost childlike, he responded, "Do you mean that you can really remember that?" Mantle was the exact opposite of Kerry. He had lots to be proud of but was very humble.

Herman Talmadge. We were quail hunting down on Mel Tolleson's place in South Houston County when I asked Senator Talmadge, "Who was your favorite president that you served with?" This long-time Democratic governor and senator's response surprised me: "Eisenhower. The world was at peace. We had prosperity. And Eisenhower operated on the premise that 'if it ain't broke, don't fix it.'" Pretty generous compliment from a Democrat about a Republican, I'd say.

Edgar ("Yellow Legs") Campbell. Billy Bledsoe, Hilt Gray, Seabie

Hickson, and I were fishing out of Cedar Key, Florida, with this legendary guide when I asked, "Yellow, do you ever take people out who know absolutely nothing about fishing?" He replied, "Yeah, y'all!"

Jimmy Carter. I served my first two years (1973 and 1974) in the state legislature during Carter's last two years as governor. During the closing days of the 1974 legislative session, I went into Governor Carter's office, and during the course of our conversation, asked him, "What are you going to do when your term is up?" Carter replied, "Run for president." To which I foolishly responded: "Of what?" This is an absolutely true account!

Aunt Lillian Maddox: I was visiting at Grandma and Papa's house in rural Washington County. I was probably about ten years old. My aunt Lillian (Daddy's sister) was also there. I got miffed about something and threatened to run away. Aunt Lillian's response: "Good. Go on." I did run away—down the dirt road and for about thirty minutes. God bless Aunt Lillian. I loved her. I think of her often.

George Steinbrenner. I was at the White House in the presidential receiving line. George Steinbrenner and a friend of his were behind me. I had a brief, pleasant conversation with Mr. Steinbrenner. As I turned away, I heard Mr. Steinbrenner say to his friend, "I like those boys from the South, they still say 'Yes, sir' and 'No, sir.'" Yes, sir, Mr. Steinbrenner, that's right.

Billy Bledsoe. Number one: "Larry, you're all right, the world's all wrong!" Number two: Every time Billy and I fished together and I caught a fish, "There must be a million of 'em out there!" Like Aunt Lillian, I loved ole Billy.

Muhammad Ali. I was with him at least four times, but all after Parkinson's disease had started taking its toll. Still, every time I saw him, his eyes sparkled and he had a wide and inviting smile as he took a boxer's stance as if he were ready to spar with me. These were the best non-conversation conversations I ever had.

Denmark Groover Jr. Denny and I were talking about a fellow House member who had made a fiery speech criticizing one of our other colleagues. I said to Denny, "Well, at least he later went to him and apologized." Denny responded, "Larry, a private apology for a public wrong is no apology at all." Amen, Brother Denny.

I've got lots more, but I'm out of space. Maybe I'll record some more sometime in the future, so if we're talking, be careful, because I'm listening and remembering, and I might put it in the paper.

CHURCH SERVICE SPAWNS MEMORIES

It was a week ago today, and I was at church services, Perry United Methodist, as guest soloist Kim Abston beautifully sang that gorgeous song "Holy Ground," to be followed shortly by our choir's outstanding rendition of "Midnight Cry." Strong. As I like to say, "Strong as new rope."

Oh, how the memories flooded my soul. Inexplicably, first it was my long-ago memory of that local production from rural Colquitt, Georgia, *Swamp Gravy*, and their, at that time, customary ending with "Amazing Grace," accompanied by uplifted, lit candles and with patrons saying, "I remember ___." The spoken memory I most recall being, "I remember Bear Bryant." Then, as the *Swamp Gravy* memory slipped away, it was people that I loved and cared for that crowded my mind.

So, today, let me share with you some of the folks I remembered last Sunday morning on holy ground, and others I have remembered this past week on regular Perry ground. While you read, I hope you'll have memories of your own.

I remembered my grandfather David Walker, Papa, and I can see him hitching up the mules and building a rabbit box for me. He was a small-of-stature, small-of-importance Renaissance man.

I remembered Denny Groover—what a lawyer, what a legislator, and what a man! WWII, Black Sheep Squadron. Denny Groover.

I remembered Tom Murphy and that money he gave to the young waif on the street in Victoria, Mexico. Complex, big-hearted Tom Murphy. He did a lot for Georgia.

I remembered Miss Ruby Hodges. She ran her business and other folks, too! She was a great political friend to me and a bad political enemy to some.

I remembered Joe Hodges and our working together. I was probably fifteen or sixteen and he was a grown man. He taught me things I didn't know but needed to know. I loved Joe Hodges.

I remembered Janice's mother, Judy. How could a little country girl from rural Alabama have such a good mind and big, generous heart?

I remembered Roy Rogers. He was probably my first hero. Roy did his business the right way. Too bad he is not around today so we could make him president of the United States. We need someone like Roy Rogers to straighten out our messes.

I remembered Celestine Sibley. There was nothing pretentious about Celestine. She was real, and folks of all kinds and from all over Georgia loved her. I was one of them.

I remembered Joe Grant. He lived on Daddy's farm and worked there and at "the tractor place." I don't think I've ever known a finer man than Mr. Grant. I'll bet his equally fine wife, Arlessie, would agree.

I remembered Herman Talmadge. He and I became good friends in his latter years, and I really enjoyed him as we quail hunted, visited, and talked politics and Georgia history.

I remembered Mr. Glea Gray. He was funny and he was fun. He was the first adult who treated young Larry Walker like an adult. I hurt, deeply, when he died. Very deeply. I say he was a "character with character."

I remembered Billy Bledsoe. Billy was my friend. It's hard, and was hard, for me to give up my fishing partner. I think of him often.

I remembered Bobby Jones, Jerry Horton ("Do-Tricks"), and Jerry Wilson. These were three wonderful guys. I remember them every day. We were all close to the same age. Why they are gone and I'm still here is hard for me to understand.

I remembered Mr. Mike Whitman—no, I actually remembered Daddy's talking about Mr. Mike Whitman and the Angus calves Daddy bought from him for his FFA boys to show. Daddy thought Mr. Mike was a good man. I do, too.

I remembered Bill Lee and his "had a little dog named Fido" and Wayne Snow and his "big red Rooster and the little red Hen." Two good guys. Two funny guys.

I remembered my grandfather Gray—Charles Powell Gray. He was probably Houston County's first Republican, and maybe its only Republican at that time. He was always neat with his dark suit, tie, white shirt, and shined shoes. Indeed, he was a neat man.

I remembered Ed Sell Jr. He was a lawyer's lawyer and I could always rely on him for good advice—kind of an original Atticus Finch. He begot a good son and my friend, Ed S. Sell III.

I remembered Richard Horne. Richard worked for our law firm for several years (excellent worker). It was only in his latter days that I learned he had been a Navy Frogman, now known as a Navy Seal. That makes him an American hero in my book.

I could go on and on, but let me close by saying it's wonderful what a good, spiritual church service can spawn.

WISE SAYINGS IN BAD TIMES

This past week I attended a Board of Regents meeting in Atlanta, and for the one night I was there, I stayed at the downtown Sheraton, just like I did for many years when I was in the state legislature.

While waiting on a ride out front of the Sheraton, I engaged the nice doorman in conversation. He had a pronounced accent and was probably from an African country or maybe the Middle East. I concluded he was very bright, and his words made me know he loved the United States.

I came to this country because I knew it was a great place, a place of great opportunity, but I do not like the way the presidential candidates are making a joke of the presidential race. Profound. It was kinda what I had been thinking, but I had never put it into words. I'd say a wise saying in bad times.

Mr. Sam Way of Hawkinsville told his son, Bob, this: *Often, the best opportunities come at the most inopportune times.* I find Sam's words very wise, especially given the difficult economic times that continue.

An obviously very wealthy man told me something that has stuck with me since. I asked him, *How did you make so much money?* He replied: *Selling out too soon and not making a big enough profit.* Indeed! I know that there are lots of people who wish they had sold out several years ago. This calls to mind another saying: *Pigs get fat and hogs get slaughtered.* Lots of hogs have gotten slaughtered since 2008.

My Daddy said lots of wise and interesting things. One of my favorites of his was, *Differences of opinions make poor land sell high.* This reminds me of a conversation I had with Daddy years ago. I was a young, struggling lawyer when I urged Daddy to buy a large tract of land with these words: *Daddy, we ought to buy this farm, there's no way it won't go up in value.* Well, in the first place the "we" meant Daddy (like, me and Pa killed a bear). And secondly, the land could go down in value and actually did. Daddy was much wiser than I was. *Differences of opinions make poor land sell high.*

Speaking of farms, who was it that first asked this question and supplied the answer: *Want to know how to make a little money farming? Start off with lots of money.* If you've got a farm and are trying to make a living with it, you will understand. What Daddy told me about "we" buying that farm comes back to my mind.

Mike Ditka said this: *Success isn't permanent, and failure isn't fatal.* I hope Ditka's words make you feel better. They don't do too much for me, but folks react differently, and perhaps his words will help some overly optimistic souls.

Try these: *To get back on your feet, miss two car payments.* That's by an unknown wit, but this one's from Ernest Haskins: *Save a little money each month and at the end of the year, you'll be surprised at how little you have.* And Elisabeth Marbury said this: *The richer your friends, the more they will cost you.* Think about Ms. Marbury's words. And think about this, something I've told clients through the years: *Be careful of going into business with partners that have lots more money than you have or lots less money than you have.* Actually, Katherine Whitehorn said it better: *The rule is not to talk about money with people who have much more or much less than you.*

I didn't start out for this to be a column about money, but it seems to have ended up this way. But it is a pervasive subject. Take the presidential debates or what they talk mostly about in Washington and Atlanta. This is my lead-in to two great quotes. The first is a simplified tax form suggested by Stanton Delaplane: *How much money did you make last year? Mail it in.* The second, which kinda relates to the first, is by Will Rogers: *The income tax has made liars out of more Americans than golf.*

Then there are the words of Paul in 1 Timothy, chapter 6, verse 10: *For the love of money is the root of all evil: which some coveted after, they have erred from the faith, and pierced themselves through with many sorrows.* Or, as Daddy used to simply say, *Money won't make you happy.* And to which I once replied, *Daddy, I notice that people who say this always seem to be those with plenty of it.* Still, as I get older, and hopefully wiser, I believe that Paul and Daddy are probably right. In fact, given the sources, I know they are.

RAY GOFF IS MY PICK

This quarterback graduated from Moultrie High School in 1973. After having been recruited by many colleges including Georgia, Florida, South Carolina, and Auburn (all of which met his requirement that he "wanted to stay in the South"), he chose UGA. It was a good day when Georgia signed this All-State and High School All-American player.

Let's see how Ray did at Georgia, where he lettered in '74, '75, and '76. He scored five touchdowns, three running and two passing, in a winning effort against Florida in 1976. (Now, isn't this timely information?)

Ray was captain of Georgia's team in '76. He was All-SEC in '76. And he was the SEC Player of the Year in '76. To top it off, he was seventh in the Heisman Trophy voting.

Ray is in the Georgia-Florida Hall of Fame (a player who scored five touchdowns in this game should be). And Ray is in the Georgia Sports Hall of Fame.

Let me repeat: it was a good day when Georgia signed Ray in 1973.

At the very young age of thirty-three, when Vince Dooly stepped down, Ray was named the head coach at his alma mater. Ray had a winning record, 46 wins, 34 losses, and 1 tie, but not a sterling record by UGA standards. My opinion: there were reasons for this that had nothing to do with Ray's recruiting and coaching ability.

Georgia was still dealing with the "Jan Kemp affair," which, as the UGA faithful know, had to do with academic improprieties involving football players. Georgia, during Ray Goff's seven-year tenure, could not sign athletes that other SEC schools could and did. In the super competitive SEC, this was deadly. Nonetheless, Ray's teams defeated Georgia Tech five out of the seven years he coached and, led by Garrison Hearst, defeated Ohio State in the 1993 Citrus Bowl.

Impressive as all of this is, frankly, it's not why Ray Goff is "my pick." Let me explain.

Chuck Byrd, my law partner at the time, and I represented Ray Goff when he was fired by Georgia in 1995. That's when I really started getting to know him. That's really when I began to learn what a fine person it was for whom I was working. But before I have my say, let me quote a few people who, like me, know Ray very well.

Jim Minter. Former sports writer for the *Atlanta Journal* and later editor of the *Atlanta Journal-Constitution*: "When my newspaper colleague Lewis Grizzard was critically ill in Emory University Hospital, he missed the G-Day game in Athens. He called the head coach to ask about it. Instead of answering over the telephone, Ray Goff got in his car, drove 60-plus miles to Atlanta, and spent two hours visiting Lewis in his hospital room. That was my first inkling of who Ray Goff really is. Since that time, I've heard and known about Ray's countless visits to his former players and coaches in times of sickness, financial trouble, or just bad luck. Ray Goff is a big man with an even bigger heart. And, as my friend and his friend Lewis Grizzard would certainly say, he is 'a Great Georgian,' a Great American, and a damn good Dawg."

Dickie Clark. Roommate of Ray's when they both played football at UGA and active with Ray in the Fellowship of Christian Athletes: "He has a heart as big as an ocean. He is a loyal and dependable friend. I've seen him help many former players with whom he played and coached."

Dink NeSmith. A long-time friend of Ray Goff's: "As a member of the athletic board, I was in the room when Ray was offered the head coaching job. We were in Jacksonville for the Gator Bowl. He had to borrow socks for the interview. I was most impressed that he never asked about pay. He just said 'I love the University of Georgia, and would be honored to coach the Bulldogs!'" By the way, his starting salary was $90,000 a year.

Larry Walker. Ray's friend: "I never dealt with anyone I thought was a finer person than Ray Goff. He's not perfect, but he treats others— rich, poor, black, white, the powerful and the meek, like you are supposed to treat your fellow man. If you don't like Ray Goff, you just really don't know him."

If you do know Ray Goff, I believe that you will join me in saying, "Ray Goff is my pick" not as a football coach, which is a job he'd now never accept, but as a great and fine human being. And many thousands of Georgians say, "Yes!"

THANKSGIVING FROM PERRY

For the big and the small, I have so much for which to be thankful. Let me share with you some of the things for which I am thankful while, hopefully, you think of some of yours.

I am thankful for:

Clean, safe, and abundant drinking water. I listen to my Mama when she says to me, "Larry, so many people in our world don't have any clean water to drink." We do. Thanks.

Comfortable shoes and clean underwear. And Janice and Mullis Brother's Cleaners who keep my clothes clean and ready to wear.

Aspirin. Metamucil. Neosporin. And occasionally a couple of Tums. I can just about make it with these miracles.

Having been born with two parents and four grandparents who loved and wanted the best for me. I won the lottery when I was born.

Shag, beach, country, big-band, blues, church, gospel, blue-grass. Just about all music except opera. And, actually, some of it is okay (in small doses and not too often).

The temperature at about 50 degrees. A hunting companion whom you like, respect, and admire. Two good dogs. A kind and competent guide. Abundant birds. Lucky shooting. And, a wonderful country meal waiting when the shooting is over. It's hard to beat a day like that.

Aging. Mellowing. Forgiveness received. Forgiveness given. Renewing and rekindling old friendships. Longevity of life. Good health. Still, a good mind. Meaningful work. A family of whom you are proud and that loves you.

A mother who is ninety-eight years of age with a bright outlook and a great spirit.

The Dawgs coming out of the tunnel in Sanford Stadium on a postcard autumn day in Athens. And living long enough to know it can be good and positive even though you don't win 'em all.

The South finally being back in the Union—and many times

leading the Union.

Memories of Papa, Grandbuddy, Grandma, Granny, and Daddy. I think about all five of them almost every day.

Fishing at Cedar Key on Yellow's boat with Mr. Hilt, Seabie, and Billy and still remembering what they said and did.

Knowing how life used to be. Let me give two examples. Grandma's wash pot. I call it Grandma's because she washed the clothes in it. And they made soap and hominy in the wash pot. I think they used the potash to help make the soap. Also, Papa's bell. It would let the "hands" and the mules know it was time for dinner (the main meal in the middle of the day), although the mules didn't need a bell. They'd just stop pulling and despite all efforts, you couldn't get them to plow anymore until the dinnertime was up. The bell was also used, when wrung loudly and for a long time, to signal trouble and that the men needed to come from the fields. I am glad that I learned about Grandma's wash pot and Papa's bell.

The "feed store" and Mr. Glea, Mr. Ed, and Joe, and all that they taught me.

The summer of '63 and the time I had with Do-Tricks, Jerry, and Bobby. I think of them every day. What a time we had in Fort Worth, Texas, and at Texas Steel Company on Hemphill Street.

Our wonderful dogs. All of them were good, but Blackie, Governor, Georgia, Tux, and the two that are still here, Hershey and Cloie, stick out. And for learning that dogs are a lot smarter than I used to think they were.

Our church, Perry United Methodist, and so many others, of all kinds of faiths, that have done and do so much. And for the forefather's guarantee of freedom of religion.

Pickup trucks. Baseball caps. Boots. Pocket knives. Marbles. BB guns. Rods and spinner reels. 28 gauge O/U shotguns and high brass shells. Maypops. Dirt roads. Bream on the bed. Large-mouth bass that could swallow a softball.

The success of the Ag Center and all the young lives that have been enhanced by this wonderful facility. It has exceeded all expectations.

Quiet workers for good: Frank Shelton, Gayle Borah, Melvin Kruger, Dicky Erwin, Jean and Ronnie Bennett, Dink NeSmith, Skeet Hulbert, Roland Fall, Bob Messer, and thousands more right here in

Middle Georgia. God's angels sometimes take unusual forms.

Learning in adversity, a new love and appreciation for David, Lynda, and Charles. I want them with me and in my foxholes for as long as I live.

Well, I'm just getting started and I'm out of space. We who live in this wonderful country all have so much for which we should be thankful. Happy Thanksgiving 2015.

REMEMBERING CICERO LUCAS

It's wrong to forget about a man like Cicero Lucas! I'm trying to help keep that from happening.

No, everybody hasn't forgotten Cicero. The folks over in the Statham, Georgia, area, where Cicero now lives, and those in the Washington, Georgia, area, where he is from, know Cicero, and I'd bet the farm that almost all of them think highly of him. Also, those who knew Cicero, or knew about him when he played football at UGA, and those who knew him when he worked at or around the Capitol remember what a great guy he was.

How did I get off on Cicero Lucas? Well, let me tell you. It sprung from my writing about Mr. Ben Fortson. If you knew "Mr. Ben," or about him, you probably knew Cicero, or about him, and let me tell you why. But first let me start at a time before Cicero worked for Mr. Fortson.

Cicero was a very good and unique football player at the University of Georgia. He was small by today's standards, but not by 1956–1958 standards when he played. He was 5 feeth 11 inches tall and weighed 185 pounds and was a fullback and a guard. He was voted Georgia's most valuable lineman in 1957 and was third-team All-SEC that same year.

But it was what they said about Cicero, which was the truth, that endeared him to the "Bulldog Nation" (which was a much smaller nation, but no less rabid, in 1957). This is what "they" said: "Coach Butts could tell Cicero to back up and try to run through that brick wall and Cicero would back up and give it his best try."

Wallace Butts, the legendary hard-nosed head coach at UGA, had to love Cicero Lucas. The Bulldog Nation loved Cicero. I heard Perry High School coach Herb St. John, an All-American at Georgia, say, on more than one occasion, "I never had any problem with Coach Butts, he told me what my job was and I did it." Cicero Lucas had to be exactly the same way. Like I say, Coach Butts had to love Cicero.

Now I'm getting to how I got to know Cicero and why I think so highly of him.

In 1960, Cicero, who is from the same part of the state that "Mr. Ben" was from, started working for Mr. Ben. Among other things, it was Cicero's job to pick Mr. Ben up and put him in his wheelchair or sit him at his desk or put him in Mr. Ben's car and then drive him to where he wanted to go. Cicero was strong. Cicero was polite. Cicero was patient. Cicero was kind. Cicero had a smile for everyone. Cicero was popular—with Mr. Ben and with everyone with whom he came into contact.

Cicero would have been any politician's dream employee, but he was especially good for Mr. Ben. In other words, Mr. Ben told Cicero what his job was and Cicero did it and, like Coach St. John, who had no problems with Wally Butts, Cicero had no problems with Coach Butts or his secretary of state, Mr. Ben Fortson.

And then in 1978, Mr. Ben was gone, but Cicero stayed on at the secretary of state's office for several years before going to the House clerk's office in 1984, where he stayed as a valued employee until he retired in 2004.

Everybody who I ever heard say anything about Cicero, from Speaker Tom Murphy to the doorkeepers at the House chambers, made it very positive. Indeed, Cicero was nice to all. And when you saw him and talked with him, he gave you a big lift, just like he gave Mr. Ben.

Cicero has to be, what, about seventy-nine years old or so? But he is still hunting—he is an excellent turkey and deer hunter—and an avid fisherman. And I know he's still nice to everyone with whom he comes into contact.

I do have two additional thoughts and then I'll close.

First, isn't it a shame that 185-pound fullbacks and guards can't play at schools like Georgia anymore. Even if they are tough as nails and disciplined as the pope, they're too small. And isn't it a shame that more people aren't like Cicero was: just do the job as you are told to do. We probably could have used a few more Ciceros in the Georgia House and Senate, and I know we could use lots more like him in the Congress of the United States.

If you once knew Cicero Lucas, don't forget him. He is worthy of your memory.

BRYOZOAS ARE IN MIDDLE GEORGIA

Indian summer was still at least sixty days away, but at 6:00 in the evening when we "put in," there was a hint of autumn in the air. The calendar said fall was here, but folks who have lived here for very long know that Southern summers hold on, like a dying oak tree, and it's still several weeks off. In some years, autumn makes only a cameo appearance, depriving me, and many others, of a favorite, glorious time of the year.

By 6:00, it had already cooled slightly, and the pond water, at least on the surface, was slick as the windshield on a brand new Lexus automobile.

With Foster's battery and my electric motor, we pushed off as quietly as a Catholic priest at prayer. Foster had two casting rods, one armed with spinner bait and the other with a plastic worm. I had two spinners with a black Torpedo and a plastic lizard. All in all, it was a good time to be alive and a good place to be—on a pretty private pond in Middle Georgia with good prospects for catching some large-mouth bass.

Larry to Foster: "Let's go to the end of the pond and then to the shady side first and fish the sunny side after it cools off." Foster, the boat driver, to Larry: "Okay." And so to the end of the pond, where the sustaining water comes in, we went, fishing the bank as we headed west.

After about twenty minutes, with several strikes, a couple of bass, and plenty of conversation, we were at the end of the pond, where neither of us had ever been before and where we could clearly see the sandy bottom and swirling water where it entered the pond. In looking to our left and right and at the headwaters, it could have been a fishing spot in Costa Rica or South America.

The fishing was promising but tough. There were logs and limbs in the water. It seemed that the fish were around the incoming water. Foster hooked a big bass but lost it when it ran under a log. I think I caught one. Maybe it was three pounds.

I was untangling my Torpedo (you do that frequently when you fish a lure with a treble hook) and looking down when I saw something in the water I'd never seen before. As I pointed, "Foster, what in the world is that?" My first thought: it's some animal, a beaver, raccoon, or armadillo, dead in the water. But it was round with something that looked like arms or extensions and about as big as a beach ball. I tried to pick it up with the paddle but couldn't get it out of the water. It made little or no movement.

Foster was perplexed and I was, too. It looked alive but made little, if any, movement. It was grayish with spots like the little dimples on a golf ball. We were astounded but moved on around the banks of this small, five-acre pond with our fishing, picking up more strikes and a few bass.

As it was getting dark, Larry to Foster, "Why don't we go back to the upper end and try it one more time?" Foster, "Okay." So we did. And much to our amazement, we saw another water monster with the same appearance, but smaller, about the size of a basketball. Foster took a picture of it, pushed it with the paddle, and it disappeared.

Of course, we talked more about these water creatures than we did the fishing and the fish. And, I couldn't wait to telephone my resident fishing expert Les Ager, who calmly responded that this "monster" was bryozoa, which I learned from the internet are a phylum of aquatic invertebrate animals (whatever that means!).

Here are some other things I've read: "They are filter feeders that sieve food particles... Most live in tropical waters...some in freshwater environments.... Over 4,000 species are known.... Some are hatcheries for fertilized eggs, and some have special zooids for defense of the colony.... They are also known as 'moss animals.'... They have been used in cancer research."

Ten days ago, I didn't even know what bryozoa was, and now I have seen two or seen something. If you've ever seen any bryozoa in Middle Georgia, tell me about it. Thanks, and happy fishing.

GEORGIA'S FAIR, PERRY'S FAIR

I wrote the next two paragraphs many years ago and called it "Pachyderms and Piccolos." Here it is.

Elephants, real live elephants, walking down Carroll, Perry's main street. And lions and tigers in cages. And the Clydesdale horses and the Heinz Hitch. When I was a boy growing up in Perry, and even when I first went to the General Assembly in 1973, if someone had told me that there would be elephants on Perry's Carroll Street, I would have probably responded: "Man, you are crazy!" But there they were. I saw them myself.

Equally impressive, even if in a different way—we are going to have the Atlanta Symphony Orchestra at the Georgia National Fairgrounds in Perry tomorrow night. The performance will be held in the McGill Exhibition Hall with doors to open at 5:00 P.M. The warm-up performance will begin at 6:30 P.M. This is big—really big. Is it as big as the Clydesdales? I don't know, but I do know the Atlanta Symphony Orchestra is known world-wide and has won eighteen Grammys. And they are coming to Perry!"

And they did come to Perry. The gray elephants and the piccolo players, and I thought it was about the most exciting thing that could ever happen to our little city—or town, or village, or hamlet. Size is relative, you know.

But let's back up with a few remembrances (out of many that should be written down and preserved before it's too late and impossible to preserve accurately).

It was probably 1988, but it could have been 1987, Joe Frank Harris was Georgia's governor, and Foster Rhodes and I were riding home late afternoon to officially deliver the news that Perry, yes, little Perry, was going to be the official site of the Georgia National Fairgrounds and Agri-Center. There was a crowd, what, perhaps 150 or so, waiting at Perry's Holiday Inn for us and a celebration, what seemed so long in coming, but now so short, because it was Perry. Not Macon, not Atlanta, not Cordele, not Tifton, but little Perry.

And as excited as I was, the words still rung in my ears: "*Boondoggle, cow barn, white elephant, doomed to failure....*" But I believed, well, I sorta believed. I wanted to believe. Was I like the little boy whistling in the graveyard? It was going to happen—thanks to Foster Rhodes, Curley Cook, Arthur White Jr., Barbara Calhoun, Joe Frank Harris, Joel Cowen, Marcus Collins, Jerry Horton, Hugh Gillis, the Beckham brothers, Ed and Billy, Henry Reaves, Tom Murphy, Gene Sutherland, Johnny Webb, Bill Roberts, Lewis Meeks, Wayne Shackleford, Emory Greene, Bill Roquemore, and many others, and with my frank acknowledgement that the omission of other names is a shame. That's one reason that a history needs to be written, and soon.

And then suddenly, it's October 6, 2016, and the expectations for the twenty-seventh successive fair are upon us.

Let me back up one more time to the first "National Fair" twenty-seven years ago. With the words "boondoggle" and "white elephant" on my mind, I drove out to US Highway 41, where Pineneedle Drive intersects, and watch traffic. And here they came, not in torrents, but enough to give hope. Maybe it will work. Maybe.

And then it's Saturday, October 15, 2016—the next to last day of the 2016 fair. And they pour down US 41 and I-75 and Courtney Hodges Blvd., and they come like agitated fire ants—from all directions. Ninety-three thousand—that's 93,000 happy people through the gates at the Ag Center. Interestingly, that's almost exactly the same number that UGA's Sanford Stadium will hold. Many of you have seen Sanford Stadium full on many occasions. It's a magnificent sight and at a magnificent site. Now think about that many people in Perry, a city now of about 15,000, and being properly accommodated. It's a magnificent sight and at a magnificent site.

By the way, there was a 536,000-plus total attendance in 2016, but to me, the 93,000-plus in one day is even more amazing. The only thing in Georgia as big, attendance-wise, that could seat this many people, is Sanford Stadium. And while UGA does have piccolo players (maybe), they don't have live elephants. But, of course, we don't have white elephants, only gray ones on occasion.

PLEASE, MARTHA, NO CHENILLE LID COVERS

Admittedly, last week's article was a little gloomy and morbid. I don't think that's me, ordinarily, and so I was thinking about something a little lighter (and hopefully funny) to give you this week. This resulted in my mind going back to March of 2005 when I wrote the below article. Bear in mind that this is more than eleven years ago. Nonetheless, the problem that I wrote about then is an even bigger problem today. Here it is:

I wouldn't put it in the same category as the Social Security/private investments debate or the budget deficit or the trade deficit, but it is still a problem. A problem that seems peculiar to men (at least as to how it affects them) as opposed to women. In fact, women seem to relish the situation, and, if I can be candid, in almost all of the cases of which I am aware, are the cause of men's perplexment and bewilderment.

Now, some of you men may think that your frustrations with this "problem" are unique to you. Think again. The next time you are in a group of men, raise the issue and you will be astounded at the universality of your male companions' first-hand experiences (and frustrations). And if there are more than six in the group, at least one or two can and will truthfully "top" anything you can tell.

What I am talking about is women's obsession with piling pillows on beds. Let me use my personal situation (and bed) as an example. Before I go further, let me say that seldom does anyone other than my wife or I go into our bedroom. Nonetheless, as the bed is made each day (and, admittedly, almost at all times by Janice), she piles eight pillows on the bed, which I remove each night, throwing them strategically around the room.

Now let me admit that I get up more in the night than I used to. And, yes, I am fearful one of her pillows will trip me, or I will trip over it. But the main problem is that I just don't understand it. What's the sense of it all?

Recently, I consulted one of my friends about this "pillow business." I got no sympathy. He said that there were twelve pillows on their bed. Round ones, square ones, oblong ones, etc. I could tell that his frustrations greatly exceeded my own. So I tried to change the subject. And with some success, though not with satisfaction. While recognizing the "pillow obsession problem" and its seemingly endless fashion duration, he told me of an even more concerning matter with which he is coping.

Like me, my friend gets up more in the night than he did when younger. Well, it seems that "Miss Martha Stewart" has placed a chenille cover on their toilet lid. The problem is that the lid won't stay up without being held up. You can see the problems that this causes. He has to walk through a minefield of twelve pillows, and if he makes it, he has a balancing task while in a semi-awake or semi-asleep state. He says, "It's a real problem." I believe him.

I thought it would die out. Like leisure suits and ducktail haircuts. But it has lasted for quite a while. And the number of pillows is never reduced. Just additions. I guess I will just have to live with it and hope I don't get smothered or trip in the night. And thank goodness we don't have a chenille lid cover. I hope that doesn't get to be a big fashion thing. Otherwise, I guess we would have to get one for me to balance and both of us to look at.

Lest you think otherwise, the contents of this article are essentially true. Names have been omitted to protect existing relationships.

And so it was with the pillows in 2005, and it doesn't appear to have changed much since then. Truthfully, I've about learned to live with it, although I really don't understand it. But Janice probably doesn't understand all those rods, reels, plastic worms, and lizards that I have! And what about my shotguns?

HUGE HUGH BROWN MCNATT

Hugh Brown McNatt. Uvalda, Georgia's, most famous son? Raconteur supreme. A Brother Dave Gardner, Atticus Finch, Jerry Clower, and Clarence Darrow all in one. A champion for children. A great friend and a bad enemy. Extraordinary trial lawyer. An atypical Georgia Power Company trial lawyer. Generous, patient, kind, and exasperating. A teacher of Sunday school and a teacher of hard-earned lessons to many that they never forget. Reverent and irreverent. Smart. Loads of common sense. A character with character. A person whom I inadvertently have in my cell phone as "Hughe," which should be "Huge." He is huge.

And so when "Huge," this stereotypical son of the South, told our Sunday school class, Pathfinders, at Perry United Methodist, of his after-death experience, I listened intently. Truthfully, I paid more attention and ascribed more credence to him and his story than had the speaker been a preacher or the holder of two divinity degrees from Oxford University.

Twenty-three days in a coma and then death and then a return to life. Amazing, especially coming from my conflicting and conflicted friend Hugh Brown McNatt. I haven't forgotten the story, nor will I ever forget it. Not from this plain-spoken (sometimes painfully, to the listeners), often irreverent man.

But even more than the death and then life again story, which, of course, is powerful coming from this man, at least to me, was his verbal recollection of the prayer he prayed during this time to his God. It went something like this: "God, if you'll help me through this, I won't bother you about little things in the future." And I believe he was good to his word. He doesn't seem to fret over small things. But he still shares them with us and he still grouses and grumbles. It's part of who he is.

Hugh has lost sight in one eye since he died and came back. This means that he no longer can quail hunt ("partridges," to Hugh), but he still goes. Takes others. Drives the bird buggy. Encourages and

LARRY WALKER

"instructs" the hunters. He's not shooting, but he's the man in charge.

He is quick with a joke, sometimes at your expense—well, often at your expense. He tells wonderful and appropriate stories. He tells inappropriate stories. He enjoys life. Just like on his quail hunts, he is in charge. He castigates and exaggerates and tells "true stories" appropriate to what is happening. He is very funny. Very. His friends want to be with him. Those who are new to him want to be with him.

As I said, and as far as I can tell, he doesn't worry God or his doctors about "the small things" anymore. Now, that's not to say that he doesn't complain to his wonderful wife, Lynn, or his friends and colleagues about small things—in fact, everything—but they take it, and understand it, and enjoy it. He wants them to enjoy it. He expects them to enjoy it. It's all a part of dealing with and being in the company of this giant personality of great capability. His legion of friends are willing to pay this small price to be with this legend, for, after all, he is really just entertaining.

I mentioned friends, his legion of friends—certainly, I do not know them all. But I do know of his friendship with Hugh (the other Hugh), Marion, Bryant, Dudley, and Bill, all of whom are judges, and too many lawyers to start mentioning. And with modesty aside, I know what will happen with this article. It's going to be read and the word will go out, "Have you read Larry's article on Hugh B.?!" And then they'll email it all over the state and even to other states. And I'm glad, because it's long overdue.

I started this article to write, once again, about feral hogs and trash throwing trash, using Hugh's promise not to worry God about "the little things" as an opening for the article, but got into Hugh and couldn't get out. I'm glad I couldn't. This huge man, Hugh McNatt, deserves this article. And they will be sending it because they love and respect him. He makes them laugh. He makes them happy. Me, too, but I think I've already written that.

245

WRITING ABOUT WHAT I'M THINKING ABOUT

It's Monday, Memorial Day 2017. I'm sitting here on our sofa, where I usually sit when I'm writing my weekly column, and I'm thinking about lots of things. So I've decided to write about what I'm thinking about. Perhaps it should be what I'm thinking "of" rather than "about," but I think about things, not of things, so that's what it will be. I hope that some of my memories cause good or important memories for you.

First, I'm thinking about Martha Ann Rhodes and that wonderful homemade vanilla ice cream I ate at "Foster's Cabin" last night. Martha Ann is an excellent cook, but she's at least equal to that in making delicious homemade ice cream, of which I ate way, way too much!

I'm thinking about what I heard Bear Bryant say to Joe Namath when the Bama team came to Sanford Stadium to practice on the Friday before the Georgia game in 1963. Ask me, and I'll tell you about it.

I'm thinking about some who went way too early: Dennis Fesmire, Hugh Lawson Jr., Stephanie Pitts, Joneal Lee, Leroy Williamson, Marvin Ragan, Larry Harkins, Ann Hunt, Pete Hunt, Charles Bridges, James Dean, John F. Kennedy, Jeff Knighton, Jean Norman, Jerry Horton, Tommie Sandefur, David Hartley, Bobby Jones, Jerry Wilson, Lee Cotten, Bobby Griffin, Janie Brockie Watson, Phyllis Anderson, Freddy Lampley, and Billy Stubbs.

I'm thinking about the 95-yard run by Pierce Staples with less than two minutes in the game that enabled Perry to beat Hawkinsville 13 to 7 in 1959. I handed the ball to Pierce. I think that was probably my "football playing" highlight!

I'm thinking about Tom Murphy and what he did for Middle Georgia and how he never got the credit for most of what he did.

I'm thinking about seeing and talking to Muhammad Ali in New York, at the state Capitol, and at the old downtown Marriott Hotel in Atlanta. And watching him spar, though he was well beyond his prime, and how his sparring partners showed him respect and exhibited forbearance.

I'm thinking about Bobby Rowan and how he made me laugh when laughter was the only cure for hurt.

I'm thinking about having to pick cotton when I was a boy and how much I despised it, but how much the picking and how much the other pickers in the field taught me.

I'm thinking about Janice Knighton moving to Perry when she and I were both in the tenth grade and how that was the most important thing that ever happened to me.

I'm thinking about Stan Carey, Uncle Ned, Liberace, the Lewis Family, the Washington Redskins, the black cat on Channel 13, and how all of this was a part of my early television.

I'm thinking about Teen Town at the Perry National Guard Armory and some of my early awkward and nervous dancing with some really nice and pretty Perry girls.

I'm thinking about Grandma, Papa, Granny, and Grandbuddy and how much I loved my four grandparents and how I felt that they loved me.

I'm thinking about June 11, 1963, and being in Selma, Alabama, the day George Wallace "stood in the schoolhouse door," and being in Meridian, Mississippi, that same night when Byron De La Beckwith Jr. shot and killed Medgar Evers, and living just off the TCU campus in Fort Worth, Texas, at the same time Lee Harvey Oswald did. I think a lot about the summer of '63. It was a tumultuous time.

I think about eating dirt, actually clay, that was dug out of one of Papa's tenant farmer's wells, and spitting it out, but how some of my playmates ate the clay and swallowed it.

I am thinking about Mr. Glea, Billy Bledsoe, Bill Lee, Celestine Sibley, Coach St. John, 'Fessor Staples, Miss Ruby Hodges, Sara Kezar, Ed Thompson, and others who enriched my life in more ways than I can recall.

I am thinking about David, my brother, and what a good man, good example, and good law partner he has been and how it would be difficult to "go on" without him.

I am thinking about Mother, now ninety-seven, and what an inspiration she is to our family.

I'm thinking about showing cows, catching fish, eating fish, shooting quail, watching Georgia football, playing basketball with two PHS greats, Dwayne Powell and Lee Martin, eating steaks as a boy with "the men" at the Perry Café in downtown Perry, going to Brazil with Connell Stafford, shooting doves in Uruguay with Clark Fain, fishing off Miami in the Intracoastal Waterway with Allan Stalvey, going all over the country and much of the world with Steve Lakis and the State Legislative Leadership Foundation, and how great all of this was.

I'm thinking about my four wonderful children and nine grandchildren and how all of them make me proud and how they are so important to Janice and me.

And, lastly, I'm thinking about it's time to quit, although I've still got lots I'm thinking about.

GREAT BOOKS YOU'VE NEVER READ

This week, it's books again. The difference is that even avid book readers haven't heard about most of these, though, in my opinion, all are excellent. Give some or all a chance this year.

Let's start with one of my all-time favorites. Yes, I've written about it before. It's *Lone Star: A History of Texas and the Texans* by T. R. Fehrenbach. Sounds dull, doesn't it? It's anything but. I've never underlined in a book as much. An example is on page 516: "The long, open border, stretching from Eagle Pass to the Gulf of Mexico, had already become a serious problem for Texas." That was in the 1850s! It's one of my all-time top-ten books.

On a somewhat similar note is *State by State: A Panoramic Portrait of America* edited by Matt Weiland and Sean Wilsey. You think it's a geography book, don't you? It's not. It's what fifty gifted authors have written about fifty different states. Two examples should whet your appetite. "Alabama" by George Packer: "Color is the oldest, deepest truth in Alabama, but it ebbs and flows..." "Tennessee" by Ann Patchett: "Shiloh.... More than ten thousand men...had died there in 1862.... If anybody tells you Tennessee has changed much, tell them to come out to Shiloh." Admit it, you're interested.

Next is *Goat Brothers* by Larry Colton. I read it in 1993. This is on the cover: "The true-life American epic of five men who meet as California fraternity brothers in the early 1960s and live out the dreams, failures, loves, and betrayals of their tumultuous generation." On page 237 of this 559-page book, the author writes about his experience playing baseball with the Macon Peaches and the team's trip on the team bus, "The Coffin," to play the Montgomery Rebels. He described the bus as the same one "which was used in the off-season to haul the Bibb County chain gang down to the Ocmulgee River to bust rocks, a sauna on wheels."

What about *The Old Man and the Boy* by Robert Ruark? A couple of quotes from the book for you to consider: "I am what you might call a monument to trial and error," and "But he (the old man) purely despised idle chitter-chatter, people that just talked without having anything to say." I am and I do, too. You've probably heard of this one, but if you haven't read it, do so before it's too late.

Now, for two books you probably haven't read or heard about: *Bacardi and the Long Fight for Cuba* by Tom Gjelten, which I finished on January 25, 2009, and about which I wrote, "I learned lots about Cuba, its people, and, of course, the Bacardi family and their rum company." And *Telex from Cuba*, a novel by Rachel Kushner and about which I wrote on February 8, 2009, "I...recommend it to anyone who wants to know what was probably going on in Cuba during Batista's time and when and after Castro took over." Two good ones.

Another good one and, in a way, similar to the Bacardi book is *The House of Gucci* by Sara Gay Forden. This is what I wrote about Gucci on May 11, 2015: "It taught me lots about family business, starting a business, and sustaining a big business once you get it established.... It also reminded me of people's foibles and how it greatly affects business, especially a big family business." A 9.25 on a 10 scale.

Now, two books about two very different Georgia legends. First, *Footnotes to History* by Griffin B. Bell, which was given to me by my friend Jim Cole in 2009. I wrote in the front of the book, "Excellent. All high school students, indeed all Americans, interested in their country should read this." You should too! And next, different, but equally compelling, is *When Men Were Boys: An Informal Portrait of Dean William Tate* by John W. English and Rob Williams. This is on the book cover: "For more than 60 years his name has been associated with the University of Georgia. But he was always more than that. Southern Apologist. Counselor. Eternal Sophomore. Wild Bill. God's Angry Man. Storyteller. Track Star. Historian. Humanist." You don't have to be old and a UGA graduate or fan to love it, but it will help!

Let me end with a quote by Joshua Ferris from the book *State by State* under "Florida": "But few know about the Flora-Bama bar, located on the border between Florida and Alabama, an area known as the Redneck Riviera. The Flora-Bama sponsors a yearly mullet toss. For a fifteen-dollar entry fee, you have the chance to stand in a ten-foot circle in Alabama and throw a dead mullet across the state line into Florida, no sand on the mullet allowed. Throwing the mullet the farthest wins you a specially designed mullet trophy." This doesn't have anything to do with anything except its great writing and reminds me of my visits to the Flora-Bama. What a place!

THE SUN GOT IN MY EYES

Most of you can't really relate to this article. Why? Well, I suspect that over half of my readers are women and most of them have never participated. As for the men readers, increasingly, most of them have, regretfully, had no "first hand" experiences. Still, as to those who can relate, they will know exactly of what I write and I believe will enthusiastically embrace and use the needed excuses. Thus, at least to my mind, enough justification for the effort.

Let me start over. Consider this as the beginning. It was four or five years ago. In December, I believe. And we—Judge Griffin Bell, University of Massachusetts president Billy Bulger, Steve Lakis, Clark Fain, and I—were down in Lee County, Georgia, bird hunting. Partridge hunting to some. Quail hunting to others. But "bird hunting" to me. It was then and there that Judge Bell, in his usual wise and colorful way, revealed that he had compiled an ever-expanding list of available excuses as to why he missed a bird that he otherwise should have killed. I seem to recall that he had forty or so excuses—excuses that went from the believable to the ridiculous—all ready for use when needed.

What brought all of this to mind after four or five years? It was a recent bird-hunting trip to Seminole County with Foster Rhodes and Clark Fain. Billy Fain was with us but he didn't shoot. Both Clark and Foster used most of these excuses—I don't recall having to avail myself of them. They may remember it otherwise. But it's my article. Here they are. I have even put them in categories.

Number One: Safety. These are the best because who can argue with being safe? Use as often as needed.

a. Afraid I would shoot a dog (this is my second favorite—it makes you appear humane).

b. Didn't want to shoot in front of you.

c. The guide was in the way.

d. The bird wagon was in the way.

Number Two: Courtesy. Like "safety," these are excellent. Makes you appear to be a nice person.

a. Was waiting on you to shoot first.

b. I've already killed my share (this can be smugly said if you didn't just shoot).

Number Three: Equipment. What commends these is that your companions cannot refute or argue.

a. My gun jammed.

b. No shell in the chamber (can only be used if you didn't fire).

c. The shell snapped (only about one shell out of 10 million doesn't fire; still, it sometimes happens).

d. Couldn't get my shells out of my jacket (again, who can question?).

Number Four: Dogs. Dogs don't talk back, do they?

a. The dogs didn't point.

b. The dogs flushed the birds.

c. The dogs didn't point in the right place.

Number Five: General. There are not the best but sometimes work when you have nothing else.

a. I thought you were going to shoot first (double-first cousin to a courtesy excuse when not coupled with a scolding or accusatory tone).

b. Birds were too close (or substitute "too far").

c. Blowing my nose.

d. Something in my eye.

e. Too much coffee this morning (necessitating appropriate relief).

Number Six: Elements. Next to safety, these are the most believable.

a. I tripped on a root (substitute "stick" or "rock" or "limb").

b. I stepped in a hole.

c. A limb was in the way.

d. It is cold and I had my hands in my pocket.

e. The sun was in my eyes (this is my favorite, although it doesn't helps if it is now a cloudy day).

Well, here they are. Just twenty-three in all. Not up to Judge Bell's numbers, but good, general, usable excuses. Maybe there are even one or two new ones for Clark and Foster in addition to the many they already have.

FIVE TONS OF CRICKET POOP

I'll bet the name of this story got your attention! I'll address this subject below. Now, for some other interesting subjects—at least I hope you find them to be of interest.

GDOT Road Signs: "GDOT" stands for Georgia Department of Transportation. I was at one of its meetings in Atlanta some time ago when someone said, "We've got five million signs on Georgia roads we have to maintain." Wow! I was astounded and somewhat unbelieving. On the Monday following that meeting, I telephoned Eric Pitts, deputy assistant maintenance engineer, to confirm. This is what he had to say: "We don't have a good inventory, but five million is probably a good number, and signs are being constantly added. The typical life of a sign is ten years, with many having to be replaced earlier because they are hit, shot, and so forth. We have daytime and nighttime inspections every year, with signs being cleaned or replaced, as needed, about every ten years." Five million! Wow!

Turkey Hill Plantation: It's near Ridgeland, South Carolina, and I was there one Saturday, quail hunting with Connell Stafford, Jim Cole, and Roland Vaughn. Turkey Hill has about 26,000 acres, and at one time was probably the largest cattle farm east of the Mississippi River. We hunted on about 2,000 of the 26,000 acres. Turkey Hill is somewhat unique in that they put their birds out in the fall of the year—18,000 of them—and you are only allowed to shoot "covey-rises." You quail hunters will understand. It was the closest thing I've seen to wild birds since I shot—well, wild birds. It was quite a day. Thanks, Connell, Jim, and Roland for your good company and for including me.

Perry Rotary Club Fishing Tournament: The seventh annual Perry Rotary Club Fishing Tournament will be had on March 28. I can't wait! The purpose of the tournament is to raise money for the Perry community and for the participants to have a good time. A team consists of up to three people, but if you have three, one must be a youth sixteen years or younger. The first year of the tournament, the requisite three bass were weighed in by the ultimate winners at the Ag Center and tipped the scales at an astounding twenty-eight pounds—and all three fish weighed over nine pounds (none of which were the "Big Fish Winner"). Needless to say, Foster Rhodes and I didn't win, but we, along with Gray Way (our youth), will be trying again this year. Think you might be interested? If so, contact Mike Gray at Walker, Hulbert, Gray & Byrd, Penny Byrd at Security Bank, or William Bailey at Planters First. I believe Gray, Foster, and I are going to do better this year and win the first prize of $1,000 for the heaviest three fish. There is also a separate prize for the biggest fish. Maybe if they had a prize for the biggest fish tale (not tail), I would have a chance.

Crickets at the Crossroads: Well, I'm getting to it—the five tons of cricket poop, that is. You're going to find some of this hard to believe. I did. Readers might recall that I wrote a story once about getting into the cricket business called "Crickets at the Crossroads." That prompted my friend Bill Kuhlke of Augusta to send me an article from *The Augusta Chronicle* by Tim Rausch called "20 People, 25 Million Crickets." This article made me realize that it's too late for me—apparently, Ghann's Cricket Farm in Martinez and its twenty employees can supply all of the needed crickets for everyone in Georgia—perhaps in the USA. Clay Ghann is a second-generation cricket farmer. His father, Aubrey, started the business in 1952 as a way to make money off of fishermen. Twenty-five million crickets surround Clay Ghann every day, but "fish bait" is only part of the business. Most of his customers buy the little critters for pet food—mainly for reptiles such as the bearded dragon, leopard gecko, turtles, and frogs. Ghann sold 180 million crickets last year. All of this is remarkable to me. But the most amazing fact is that the twenty million crickets make five tons of cricket poop (Mr. Rausch called it "poo"—is it poo or poop?) per week. That's not a typo—yes, five tons per week.

Note: I've decided against getting into the cricket business, but I am wondering if I could get some of that cricket manure to put on our lngleaf pines.

MY FIRST WORD WAS "READ"

Mother says that the first word I ever said was "Read." I would get the *Atlanta Journal-Constitution*, point at the funny papers (cartoons), and say to my father, "Read." And read he would, with me sitting in his lap. It was the start of a lifelong love of books and reading. It is as if I never have enough time to do the reading I want. Also, I've noticed that my eyes don't last as long as they used to.

Have you read *John Adams* by David McCullough? If not, and you like to read, get it and read it. It is not an easy read—651 pages—but it is well worth the effort. You will learn much about the birth of our wonderful country and the people most responsible for the way we were formed. Incidentally, McCullough also wrote *Truman*, for which he received the Pulitzer Prize. More about *Truman* later.

Let me also recommend the Pulitzer prize-winning *Founding Brothers*. This is a wonderful book, and you will learn how greatly gifted but flawed individuals—Hamilton, Burr, Jefferson, Franklin, Washington, Adams, and Madison—chartered the course that our country follows even to this day. If you are going to choose between *John Adams* and this book, go with the shorter (248 pages) *Founding Brothers* by Joseph J. Ellis. Recently, I read *The Rise of Theodore Roosevelt* (782 pages) by Edmund Morris and liked it so much that I am now reading Mr. Morris's *Theodore Rex* (555 pages). The first book is about Teddy Roosevelt's early days before he became president, and *Theodore Rex* starts about the time President McKinley was assassinated in 1901—resulting in Roosevelt's becoming president—and then covers Roosevelt's presidency and the rest of his life. Roosevelt was one of the most interesting people this country ever produced, and Edmund Morris has done a magnificent job with both books. Incidentally, Morris won the Pulitzer Prize for his first book on Roosevelt.

Earlier, I mentioned McCullough's book on John Adams. I am also reading his book *Truman*, which was a national best seller. This book is

992 pages and I am on page 315. Do you think I will ever finish it? This is an excellent account of Truman's life and is a superb biography. I will finish it. I like the book, Mr. McCullough's writing, and Mr. Truman that much.

While reading *Truman*, I am also reading *The Path to Power* (768 pages), which covers Lyndon Johnson's life from his birth to his being a United States congressman and his defeat in his first bid for the United States Senate. I am on page 480. When I finish the book, I will read *Master of the Senate* (1,040 pages). Both of these books are by Robert A. Cairo.

While writing this story, I realized that much of my reading of late has been biographies, and six of the books have been about three of our most interesting presidents—Teddy Roosevelt, Harry S. Truman, and Lyndon Johnson. Notice I said "interesting" and not "greatest." I have done more reading recently, more than I realized (some 2,500 pages), but with the books I write about herein, I am committed to some 2,000 additional pages. Throw in *Andrew Jackson and His Indian Wars* by Robert V. Remini and *Then Sings My Soul* by Sonny Sammons, both of which I want to read, and I now understand why my eyes sometimes hurt.

Let me rate the top three books I have recently read and am reading. I recommend the books to you in this order: 1) *Founding Brothers*, 2) *The Rise of Theodore Roosevelt*, and 3) *Truman*. *John Adams* is a close fourth—and then, again, it could be *The Path to Power*. I like all of them. I hope you do too! Happy reading.

ABOUT THE AUTHOR

Larry Walker, a native of Georgia's gnat line, graduated from Perry High School in 1960 and then attended the University of Georgia, where he earned a bachelor's degree in business administration and his Juris Doctor degree (making him a Double Dawg) before returning to Perry to practice law in June 1965.

While at UGA, he married his high school sweetheart, Janice Knighton. They have four children, all of whom live in Perry, and nine grandchildren.

In January 1966, at age 23, Walker was appointed as Perry's municipal court judge, a part-time job he held for six years before being named Perry's city attorney, another part-time job, and a role Walker and his firm has held continuously since 1972.

In 1972, Walker was elected to Georgia's House of Representatives, taking the seat held by Perry's Sam Nunn, who was elected to the United States Senate on the same day Walker was elected to the State House.

In his thirty-two-year tenure, Walker served for four years as administration floor leader for Governor Joe Frank Harris and for sixteen years as House majority leader. At the request of Governor Zell Miller, and as agreed to by Speaker Tom Murphy, Walker served as both House majority leader and Governor Miller's floor leader in the House during the last four years of the governors term. Walker also served for four years as chair of the State Legislative Leaders Foundation, a nationwide organization of legislative leaders.

Walker retired from the legislature in 2004 after thirty-two years of service. He was subsequently elected by legislative colleagues to the State Board of Transportation, serving two and a half years before being appointed to the Georgia Board of Regents by Governor Sonny Perdue and then being reappointed for a full seven-year term by Governor Nathan Deal. Walker retired from the Board of Regents in 2018.

Walker has practiced law in Perry for more than fifty-three years and in 2014 was honored by the American Bar Association as one of the outstanding small law-firm practitioners in the United States.

Walker wrote a weekly newspaper column for the *Houston Home Journal* and then for *The Macon Telegraph* for more than sixteen years.